Pathways of Power

Pathways of Power

The Dynamics of National Policymaking

Timothy J. Conlan
Paul L. Posner
David R. Beam

GEORGETOWN UNIVERSITY PRESS
Washington, DC

Library of Congress Cataloging-in-Publication Data

Conlan, Timothy J.
  Pathways of power : the dynamics of national policymaking / Timothy J. Conlan, Paul L. Posner, David R. Beam.
      pages   cm
  Includes bibliographical references and index.
  ISBN 978-1-62616-039-2 (pbk. : alk. paper)
  1. Policy sciences. 2. United States—Politics and government. I. Title.
  H97.C656 2013
  320.60973—dc23

                                                    2013026130

♾ This book is printed on acid-free paper meeting the requirements of the American National Standard for Permanence in Paper for Printed Library Materials.

15 14   9 8 7 6 5 4 3 2 First printing

Printed in the United States

Contents

Preface

This book draws upon three sources of inspiration. First, several of its themes or elements first emerged in our previous research on the politics of tax reform, the federal budget, federal grants-in-aid and federal mandates. We wished to build on our earlier insights about the complex dynamics and changing character of federal policymaking in a more systematic and thorough way in this book. The result spans thirty-two years of policy history. Second, both our earlier research and the present book have been informed by our experiences in government, where each of us served for periods ranging from five to over twenty-five years. Among us, we have worked in both the executive and legislative branches of the federal government, as well as at the state and local levels. From this perspective, we feel that too many existing treatments of public policy fail to fully convey the dynamism and changeability of the policy process. We faced a similar frustration in our search for literature to assign our students in graduate and upper-division courses on public policymaking and the policy process. We like and use much of the existing literature in these courses but, as we explain in chapter 1, all seem lacking in portraying the dynamic interactions and energy that characterizes policymaking today. Having tested the framework developed in this book on both full-time students and part-time working professionals in our MPA program, as well as graduate and undergraduate students in political science, we are convinced that students at all levels like it and learn from it.

The audiences for this book mirror its sources of inspiration: our students, our colleagues in the academic research community, and our professional colleagues in government. Such diverse audiences inevitably necessitate striking a balance between divergent needs and perspectives. The level of sophistication appropriate for our colleagues in academia and government risks confusing students with less grounding and knowledge about the policy process and specific cases of policymaking. At the same time, providing students with the foundation they need to understand the arguments can become tedious to knowledgeable scholars and bureaucrats. But many academic works encounter this tension, and we hope and believe that we have struck the right balance.

Finally, and most sadly, we want to note that this book is dedicated to the memory of our friend and coauthor, David Beam. Dave passed away on August 14, 2012, after several years of poor health. He was instrumental in our earliest thinking about the pathways framework, which grew out of themes first explored in *Taxing Choices*, our book with Margaret Wrightson on the politics of the Tax

Reform Act of 1986. Subsequently, Dave collaborated on and coauthored several conference papers and articles that became the basis for some of our book chapters. Although Dave participated less in writing the actual chapters contained in this book, he was a constant intellectual presence and contributor to many of the underlying ideas—and he served as an effective critic and editor until the end. We will miss him greatly.

Acknowledgments

We would like to thank the students and graduate research assistants who contributed background research for some of the cases drawn upon in this book, especially Asif Shahan, William Clark, Jamie Henkle, and Julie Fairfax. Several portions of this book have been presented earlier as conference papers or book chapters, and in the process we have benefited from the comments, critiques, and suggestions of many reviewers and colleagues. We wish to thank them all. At Georgetown University Press, we would like to thank Don Jacobs for his support, as well as the extremely helpful suggestions of two anonymous reviewers. Finally, we would like to thank our wives Arlene and Marge for their patience and encouragement throughout the long process of writing this book.

CHAPTER ONE

Introduction

- In 1997, Congress enacted cost-cutting reforms to Medicare that reflected expert consensus about the best ways to moderate growth trends in health care costs, such as limiting overly generous reimbursements to health maintenance organizations and home health providers. The legislation also established a "sustainable growth rate" formula for reimbursing doctors under Medicare, as well as a new program to support health services to the children of low-wage workers. This latter program—the State Children's Health Insurance Program (SCHIP)—also reflected expert consensus on the long-term benefits of improving health outcomes for children. The legislation passed with broad bipartisan support in both houses of Congress.

- Beginning in 1999, and in virtually every subsequent year for the next decade, provisions of the 1997 Medicare reforms were trimmed back in the face of vigorous lobbying by health care–provider groups. Bipartisan majorities in Congress passed revisions in 1999 that were estimated to increase Medicare spending by $27 billion over ten years, followed by legislation in 2000 that was estimated to increase spending by $82 billion in the next decade. Although doctors failed to eliminate the sustainable growth-rate formula, aggressive lobbying by the American Medical Association and other physicians' groups led Congress to pass "doc fix" legislation every year between 2003 and 2009, which temporarily suspended the limits and raised doctors' fees under Medicare.

- In 2010, President Barack Obama signed legislation that extended health insurance coverage to millions of uninsured Americans. This law marked the culmination of decades of Democratic efforts to establish a program of universal health insurance. Hence, President Obama's success at passing the Patient Protection and Affordable Care Act was considered a major political victory, particularly in light of President Bill Clinton's failure to pass a reform bill in 1994. It was also an exceedingly partisan accomplishment. Not a single Republican voted in favor of the act in either the House or the Senate. Moreover, both real and imagined provisions of the bill—such as the requirement that all individuals carry health insurance and populist concerns about supposed "death panels"—alarmed many citizens, rallied conservatives, and contributed to Republican victories in the 2010 midterm elections. These victories spawned efforts in the 112th Congress to repeal the law.

As these examples show, the federal policy process can vary widely from one enactment to the next, even within a single field such as health care. The process may be guided by the norms of technical experts in one case, dominated by narrow interest groups in another, led by the president and party leaders in a third, or driven by populist sentiment in a fourth. Some policies race through the process at breakneck speed, while others become stuck in a policy quagmire for years or decades. Some emerge fully grown almost overnight, while others evolve in slow, incremental stages. Some are shaped in the glare of public visibility while others are crafted in the shadows by obscure subcommittees and bureaucratic agencies.

Conventional treatments of the policy process have difficulty accommodating this complexity. Civics texts portray a single, idealized model of "how a bill becomes law," journalistic treatments tend to emphasize the role of special-interest lobbying and campaign contributions to Congress, and many college textbooks describe a common set of stages through which all policies progress, from agenda setting to policy implementation. While these approaches have their merits, they fail to convey—much less explain—the great diversity in political processes that shape specific policies in contemporary Washington.

Rather than describing a single route along which all policies progress, this book argues that the policy process is best understood as a set of four distinctive pathways of public policymaking, each of which requires different political resources, appeals to different actors in the system, and elicits its own unique set of strategies and styles of coalition building:

- The traditional **pluralist pathway**, where policies are constructed largely by the processes of mutual adjustment among contending organized interests, through bargaining, compromise, and vote trading. Unorganized, poorly represented interests, which may include the public at large, typically exert less influence here. Policy outcomes that emerge from the pluralist pathway are prone to be modest and incremental in nature.
- The **partisan pathway** has long provided the traditional route for large-scale, nonincremental policy changes. In this model a strong party leader—typically a president—sweeps into office with large, unified party majorities in Congress. This leader mobilizes the resources of office to construct a coherent legislative program and rallies the public and the party followers behind it. Under such circumstances, the legislative backlog of a political generation may be disposed of in a few months. But such periods of unity tend to be brief, as

party coalitions generally succumb to internal, centrifugal forces or to subsequent electoral losses.

- In more recent years especially, an **expert pathway** has developed, which provides a route for both incremental and nonincremental policy change. This pathway is dominated by a growing cadre of policy experts and professionals in the bureaucracy, academia, and Washington think tanks. Their influence derives from the persuasive power of ideas that have been refined, refereed, and perfected within specialized policy communities. Especially where policy experts have achieved a broad degree of consensus, they can serve as effective reference points for the mass media, decision makers, and other nonspecialists in the policymaking arena.

- Finally, a **symbolic pathway** has become increasingly prominent in recent years. Like the expert pathway, it too is built around the power of ideas. But symbolic ideas tend to be simple, value-laden beliefs and valence issues whose power lies in their appeal to commonsense notions of right and wrong rather than expert appeals to efficiency and empirically demonstrated effectiveness. The symbolic pathway relies heavily on policy entrepreneurs and communication through the mass media to bridge the gap between policymakers and the general public.

Overall, these four distinctive pathways are distinguished from one another along two critical dimensions, graphically portrayed in table 1.1. One dimension is the *scale of political mobilization*. Does the policy in question elicit attention from a narrow and specialized audience, or is it the focus of attention and concern by a large-scale mass audience? Ever since the publication of E. E. Schattschneider's small but influential book *The Semi-Sovereign People*, political scientists have paid attention to the fact that the scale of political mobilization—what Schattschneider called the "scope of conflict"—could have an important and systematic impact on the politics of an issue. In Schattschneider's words, "every change in the scope of conflict has a bias. . . . That is, it must be assumed that every change in the number of participants is about something that the newcomers have sympathies or antipathies that make it possible to involve them. By definition, the intervening bystanders are not neutral. Thus, in political conflict, every change in scope changes the equation."[1]

The second important dimension, and one that more recent scholarship has directed attention to, involves the principal *method of political mobilization*. What is the predominant form of coalition building involved in enacting a given policy? Is support constructed primarily through organizational methods—principally through the efforts of specific interest groups or political parties—or is support gathered primarily through the construction and manipulation of ideas?

Table 1.1. The Four Pathways of Power
(with prototypical examples)

	SCOPE OF MOBILIZATION	
	SPECIALIZED	*MASS*
	Expert	*Symbolic*
IDEATIONAL	Tax Reform Act of 1986 Airline Deregulation CFO Act	Megan's Law Social Security "Lockbox" "Death Tax"
FORM OF MOBILIZATION	*Pluralist*	*Partisan*
ORGANIZATIONAL	2002 Farm Bill ISTEA	2001 Bush Tax Cuts 2010 Health Care Reform

Traditional politics—and traditional political science models—emphasized organizational methods of coalition building. As far back as the *Federalist Papers*, American politics have been viewed as a battle between contending "factions" and interests. Over time, the understanding of factions took note of more complex forms: political organizations, social movements (such as the abolitionist and prohibition movements of the nineteenth century), and the established farm, business, and labor groups of the twentieth century. Enveloping, embracing, and competing with interest groups were political parties, which formed the backbone of American electoral politics from the early nineteenth century on. Parties by the late nineteenth century were described as mass, militant armies of (white male) citizens, which dominated political communication, mobilized the electorate, and organized the government. Thus by the mid-twentieth century, American politics were encapsulated by the twin organizations of "parties" and "pressure groups."[2] These organizations remain important political actors today, as evident by the tremendous growth of Washington interest groups and the renewed strength of national party organizations and party leadership in Congress.

However, many modern analyses of public policymaking have tended to emphasize the power of ideas over that of traditional organizations. Scholarly books analyzing the politics of deregulation, tax reform, and welfare reform all identified the politics of ideas, rather than parties or interests, as the critical dynamic leading to enactment.[3] In one sense, of course, this is nothing new. Plato plumbed the intersection of ideas and politics in *The Republic*, while in the modern era the potential power of political ideas was captured in Victor Hugo's nineteenth-century aphorism "Greater than the tread of mighty armies is an idea whose time has come." But like many aphorisms, the concept was widely acknowledged and unevenly developed. Our examination of contemporary policymaking indicates that the politics of ideas are increasingly important and that they come in the two very distinctive flavors identified above: the expert and the symbolic.

A Prima Facie Case for the Pathways of Power Framework

Although this simple model of four policymaking styles has intuitive appeal, does it really describe or help explain observable forms of federal policymaking? Ultimately, that is the question to which this entire book is devoted. But a crude, prima facie case for the pathways of power framework is suggested in table 1.2, which compares important features of sixteen different policies—or related groups of policies—drawn mainly from the last half century. Four policies, or sets of policies, were selected as exemplars of each policy pathway and compared along several different dimensions: sponsorship, enactment speed, public salience, degree of conflict, and level of partisanship. Because they were not drawn as a random or representative sample of all federal policies, these cases are intended to be only illustrative. They do not provide a definitive test of the pathways framework or all of the critical variables that distinguish pathways from one another. However, the very different patterns of political behavior elicited by these archetypes suggest the value of exploring the pathways-of-power model in greater depth and rigor in the remainder of this book.

For example, if one examines their legislative sponsorship in Congress, distinctive patterns emerge between the four policy types. The chief legislative sponsors of the four pluralist policies examined in table 1.2 were the chairmen and/or ranking minority members of the authorizing committees with jurisdiction in Congress. The same was true of the four examples of the expert pathway. In both cases the narrow scope of political mobilization coincided with a dominant role assumed by leaders of the relevant policy subsystem. In contrast, policy leadership in the partisan pathway was typically exerted by the president and/or congressional party leadership. Committee leaders are often deeply involved in crafting the legislative details in these instances, but the basic framework of the response, as well as its driving energy, ultimately come from those at a higher pay grade. Chief sponsorship of symbolic policies, in contrast, is highly variable in the four cases examined here, with leadership coming from individual policy entrepreneurs in the case of Megan's Law (which required public notification of sex offenders'

Table 1.2. Archetypes of Pathway Politics

Program and Policy Type	Chief Sponsor	Public Salience	Enactment Time	Degree of Consensus	Partisanship
PLURALIST	Authorizing Committee	Relatively Low	16 months	High	Low
FIFRA[1]	Chairs and			House: 372-37	
CDBG[2]	Ranking			Senate: 86-6	
ISTEA[3]	Members				
FIRE Act[4]					
PARTISAN	President and	High	5 months	Low	High
	Congressional				
Great Society[5]	Party				
Contract w/	Leadership			House: 267-152	
America					
Bush Tax Cuts				Senate: 64-30	
Affordable Care Act					
EXPERT	Committee	Highly Variable	22 months	High	Low
	Chairs and				
Tax Reform Act[6]	Ranking				
Airline	Members			House: 324-71	
Deregulation Act[7]					
CFO Act[8]				Senate: 71-14[9]	
FAIR Act[10]					
SYMBOLIC	Variable:	Relatively High	107 days	High	Low
	Individual				
NEPA[11]	Members to			House: 388-33	
Megan's Law	Leaders			Senate 98-1[12]	
Afghanistan War					
Emergency					
Resolution and					
Appropriation					
USA PATRIOT Act					

1. Federal Insecticide, Fungicide, and Rodenticide Act of 1947.
2. Community Development Block Grant Program, 1974.
3. Intermodal Surface Transportation Efficiency Act of 1991.
4. Firefighter Investment and Response Act of 2000.
5. Elementary and Secondary Education Act and Medicaid of 1965.
6. Tax Reform Act of 1986.
7. Airline Deregulation Act of 1978.
8. Chief Financial Officer and Federal Financial Reform Act of 1990.
9. House and Senate votes reflect the Tax Reform Act and the 1996 Farm Bill; the airline deregulation and CFO acts passed on voice votes.
10. Federal Agricultural Improvement and Reform Act of 1996.
11. National Environmental Policy Act of 1969.
12. Votes on the Afghanistan War Resolution and PATRIOT Act. NEPA and Megan's Law passed on noncontroversial voice votes.

residence in a community), from subsystem leaders in the National Environmental Policy Act, and from party leadership in the post-9/11 Afghanistan War resolution and emergency supplemental.

Patterns of policy incubation and enactment also vary systematically among the four pathways, as represented by these archetypal policies. In the four examples of pluralist policymaking, the incubation period—or time between the first serious discussion of the issue and its enactment—averaged several years. In the session of Congress when each program was finally enacted, the period of congressional consideration averaged sixteen months from introduction to final decision. In contrast, the four archetypes of the partisan pathway had incubation periods that could extend beyond ten years.[4] When these programs were finally enacted by Congress, however, they typically raced through in a matter of months, often on the wave of a landslide election victory that gave the victorious party claim to a popular "mandate." The average enactment time for several major programs of Lyndon Johnson's Great Society agenda of 1965, the Republican Contract with America in 1995, and the Bush-era tax cuts of 2001 was five months, not far off the goal of a hundred days established by President Roosevelt in 1933. The true speed record was set, however, by the four examples of symbolic policymaking in table 1.2. These programs truly did race through Congress in about a hundred days from introduction to enactment. Most remarkably, their incubation period was practically identical to their enactment phase, indicating that these ideas jumped onto the fast track to adoption practically the first moment they were seriously proposed. This is in stark contrast to the slow and steady progress of persuasion that marks expert-driven legislation in the expert pathway.

Finally, when measured by the comparison of "ideal types," the four pathways appear to elicit demonstrably different levels of salience, conflict, and partisanship in the legislative process. Pluralist policymaking is characterized by low levels of public salience, conflict, and partisanship. The four pluralist cases examined in table 1.2 were obscure to most members of the general public, and yet they passed by an average vote of 372-37 in the House and 86-6 in the Senate. In sharp contrast, the partisan pathway is typically marked by high levels of salience, conflict, and partisanship. Six specific pieces of partisan legislation—including two each from the Great Society and the Contract with America—passed on average votes of 267-152. All were subject to enormous media attention and passed on divisive, party-line votes, although with some defections from the minority party in Congress. Although the four cases of expert policymaking were largely consensual—with muted partisanship and frequent use of noncontroversial voice votes in Congress—the four examples of symbolic policymaking were even more so. All but one of these programs passed with virtual unanimity in both the House and the Senate, either on voice or recorded votes.[5] For example, only one House member opposed the emergency resolution authorizing US intervention in

Afghanistan following the September 11 terrorist attacks in 2001, even though this gave the president sweeping powers to combat terrorism and led to over a decade of military involvement in Afghanistan.

Based on this admittedly select and limited number of cases, we suggest that the pathways-of-power framework has significant value as a descriptive and explanatory tool. On the other hand, one could seek to explain some or all of these cases based on a number of alternative models of the policymaking process. Indeed, we have drawn insights from several alternative models that we have found helpful in our own experience and research. Thus, one might well ask, "Do we really need another model of the policymaking process?" Our experience participating in, conducting research on, and teaching about the policy process says, "Yes, we do." Both we and our students have found the pathways framework to be a useful lens for understanding the national policy process.

But this is a question that deserves more careful consideration before developing the pathways framework in more detail. Accordingly, the following section examines some of the most influential current models of the policy process and how the pathways approach can improve or supplement their insights. We then elaborate the research questions and hypotheses that drive our own approach, as well as the methodology we employ to address them. Finally, the chapter concludes with a brief roadmap for the remainder of the book.

Existing Models of the Policy Process

Existing policy models might be classified into three groups: those that focus on *stages* of the policy process, those that emphasize the *institutions* of policymaking, and *integrative frameworks* that seek to classify policies and associate them with distinctive forms of policymaking behavior. All of these approaches have their merits, and we have drawn upon many of them in our own research. Yet, in our view, each has difficulty fully capturing or adequately explaining the complexity of the contemporary national policymaking process, or they have overlooked one or more critical features of that process.

The most common approach to analyzing public policymaking, and the approach that has been adopted by most texts on the subject, organizes the topic around major stages of the policymaking process.[6] This approach seeks to cover the policy cycle from beginning to end: from problem definition and agenda setting to policy formulation, legitimation, and adoption, and on through policy implementation, evaluation, and modification. Growing initially out of systems theory, the policy-stages approach has the great virtue of being very comprehensive. It can be employed to describe virtually all policymaking in all political systems. But that comprehensiveness comes at an analytical price. The same series of stages can be utilized to explain the development of educational policy in the state of Virginia, defense policy in the former Soviet Union, and communal grazing restrictions in rural African villages.

To accommodate such breadth and adaptability, the complexities of the policy process within any one stage in any one policy system must be compressed. The diversity of policy pathways and politics described in this book can largely be collapsed into the single stages of policy formulation and legitimation, for example. Thus, in one sense, the pathways approach can be viewed as a complementary perspective with the policy-stages approach, devoting more detailed and sustained analytical attention to the initial stages of the policy process. It can easily be teamed with other works focusing on other phases of the process, such as those by John Kingdon or Frank Baumgartner and Bryan Jones that deal with agenda setting and those by Jeffrey Pressman and Aaron Wildavsky, Daniel Mazmanian and Paul Sabatier, Paul Peterson, Barry Rabe, and Kenneth Wong, or Paul Manna that analyze implementation.[7]

Institutional analyses provide another approach to the study of policymaking. Such works focus on the distinctive roles that different policymaking institutions play in the policy process. This approach has great utility for highlighting the importance that institutional structures, rules, and resources play in policy design and system performance, and some institutional works have paralleled our findings about the evolving diversity of federal policymaking processes. Barbara Sinclair, for example, has analyzed changes in the legislative process over recent years and demonstrated that there are now a variety of unorthodox congressional processes that differ widely from the textbook model of "how a bill becomes law."[8] Many of her observations reinforce the findings in this book.

Ultimately, however, institutional analyses are limited by their own strengths. By delving deeply into the behavior of individual institutions—be it Congress, the presidency, or the bureaucracy—they inevitably establish a degree of isolation between different institutional players in the policy process. The approach has difficulty accommodating all of the nuanced interactions between institutions that are critical to the formation and adoption of public policies—interactions that are a central focus of *Pathways of Power*. Partly for this reason, institutional studies serve as valuable and often indispensable sources for integrative studies and approaches such as this one but not as substitutes.

Integrative models constitute the final approach to understanding the making of public policy. Various scholars have developed unique frameworks for explaining behavior and variability in the policy process—frameworks that typically show both similarities and differences with the pathways framework. In crafting this model, we have learned and benefited from many of them. Prominent examples include models developed by Theodore Lowi, James Q. Wilson, and Paul Sabatier.

In the 1960s, for example, Lowi developed an influential scheme that classified public policies into three distinct categories: regulatory, distributive, and

redistributive.[9] Each type, he wrote, had a unique pattern of historical development and a unique political economy. For example, Lowi argued that regulatory
politics tended to be characterized by interest-group conflict, whereas redistributive policies elicited broad party and class coalitions.

Lowi's model has considerable utility for understanding the historical evolution of federal policies, and it has had widespread influence and analytical appeal.
But we and others have found that it often fails to capture the complexities of
contemporary policymaking. Many pieces of modern legislation combine features
of two or three policy types, raising questions as to which policy type should determine the politics. In many other cases, the observable patterns of policymaking
simply depart from the model's predictions. For example, the Family Educational
Rights and Privacy Act (FERPA), the Clean Air Amendments of 1970, and the
Financial Services Modernization Act of 1999 all involved government regulation,
but their politics ranged from entrepreneurial leadership in the first case, to partisan competition for political credit in the second, to Lowi's expected pattern of
interest-group conflict in the third.

Our approach in this book has also been influenced and informed by James Q.
Wilson's model of policymaking, which is built around the distribution of policy
costs and benefits.[10] There is much to admire in Wilson's elegant, parsimonious
model of the politics of public policymaking, and the pathways model shares certain features with it. Our partisan pathway is similar to the politics of diffused
costs and benefits, for example, and pluralist politics has much in common with
the politics of concentrated costs and benefits. But our appreciation for the politics
of ideas makes us uneasy with a model based entirely on the distribution of policy
"costs" and "benefits." Although the politics of "who gets what, when, and how" is
absolutely central to understanding policymaking in many instances, our studies
of and experience with contemporary policymaking lead us to give stronger emphasis to the power of ideas in other cases.[11]

Ideas and values often trump interests in contemporary policymaking. This
is an especially important point for American students to understand, because
our political culture of liberalism, reinforced by popular treatments of politics—
from muckraking journalists to public-choice economists—generates an implicit
presumption by most Americans that politics and policymaking are based almost
entirely on self-interest. While this is often true, we know of no better spokesman
for the limits of interest-based models of politics than Wilson himself. He argued
in his address upon accepting the 1989 Madison Award from the American Political Science Association:

> What would the intelligent lay person make of a political science profession that can
> explain the outcomes of elections but not why people vote; can explain the influence
> of large associations but not why people join them; can explain the struggle for

material advantage but not that for ethnic advancement, religious salvation, or public morality; can explain the distribution of regulatory benefits to powerful clients but not the withdrawal of those benefits by means of deregulation. The world today is convulsed with religious, nationalistic, and ethnic movements; black people in Harlem dance in the streets when a South African man whom they have never met and who can do nothing for them is released from prison; unarmed East Europeans fight the secret police and the armed forces of their puppet governments and we say—what? That this is to be explained by people calculating the net present discounted value of their future benefits?[12]

We agree entirely with Wilson's point and have endeavored in the pathways model to underscore the conditions under which ideas, beliefs, and values can play a leading role in the politics of public policymaking.

One other influential model that seeks to highlight the importance of substantive ideas and belief systems in the policymaking process is the "advocacy coalition" model developed by Paul Sabatier and Hank Jenkins-Smith.[13] This model emphasizes the role of coalitions of policymakers, advocates, and analysts working to accomplish change within discrete policy subsystems. In doing so, the model has much in common with what we describe as the expert and pluralist pathways. Our description of macro-level policymaking in the partisan and symbolic pathways is distinctive, however. For example, emphasizing the role of advocacy coalitions can be misleading in certain cases of symbolic policymaking such as Megan's Law. The enactment of this law depended far more on the symbolic appeal of a generalized idea than on the efforts of a sustained political coalition. Indeed, one is hard pressed to find evidence of any coalition at all in the history and passage of this law or others like it.

The Dynamic Character of Contemporary Policymaking

Quite apart from the pros and cons of alternative typologies for categorizing and analyzing public policymaking, one of our principal motivations in developing the pathways framework was to capture the dynamism of contemporary policymaking. A prominent feature of most existing models is that they are relatively static. Although advances have been made in modeling the long-term evolution of public policy, we want to draw equal attention to the fluidity of the process in real time.[14]

Many public policies—and perhaps most of them—do not fit neatly into the analytical categories that we or other scholars have devised. Although we believe it is analytically useful to conceptualize four styles of policymaking arrayed across the dimensions of scale and form of political mobilization, the notion of "pathways of power" is designed as well to evoke quite a different concept: that power in Washington flows through distinctive policymaking channels that exist simultaneously and often in competition with each other.

Thus the pathways framework emphasizes the importance of looking at the policymaking system strategically, from the standpoint of actors trying to build a coalition of support for their policy proposals. The four pathways do not represent isolated and distinct political categories. They are navigated by restless, purposeful individuals who devise and modify strategies of coalition building as they seek to reach or build support for their policy objectives. While often it is accurate to characterize a particular strategy as "mostly" partisan or "chiefly" pluralist, others resist being pigeonholed so neatly. More than one may be in play simultaneously as different actors jockey to move consideration of an issue onto the terrain most favorable to them. A veteran subcommittee chairman may seek to defend his turf and contain an issue within the familiar confines of the pluralist pathway, while an upstart policy entrepreneur may offer hot-button floor amendments or engineer a media spectacle in hopes of jumping tracks onto the symbolic pathway. In short, policies are often fought over by different actors in the political system who strive to gain control over the process by routing consideration of the policy onto a pathway that maximizes their resources and position in the system. In the process, the style of politics and the distribution of influence can change dramatically.

This perspective raises a number of research questions that are explored throughout the remainder of this book. How do the different pathways function in our complex policymaking environment? Who are the central policy actors in each, and what characterizes their approach to building successful legislative coalitions? How can the four pathways be distinguished from one another in terms of the source of policy ideas, issue salience, and scope of conflict? Do the pathways tend to differ systematically in their policy outputs, such as the magnitude of policy change or its sustainability over time?

Moreover, we are interested in potential life-cycle effects in the politics of pathways policymaking. How do issues evolve over time? Once a policy is enacted along a single pathway, do future enactments or clusters of related issues, such as health care or farm policy, tend to remain in that pathway, or are subsequent or related issues likely to jump from one pathway to the next? In short, is there evidence of "pathway dependence," or could there be a pathways dialectic that favors the succession of one pathway to another over time. Finally, from a macro perspective, have there been any evolutionary effects in the frequency and use of different pathways over time? The policy literature suggests movement toward a more polarized party system over the past several decades, while other indicators suggest the rising institutionalization of experts in the national policy process. How are these institutional developments manifested in the prevalence of the various pathways over time?

In the remainder of this book we deploy a three-part methodology for exploring these research questions. First, we utilize qualitative methods to develop an empirically grounded typological analysis in chapters 2 through 5.[15] The mutually exclusive categories in our typology allow us to systematically define and analyze the characteristics and dynamics of each policy pathway. Central actors, processes, and exogenous variables influencing each pathway are described and analyzed, drawing from numerous policy cases for each, as well as the existing policy literature.

Second, in chapter 6 we employ a "medium-N" longitudinal analysis of forty-two major policies in eight different issue areas. This enables us to track policy changes over a period of thirty years, as well as to identify systematic patterns of variation between the pathways in terms of policy origins and sustainability over time. The medium-N approach allows us to combine the advantages of generalizability common to large-N studies with the fine-grained, nuanced knowledge that can be obtained from well-designed case studies. As detailed in the appendix, the forty-two policy cases reflect a two-part screening process. We have chosen what we believe to be the most important policy decisions in eight domestic policy fields since 1980 (when idea-based politics became recognizably more prominent), supplemented as needed by a stratified selection of cases that permits adequate representation of each pathway. This generates a nonrandom but systematic sample of policies reflecting the application of expert knowledge of multiple cases in eight policy arenas.

Finally, in chapters 7 through 9 we employ an issue-domain analysis of pathway dynamics. Specifically, in three major issue domains—federal budgetary process, federal tax policy, and intergovernmental policy—we utilize the pathway framework as a tool for understanding the politics and evolution of related sets of policy issues. This helps us to analyze and explain both patterns and apparent paradoxes of political behavior among seemingly related sets of public policies.

The Plan of This Book

Chapters 2 through 5 examine the individual pathways of power in more detail. Chapter 2 begins with the pluralist pathway, arguably the oldest and most fundamental route of legislative policymaking, followed by partisan policymaking in chapter 3. Chapters 4 and 5 examine the two ideational models of policymaking, expert and symbolic. Each chapter includes a brief case study illustrating the pathway in operation.

Chapter 6 focuses on policy change and evolution, as well as patterns of behavior that can be observed among our sample of forty-two legislative enactments. Chapters 7 through 9 apply the pathways framework to specific fields of public policy in order to demonstrate how the contours of public policy in each field have been shaped by contending pathways. Chapter 7 examines federal budget policy, showing how pathways can be used to understand the dynamics of federal spending and budget process reform. Chapter 8 examines federal tax policy, examining the pathway politics of tax cuts, tax expenditures, and comprehensive tax reform. Chapter 9 focuses on intergovernmental policy and how the pathways model can help explain the differing politics of federal grants, unfunded mandates, and waves of federalism reform attempts.

Finally, chapter 10 presents our conclusions and outlines several promising avenues of further research. It elaborates on some of the most compelling and complex issues of pathways competition and interaction, and it raises questions about the direction of policymaking in twenty-first-century America.

Notes

1. E. E. Schattschneider, *The Semi-Sovereign People: A Realist's View of Democracy in America* (Hinsdale, IL: Dryden, 1960), 4–5.

2. See, for example, the many editions of V. O. Key's classic text, *Politics, Parties, and Pressure Groups* (New York: Thomas Y. Crowell, 1942–1964).

3. Martha Derthick and Paul Quirk, *The Politics of Deregulation* (Washington, DC: Brookings Institution Press, 1985); Tim Conlan, Margaret Wrightson, and David Beam, *Taxing Choices: The Politics of Tax Reform* (Washington, DC: CQ Press, 1990); Larry Mead, *Government Matters: Welfare Reform in Wisconsin* (Princeton, NJ: Princeton University Press, 2004); and Daniel Béland and Alex Waddan, *The Politics of Policy Change: Welfare, Medicare, and Social Security Reform in the United States* (Washington, DC: Georgetown University Press, 2012), 175.

4. Because broad agendas such as the Great Society and the Contract with America encompassed many different programs, precise averages are difficult to ascertain.

5. The Uniting and Strengthening America by Providing Appropriate Tools Required to Intercept and Obstruct Terrorism Act of 2001 (aka the USA PATRIOT Act) passed overwhelmingly but not unanimously in the House (357-66) and nearly unanimously in the Senate (98-1).

6. See, for example, James Anderson, *Public Policymaking: An Introduction* (Chicago: Houghton Mifflin Harcourt, 1997); Thomas Dye, *Understanding Public Policy* (Englewood Cliffs, NJ: Prentice Hall, 2007); Dennis J. Palumbo, *Public Policy in America: Government in Action* (New York: Harcourt Brace, 1994); and B. Guy Peters, *American Public Policy: Promise and Performance* (Washington, DC: CQ Press, 2007).

7. John Kingdon, *Agendas, Alternatives, and Public Policies*, 2nd ed. (New York: Longman, 2003); Frank Baumgartner and Bryan Jones, *Agendas and Instability in American Politics*, 1st ed. (Chicago: University of Chicago Press, 1993); Jeffrey Pressman and Aaron Wildavsky, *Implementation: How Great Expectations in Washington Are Dashed in Oakland; Or, Why It's Amazing That Federal Programs Work at All, This Being a Saga of the Economic Development Administration as Told by Two Sympathetic Observers Who Seek to Build Morals on a Foundation of Ruined Hopes* (Berkeley: University of California Press, 1973); Daniel Mazmanian and Paul Sabatier, *Implementation and Public Policy* (Lanham, MD: University

Press of America, 1989); Paul Peterson, Barry Rabe, and Kenneth Wong, *When Federalism Works* (Washington, DC: Brookings Institution Press, 1986); Malcolm Goggin, Ann Bowman, James Lester, and Laurence O'Toole, *Implementation Theory and Practice: Toward a Third Generation* (Glenview, IL: Scott Foresman, 1990); and Paul Manna, *Collision Course: Federal Education Policy Meets State and Local Realities* (Washington, DC: CQ Press, 2011).

8. Barbara Sinclair, *Unorthodox Lawmaking: New Legislative Processes in the U.S. Congress*, 3rd ed. (Washington, DC: CQ Press, 2007).

9. Theodore Lowi, "American Business, Public Policy, Case-Studies, and Political Theory," *World Politics* 16, no. 4: 677–715.

10. James Q. Wilson, *The Politics of Regulation* (New York: Basic Books, 1980), chapter 10.

11. Conlan, Wrightson, and Beam, *Taxing Choices*; see also Deborah A. Stone, *Policy Paradox and Political Reason* (New York: Norton, 2011); and Derthick and Quirk, *Politics of Deregulation*.

12. James Q. Wilson, "The James Madison Lecture: Interests and Deliberation in the American Republic," *PS: Political Science and Politics* 23 (1990): 558–62.

13. Paul Sabatier and Hank Jenkins-Smith, *Policy Change and Learning: An Advocacy Coalition Approach* (Boulder, CO: Westview, 1993).

14. See Baumgartner and Jones, *Agendas and Instability in American Politics*; and Sabatier and Jenkins-Smith, *Policy Change and Learning*.

15. See Kenneth D. Bailey, *Typology and Taxonomies: An Introduction to Classification Techniques* (Newbury Park, CA: Sage, 1994); and Susann Kluge, "Empirically Grounded Construction of Types and Typologies in Qualitative Social Research," *Forum: Qualitative Social Research* 1, no. 1 (2000).

CHAPTER TWO

The Pluralist Pathway

- In 1971, President Richard Nixon proposed a sweeping reorganization of federal aid programs to state and local governments. Among other changes, he recommended consolidating 130 existing grant programs into six broadly defined block grants. Yet, despite heavy administration lobbying and pressure, the only block grants that passed Congress, after years of effort, were the two that enjoyed strong support from key clientele groups. The remaining four went nowhere in the face of heavy opposition from affected interest groups, who viewed them as a threat to their core policy goals and established lines of federal funding. Such groups—whether in transportation, education, rural development, or law enforcement—publicly attacked the proposals, secretly sabotaged them, and collectively organized to block them.[1]
- A 1996 bill increasing the federal minimum wage was publicly touted as a helping hand to the working poor, but it doled out significant benefits for business as well. When the bill emerged as the "last train to leave the station" before the 1996 election, lobbyists fought to get provisions favoring their clients on board. The final "minimum wage" bill included $16 billion in business tax cuts, including millions of dollars of special benefits for the newspaper industry, the life insurance industry, and individual companies such as Citicorp, Rhône-Poulenc Rorer (pharmaceuticals) and Hercules (chemicals).[2]
- In 2004, Congress passed the American Jobs Creation Act. It began when President George W. Bush, in response to an adverse international trade ruling, urged Congress to eliminate two existing tax subsidies for companies involved in international trade and replace them with a limited program of compensatory tax cuts to the affected corporations. The opportunity to pass new corporate tax legislation produced a scramble among competing business interests to advance legislation favorable to them. The final legislation provided an array of new tax preferences that far exceeded the value of the original tax subsidies, benefiting information technology companies that outsourced production overseas, multinational firms that manufactured goods in the United States, the domestic makers of archery equipment, the alcoholic beverage industry, owners of federal tobacco quotas, American racetracks and gambling interests, and others.[3]

Each of these episodes, which occurred in different decades and in different policy arenas, illustrates the influence of interest groups in the federal policymaking process. For most Americans, such influence is taken for granted. In the view of many, it is simply the way the system works—or fails to work properly. Through reports in the news media, the accusations of political reformers, and in their own casual observation of the political process, Americans have been accustomed to seeing interest groups at the very heart of American politics and policymaking. As one report by the citizen reform group Common Cause put it, "the Special Interest State is a system in which interest groups dominate the making of government policy. The interests legitimately concentrate on pursuing their own immediate—usually economic—agendas, but in so doing they pay little attention to the impact of their agendas on the nation as a whole."[4]

Appreciation for the power of group politics extends beyond the preserve of average citizens and citizen activists, however. For much of the past century, most scholars of American politics looked upon interest groups as critically important actors—often the most important actors—in the political system.[5] As the early-twentieth-century political scientist Arthur Bentley put it, the entire political process can be regarded as "the equilibration of interests, the balancing of groups." Bentley went so far as to argue that "there are no political phenomena except group phenomena." Society itself should be viewed, in his words, as "nothing more than the complex of groups that compose it." When the actions of such groups are fully analyzed, Bentley argued, "everything is stated. . . . When I say everything, I mean everything."[6]

The political science literature increasingly accepted this view of policy as the product of competing group interests after World War I. The popularity of this doctrine was increased further by the widespread acceptance of pluralist theory in the 1950s. The pluralist paradigm viewed American politics as a process of adjustment among a multiplicity of distinctive and crosscutting social, economic, and cultural groups and interests in society. Pluralists argued that this proliferation of groups and interests served to disperse political power in society and enabled virtually every organized and determined interest to gain influence over political decision making at some stage and in some arenas. The pluralist view was forcefully expounded in works such as David Truman's *The Governmental Process*, Robert Dahl's *Who Governs?*, and Charles Lindblom's *The Intelligence of Democracy.*[7] In 1952, Earl Latham spelled out the policy implications of such pluralist theory in the starkest terms: "What may be called public policy is actually the equilibrium reached in the group struggle at any given moment, and it represents a balance which the contending factions or groups constantly strive to tip in their favor. . . . The legislature referees the group struggle, ratifies the victories of the successful coalition, and records the terms of the surrenders, compromises, and conquests in the form of statutes."[8]

Few political scientists would accept such an extreme interpretation today. On the contrary, a good deal of modern scholarship has focused attention on the challenges of interest group formation and on the public policy biases that spring from differential incentives for interest mobilization.[9] The economic or exchange model of interest group politics challenges in particular the pluralist assumption that all social groups and economic interests are likely to be represented in the public policy process.[10] At the same time, much contemporary scholarship on interest group involvement in the policy process lends support to many of the classic elements of the pluralist paradigm. Among other things, neopluralist scholarship finds that a multiplicity of groups—representing a broad range of social and economic interests—tends to be involved in the policy process, that many groups focus their activities within particular policy domains or niches, and that the status quo tends to reflect the existing balance of power among contending interests, making policy change difficult and favoring marginal or incremental adjustments.[11]

Consequently, the conviction that interest groups, within a pluralistic policy environment, remain important political actors and shapers of public policies remains widespread among academics, participants in the policy process, and the general public. This chapter explores the dynamics of group-centered, pluralist policymaking in detail. It identifies the major participants and processes involved in the pluralist pathway, and it explores the evolution of pluralistic policymaking and its role in contemporary politics.

Origins of Pluralist Policymaking

The conceptualization of American society as a multiplicity of contending groups and interests, and concern that these narrow special interests might play too great a role in the design of public policy, are as old as the American republic. As James Madison wrote in *Federalist No. 10*:

> The friend of popular governments never finds himself so much alarmed for their character and fate, as when he contemplates their propensity to this dangerous vice [of faction]. By a faction, I understand a number of citizens . . . who are united and actuated by some common impulse of passion, or of interest, adverse to . . . the permanent and aggregate interests of the community. . . . The latent causes of faction are . . . sown in the nature of man; . . . a zeal for different opinions concerning religion, concerning government, and many other points. . . . But the most common and durable source of factions has been the various and unequal distribution of property. . . . A landed interest, a manufacturing interest, a mercantile interest, a moneyed interest, with many lesser interests, grow up of necessity in civilized nations.[12]

Madison justified the extended sphere of the new national Constitution as a device for controlling the "mischiefs of faction." Yet, since his time, the involvement of special interests in the policy process has continued and been magnified by the structural, cultural, and institutional features of American government and society.

As Madison suggested, the foundation of factions and interest groups lay in the social and economic pluralism of a heterogeneous society. Economic development and modernization create increasingly specialized economic activities and particularistic interests. What in Madison's day could be called "a manufacturing interest" is now viewed as a complex array of competing and overlapping producers: automobile manufacturers, computer makers, software developers, electricity generators, chemical producers, telecommunications companies, and so forth. This proliferation of distinctive economic interests encourages the formation of new organizations and associations to represent the new interests in the formation of public policy. V. O Key described the process in a classic postwar text on American politics: "The great proliferation of organized groups came in the twentieth century. Our complex array of private organizations sprang from changes in the social order that created [new] political needs. . . . Chief among these changes were the diversities introduced by specialization in the production and distribution of goods and services."[13]

Economic modernization and specialization also create dense networks of interdependent relationships between different interests, and these interdependencies tend to increase the demand for governmental services and regulation and the potential for conflict over their scope and design. To quote Key again: "This multiplication of specialized segments of society threw upon government an enormous new burden. Specialization has as its corollary interdependence; independence has as its consequence friction. . . . Increased specialization almost inevitable means increased governmental intervention to control relations among groups."[14]

In the United States, moreover, the multiplicity of interests created by economic modernization was supplemented by extraordinary social pluralism. Waves of immigration over the course of American history produced a bewildering diversity of ethnic communities, each with its own language, religious practices, and cultural heritage.[15]

American culture and the structure of its institutions accentuated the tendency to express social and economic diversity through the formation of organized groups. As Alexis de Tocqueville observed in the 1830s, Americans showed a cultural propensity to form groups and associations of all types: "In no country in the world has the principle of association been more successfully used, or applied to a greater multitude of objects, than in America. . . . Associations are established to promote the public safety, commerce, industry, morality, and religion.

There is no end which the human will despairs of attaining through the combined power of individuals united into a society.""[16]

De Tocqueville's observations have found considerable support in modern scholarship, which has also emphasized the supportive role played by our political institutions. As Theda Skocpol has argued, "communities of all sizes established voluntary groups with remarkable simultaneity [in the nineteenth century]. . . . Politics, religious freedom, and republican government lie at the heart of the answer."[17]

To be sure, contemporary trends in civic engagement are hotly debated today, with some scholars pointing to decline and others to continued activism.[18] Yet Americans' cultural tendency to join associations and support groups that are active in civic affairs continues to be strong by comparative standards.[19] When it comes to public policy, moreover, there has been a dramatic increase in the number of interest groups in Washington and seeking to influence federal policy in the period after 1960.[20] New public policy, in turn, begets new groups and more lobbying.[21]

Finally, the structure of American political institutions has promoted interest-group involvement in the public policy process. Both the decentralization of American government and the separation-of-powers system have enhanced the ability of special interests to gain access to public decision making and to influence public policy. Groups and interests that are unable to gain presidential recognition of, or support for, their policy position can turn to one of two chambers of Congress, semiautonomous executive agencies, the judiciary, or one or several of the fifty states. As Allan J. Cigler and Burdett Loomis note in their classic treatment of group politics, "the decentralized political power structure in the United States allows important decisions to be made at the national, state, or local levels. Even within governmental levels, there are multiple points of access. For example, business-related policies such as taxes are acted upon at each level and interest groups may affect these policies in the legislative, executive, or judicial arenas."[22]

This multiplicity of access points can help groups find a receptive audience for their ideas and a forum for possible experimentation and demonstration of a policy's merits. On the other hand, a multiplicity of access points can also be construed as a multiplicity of veto points.[23] A majority in a single legislative committee may be all that is required to block a policy from becoming law. Thus interest groups have a particular incentive to organize and become legislatively active in a separation-of-powers system because the fragmentation of the policymaking process heightens their potential for at least negative influence. It is no accident, for example, that political science texts and commentators once routinely referred to interest groups as "veto groups." It is emblematic of one way in which political institutions in the United States have promoted pluralist policymaking.

The Dynamics of Pluralist Policymaking

At the national level, pluralist policymaking has several distinctive characteristics. As discussed above, it is characterized by a multiplicity of both actors and decision-making arenas. Each of these decision-making arenas enjoys a degree of autonomy, giving rise to a segmented policymaking environment. Politicians' traditional role in this system is to act as brokers for and between the multiple contending interests, seeking political compromises that will enable them to piece together majority coalitions. These majorities can be built up through a variety of coalition-building techniques, but the most common pluralistic techniques are bundling, bargaining, and reciprocity.[24]

Segmented Policymaking

The pluralist paradigm gives rise to a fragmented and dispersed policymaking environment. This characteristic has long been recognized in the policy literature. As early as 1939, Ernest Griffith described what he called "whirlpools or centers of activity focusing on particular problems," composed of "legislators, administrators, lobbyists, scholars."[25] Subsequent studies in the 1950s, 1960s, and 1970s variously referred to this same phenomenon as policy "subsystems," "subgovernments," "iron triangles," and "issue networks."[26] Although the names and connotations given to the phenomenon vary—especially in the degree of policymaking autonomy and insulation granted to these policy subsystems—the underlying premise in all of these analyses holds much in common. Baumgartner and his colleagues observe that

> despite the sharp differences between the subgovernments of old and contemporary
> issue networks, there is continuity too. . . . Heclo describes an issue network as
> a "shared knowledge group," but he failed to acknowledge that this was true of
> subgovernments as well. The participants in a subgovernment were experts in their
> policy area, and this eased negotiations. Another point of similarity is that, just like
> subgovernments, today's policy communities push Congress toward equilibrium. That
> is, the very structure of policy communities, which include key congressional policy
> makers and staffers as well as lobbyists, works in favor of the status quo.[27]

All agree as well that there is a substantial degree of segmentation in the making of public policy in Washington. J. Leiper Freeman wrote in the mid-1960s: "Policy making is often left to essentially subordinate units of the Administration and Congress. Similarly, the parties often leave issue politics to interest groups. In this sense, such sub-units of the political setting, encouraged by diffused power and functional specialization of political expertise, tend to enjoy a relatively wide range of autonomy. Policy tends to be 'farmed out.'"[28]

The reason is simple. There are far too many policy issues—many of which are technically or contextually complex—with too many real and potential ramifications, for any one set of political decision makers to master. A handful of executive and legislative leaders would simply be unable to handle them all, physically or intellectually. As Frank Baumgartner, Jeffrey Berry, Marie Hojnacki, David Kimball, and Beth Leech note, "a government institution, like Congress, has limited capacity and can process only some of what is brought before it. Despite its enormous resources, many issues languish while Congress focuses on a small subset of problems."[29] Consequently, many issues must be, as Freeman put it, "farmed out" to smaller subunits.

For example, on a single fairly typical day in May 2003, various House and Senate committees and subcommittees in Congress held thirty-one separate hearings, meetings, and legislative markups on issues as diverse as stem cell research, broadband access in rural areas, the regulation of equity markets, highway safety, postwar reconstruction in Iraq, and federal crop insurance programs.[30] During the entire 112th Congress (2011 to 2012), 10,439 bills were introduced in Congress and 1,744 total measures were adopted.[31]

Because a small set of leaders, or the entire Congress acting collectively, is unable to adequately address all the policy issues before the government at any one point in time, issues are winnowed in the agenda-setting process, and a small subset of issues that are deemed to be of greatest or most immediate importance are elevated to the level of leadership and collective decision making.[32] The vast majority of policy decisions, which are mostly considered to be of less general importance, are decided by smaller sets of decision makers within one of the policy subsystems or issue networks described above because they are relatively routine, incremental, technically complex, or thought to affect fewer people or interests. These decisions may be made by career government officials or congressional subcommittee members or their staffs, or even by interest group representatives who are asked to propose specific language to deal with an issue. Their decisions are not technically final. They are typically subject to review and revision by upper-level executive branch officials or by the full Congress and/or by the courts. But in fact, in the vast majority of cases, they are the final decisions rendered by the formal institutions of government, at least for a given time. Priorities are made and attention goes elsewhere.

None of this means, moreover, that such policy decisions are unimportant. Taken collectively, they constitute the bulk of what government does on a day-to-day basis. Moreover, individual decisions are often vitally important to those most directly affected by them. Even issues of apparently modest significance may ultimately prove to be of great significance to the broader community, although their importance may not always be recognized in the short term.

For example, in the 1940s and 1950s federal policy governing the use and regulation of powerful new classes of chemical pesticides and herbicides, such as DDT, was dominated by "those perceiving direct and largely economic policy stakes in the use of pesticides."[33] According to John Blodgett, the fundamental aim of those who formulated and pushed the Federal Insecticide, Fungicide, and Rodenticide Act (FIFRA) of 1947 was to "protect the farmer from adulterated, ineffectual, or unsafe products," thus promoting the new chemical age in agriculture by ensuring confidence in the safety and efficacy of the new products.[34] Christopher Bosso described the policy process in FIFRA as "classic clientele politics": "The pesticides issue was not salient to any but those directly benefitting from pesticides, and the scope of debate was severely limited to those most intimately involved. Furthermore, relationships among these players were clearly accommodative in tone. The configuration of central players also approximates a classic 'iron triangle,' with decision making among congressional committee members, mid-level USDA bureaucrats, and those representing a few, well-organized interests—all sharing a relatively common perspective on the issue."[35]

As the scope of government expanded in the postwar era and similar communities of specialized interest proliferated across government, segmentation became more pervasive. Federal departments were likened to "holding companies"—diverse agglomerations of semiautonomous fiefdoms, each with unique political histories, customs, clienteles, and concerns, rather than unified hierarchies for coordinated policy decision making and implementation.[36] Congressional committees and subcommittees are also capable of acting as semiautonomous centers of policymaking, whose members typically self-select committee assignments to correlate with individual policy interests and constituency needs.[37] The result is a legislative architecture in which farm state members dominate the agriculture committees (and, within agriculture, southerners rule over cotton and peanuts, Plains states members seek jurisdiction over feed grains, etc.), urban members fill the Committee on Banking, members whose states or districts contain large military bases and defense contractors dominate the armed services committees, and so forth.[38]

Segmented Policymaking in Action

The often predictable results have been seen countless times when Congress confronts presidential attempts to reorganize federal programs and agencies and upsets these established clusters of policy relationships. Congress's reactions to President Richard M. Nixon's "special revenue sharing" proposals in the early

1970s illustrate the point. The president's proposal to combine numerous highway and transit grants into a single transportation revenue–sharing program attracted so much opposition that his bill was never even introduced in the House. Not a single Republican would sponsor President Nixon's proposal. When no Senate Republican stepped forward to introduce the bill in that chamber either, the chairman of the Senate Commerce Committee, Sen. Warren Magnuson (D-WA), agreed to introduce it "by request," a legislative courtesy signifying no endorsement of the bill. Once introduced in the Senate, it was soon forgotten. No hearings were ever held and no action was ever taken.

This frosty response to a high-profile presidential initiative reflected vigorous opposition to the plan from interest groups involved in trucking and road construction. The president of the American Trucking Association called the plan "an elaborate device to arrive at a simple unjust end—a large scale raid on the federal Highway Trust Fund," and he declared the truckers' "revulsion" toward this aim.[39] The American Road Builders Association was strongly opposed for the same reason. Likewise, an official of the Air Transport Association said the plan posed a "great danger" to the airline industry.[40] In addition to strong interest group opposition, members of Congress had their own reasons to oppose the plan. Many feared losing control over the allocation of transportation projects if existing programs were devolved to the states in the form of a broad formula-based block grant. Undersecretary of Transportation James Boggs declared: "Our categorical programs are nearer and dearer to Congressmen's hearts than any others. They are the porkiest of the pork, and Congress guards them very jealously."[41]

The close ties that build up within policy subsystems, particularly relationships among program specialists in the agency, Congress, and associated interest groups, could also be seen in the case of education revenue sharing. According to one congressional staffer, many agency bureaucrats considered Nixon's proposals to be "a means to abolish their jobs," since, once programs were consolidated, fewer federal personnel would be needed to administer them.[42] Consequently, both interest group and congressional staff reported receiving timely inside information on administration planning, which they were able to use to undermine the president's proposals. One education lobbyist said: "I never knew what my mail would bring. I would receive . . . the schedule of a secret meeting or conference about the battle front. There would be no name. These people were unsung heroes, providing us with all sorts of information." On Capitol Hill a staffer for the Senate Education Subcommittee agreed that leaks were rampant: "I saw those [reform] proposals before [the agency head] did."[43]

Even the Nixon block grants that were adopted support the pluralist model, since they occurred in areas where the policy communities involved were already supportive of program consolidation and simplification: community development and job training. The Democratic general counsel of the House Urban

Affairs Subcommittee was working on block grant legislation even before Nixon announced his proposals, and the lobbyist for the National League of Cities even claimed that "it almost passed without the administration. There was never any concerted opposition to the block grant, if you stripped away the politics of Nixon's New Federalism. Most of the opposition came from the stinko placed on [the block grant idea] by Nixon."[44]

Multiplicity of Actors

As noted earlier, one of the defining characteristics of pluralism is the notion that large numbers of different groups and individuals are actively or potentially involved in the policymaking process. This emphasis on a multiplicity of policy actors is one of the chief features that distinguishes pluralist theory from alternative conceptions of class politics and elite theory.[45]

This multiplicity of actors is abundantly evident in the modern interest group environment in the nation's capital. Precise numbers of groups and lobbyists are difficult to ascertain for many reasons. Individual groups come and go, they move, they expand and contract their political activities, and so on. There is no central registry of groups or lobbyists. Moreover, definitions of what constitutes an interest group vary. Should the Catholic Church be considered an interest group? If so, does it constitute a single group, or is it more accurately considered a collection of many different groups with varied policy and group interests, such as the Council of American Bishops, the Maryknoll nuns, Catholic Charities, and so forth? Should political action committees be considered separate entities or merely the financing arms of affiliated organizations like the National Association of Home Builders or National Education Association?

In short, there are many complexities and ambiguities, but some things are unmistakably clear. First, thousands of interest groups are based in and around the nation's capital. By one count, there are nearly 750 advocacy groups in the health care field alone.[46] Such groups are supplemented by thousands of independent lobbyists and law firms representing clients both in and out of Washington. In addition, the numbers of both groups and lobbyists have grown dramatically in recent decades. One study found that 40 percent of all groups with offices in the Washington area in 1980 had been founded after 1960.[47] Similarly, the number of political action committees grew 49 percent between 1980 and 1998, from 2,551 to 3,798.[48]

The diversity of interest groups has increased over time, as well. The 1960s and 1970s saw a tremendous expansion in the types of interests represented in Washington. By all accounts there was a dramatic increase in the numbers of groups representing the socially and economically disadvantaged, broad interests such as consumer advocacy, and the ideologically committed.[49] According to one 1986 study, for example, 57 percent of all citizens groups represented in Washington, 46 percent of all civil rights groups, 51 percent of all social welfare groups, and 43 percent of groups representing special demographic groups such as the elderly and women were founded during the 1970s.[50] These percentages were far higher than those for trade and professional associations, for example, which tended to have far longer life spans.

Data indicating that there are many more groups and a wider array of interests represented in Washington today tend to support the pluralist presumption that all major interests will have some effective degree of access to the political system. Moreover, the tremendous proliferation in the numbers of groups suggests that the relative influence of any single interest group has diminished in this new environment.[51] Nevertheless, the pluralist pathway does not assume that all interests will be equally represented or that all interest groups will be influential in all policy domains. Far from it. As Kay Lehman Schlozman and John T. Tierney have argued, the chorus of lobbyists sings with a business and upper-class accent.[52] This is because different interests can have very different incentives to organize, and different groups will confront varying levels of resource constraints. Mancur Olson has argued, for example, that groups organized around specific material interests and able to deliver tangible material benefits to their members enjoy significant advantages in forming and maintaining themselves. Groups unable to provide specialized benefits to their members face a "free rider" problem that makes it challenging to organize in the first place and difficult to persist and retain their members.[53] Consequently, some groups, such as the National Association of Realtors, AARP, and the National Education Association, can afford to employ teams of full-time lobbyists by drawing upon the financial and political resources provided by thousands of dues-paying members in every state, while others limp along with few members, few resources, and little staff.[54]

Once organized, moreover, rationally behaving groups will have to make priorities about the policy areas and specific issues on which to concentrate. Some will have stronger incentives to influence policy and decision making in one area; others will focus elsewhere. Environmental groups are drawn to certain agencies and committees in Congress, banks and investment firms to others, and doctors and health insurance groups to a different set still.

But such uneven representation does not mean that other voices can't be heard or are simply frozen out. Former Senate majority leader Bob Dole once famously observed that "there aren't any poor PACs, or Food Stamps PACs, or Nutrition PACs or Medicare PACs."[55] Yet the federal government spends hundreds of billions of dollars annually on Medicare, food stamps, child nutrition, and programs for the poor. In part this is because medical, elderly, farm, and social welfare groups benefit from these programs and *do* lobby strenuously for them. In part it also reflects the behavior of foundations and wealthy benefactors, who have proved to be important sources of financial support for many public-interest, consumer, and environmental groups that lack selective benefits with which to attract dues-paying members.[56] It also reflects the fact that political support for certain programs benefiting poor or disadvantaged clients can be marshaled without reliance on campaign contributions and heavy lobbying.[57] Convincing arguments can be made by individual scholars and researchers, as well as representatives of major interest groups. Finally, and most important from a pathways perspective, many policies are adopted through the partisan, expert, and symbolic pathways, making them far less dependent in their initial stages on group representation in the pluralist realm. Thus the earned income tax credit originated and grew in the expert and partisan pathways, beginning with economists' gradual consensus in favor of a negative income tax and expanding significantly in omnibus budget deals during the Clinton administration.

Partly for this reason, the old image of the impregnable iron triangle has been largely replaced by the more permeable concept of the "issue network." As Hugh Heclo explained it, "the iron triangle concept is not so much wrong as it is disastrously incomplete. . . . Looking for the closed triangles of control, we tend to miss the fairly open networks of people that increasingly impinge upon government."[58] In addition, the environment of a policy issue can be dramatically altered by external events, the activities of new policy actors, or simply the passage of time and technological change. All of these can act to suddenly lift an issue out of its familiar policy environment and place it onto a partisan or symbolic policy pathway.

For example, FIFRA's client-oriented policy framework—which had remained remarkably stable for almost twenty years—was altered abruptly in the 1960s and 1970s when growing evidence of serious environmental and health concerns recast the context of pesticide policy, introduced new actors into the decision-making process, and dramatically changed the dynamics of policymaking in this domain. During the late 1960s, Rachel Carson—an individual author and scientist who wrote a devastatingly effective book on the effects of DDT on birds and wildlife—probably had more influence on the direction of environmental policy in this field than any of the major chemical firms or interest groups in the area. In essence, pesticides policy jumped tracks from pluralist to symbolic policymaking during this period and proceeded along a very different policymaking pathway.

Even when policies remain within the cozy confines of pluralist policymaking, this does not mean that everyone within a policy subsystem stands in agreement on major issues. Such consensus is implied by the iron triangle metaphor, and it was a relatively accurate depiction of the agricultural policy domain in the 1940s and 1950s described by Bosso. Other early studies of the policy subsystems in water policy and Native American affairs suggested comparably insulated and consensual domains.[59] Yet many other policy communities and subsystems are frequently rocked by brutal conflicts between contending interest groups. The railroad and trucking industries routinely battle over surface transportation subsidies and regulations.[60] The banking, securities, and insurance industries brawl over financial services access and regulations, telecom companies fight with each other and with the cable industry over telecommunications issues, and so forth.[61] Consequently, James Q. Wilson has argued that in regulatory policy, "interest group politics" are defined by group conflict between narrow, organized bands of winners and losers.[62] Theodore Lowi similarly characterized regulatory politics as the setting for interest group conflict.[63]

As a result, research in the pluralist paradigm has generally assigned politicians the role of policy brokers, rather than powerful, autonomous leaders or policy entrepreneurs. The broker's irreplaceable role is to mitigate and manage intergroup conflicts and to search for compromises that all—or a comfortable majority of—conflicting parties can accept. Dahl and Lindblom explain: "The politician is a key figure . . . for the politician is, above all, the man whose career depends upon successful negotiation of bargains. To win office, he must negotiate electoral alliances. To satisfy his electoral alliance he must negotiate alliances with other legislators and with administrators, for his control depends upon negotiation. . . . And if the politician frequently neglects the substantive issues of policy in order to maintain, restore, or strengthen his alliances, this is a part of the price a bargaining society must pay for a modicum of social peace."[64]

Similarly, Latham described legislators as "referees [of] the group struggle." The "principal function" of legislatures and other official policymaking bodies was, he wrote, "to provide various levels of compromise in the writing of the rules. . . . Every statute tends to represent compromise because the very process of accommodating conflicts of group interest is one of deliberation and consent. The legislative vote on any issue thus tends to represent . . . the balance of power among the contending groups at the moment of voting."[65]

Coalition Building

For those policymakers whose goal is to prevent legislative action from taking place, the fragmentation of pluralistic politics can be a great advantage. As Frank Baumgartner and his colleagues say in *Lobbying and Policy Change*, "defenders of the status quo usually win in Washington."[66] Oftentimes blocking a proposal at a single legislative checkpoint is all that is needed to derail it. Positive initiatives are another matter. A highly pluralistic environment poses substantial challenges for policymakers who are seeking to initiate new programs or policies or who wish to make major changes in existing ones. Reversing the obstructionist scenario, positive initiatives require building a series of majority—or supermajority— coalitions in both the House and Senate. New enactments typically must clear one or more authorizing committees (and subcommittees) in each chamber, the House Rules Committee, the majority party leadership in each chamber, a House-Senate conference committee if the issue involves major legislation, and, finally, the president's signature. If the policy requires discretionary spending in order to be implemented, then the entire process is repeated a second time through the appropriations process. It is no wonder that a prominent book on the legislative politics of federal aid to education in the early 1960s was titled *The Obstacle Course on Capitol Hill.*[67]

Different coalition-building strategies are available to cope with these obstacles in the pluralist pathway, but they all tend to favor relatively modest, noncontroversial, and incremental initiatives. One classic strategy is reciprocity. Reciprocity can be as simple as the naked exchange of support for wholly unrelated initiatives: "You scratch my back, and I'll scratch yours." As simple as it appears on the surface, little legislation would ever be produced if this were the principal mechanism of coalition building, however.[68] The transaction costs involved in engineering multiple second- and third-order trades among hundreds of legislators in order to navigate the complex and lengthy legislative process outlined above are simply too high.

A much more efficient form of reciprocity is based upon deference to specialized expertise. In a segmented, pluralistic policy environment, centers of specialized knowledge are inevitably created. A decision rule to defer to the judgments reached in other committees or subcommittees in the expectation that similar deference will be shown to your (sub)committee's decisions was a hallmark of congressional behavior in the pluralist epoch of the 1950s.[69] Unlike logrolling, deference to expertise assumes that a concept of public interest underlies the reciprocal behavior, rather than a mere exchange in pursuit of independent selfish interests. It is premised on a belief that "if you knew all that we know, you would reach the same decision that we have." Like logrolling, however, deferential reciprocity breaks down if the decisions are highly controversial. Decision makers lose their willingness to blindly trust and defer to others if their core goals or beliefs appear to be challenged by the exchange.

Bundling is another classic technique of pluralistic coalition building. The underlying premise behind bundling is similar to that of reciprocity—in which policymakers defer to each other's related or unrelated proposals—but the time sequence is altered. Reciprocity typically involves a sequential process in which reciprocal actions occur asynchronously, whereas bundling builds coalitions by including all the reciprocal deals into one large package. It says, in essence, "You can't get yours unless you accept ours." Sen. Daniel Patrick Moynihan remarked during a Senate Public Works Committee debate over an economic stimulus package in the early 1980s, "There will come a time in this body when either all members in this body will see our interests served or else none of us will."[70]

This bundling strategy is commonly used in making distributive policy such as public works, appropriations (which often results in omnibus spending bills), and tax legislation. As projects are added for more members, the supporting coalition grows as well. This was a factor behind the explosion of legislative earmarking that took place in Congress during the 1990s and early 2000s. Earmarks direct the expenditure of funds to specific, often tangible projects, such as the improvement of a particular highway interchange or bridge-repair project, and thus are often championed by members of Congress seeking to assure priority attention to projects in their districts. For example, the 2005 federal highway bill—the Safe, Accountable, Flexible, Efficient Transportation Equity Act: A Legacy for Users (SAFETEA-LU)—contained more than six thousand earmarks.[71] In social policy, Barbara Sinclair described an example of bundling as a technique of coalition building in her analysis of the politics of President Bill Clinton's national service legislation in 1993: "Chairman [William] Ford (D, MI) offered his 'nondivisible en bloc amendments' and after a short debate they were adopted on a voice vote. Included were some modifications he had worked out with members of the committee minority and number of the amendments proposed by House members not on the committee. By rolling these noncontroversial changes into a package, Ford saved floor time and bolstered support for the bill; the members whose amendments were incorporated in the bill had, as a result, an added incentive to support the legislation."[72]

As the national service legislation case suggests, bundling is most effective when the measures included are of low or modest controversy. Spending a few dollars more or a few dollars less for Department of Agriculture programs or adding several new bridges and overpasses to a federal transportation bill is unlikely to be viewed as a deal breaker by other members of Congress. If the added projects result in more votes for the whole package, so much the better. Consequently, federal appropriations for agencies that deliver tangible programs and projects to large numbers of congressional districts have been found to fare better in times of budgetary cutbacks than do bills that fund indivisible public services.[73] In contrast, passage of the appropriations bill for the Departments of Labor and Health and Human Services is typically held up until the very end of the budget year because of disputes over highly controversial issues that do not lend themselves to "split-the-difference" decision making, such as federal funding of stem cell research or of abortions and family planning.

Incremental Outcomes

The outcomes of pluralist policymaking tend to be incremental in character. Incrementalism emphasizes that most new policies, most of the time, involve only small departures from their predecessors. In part incrementalism results from human cognitive limitations: No individual policymaker can rationally evaluate all the alternative means to multitudinous ends they might favor. As Lindblom put it, "decision makers do not attempt a comprehensive survey and evaluation. In the examination of the consequences of possible alternative policies they do not investigate all of them, but only, at most, those with respect to which the policies are thought to differ. . . . Attention is focused on increments by which social states and policies differ."[74] Small, simple changes—various marginal adjustments—are more readily understood.

Incrementalism also has a strong political rationale. It is normally the path of least resistance where there is a pluralistic distribution of political power. Since the existing allocation of benefits should conform to the allocation of political influence—and typically have been spread widely in a "distributive" pattern—any attempt to revise policies dramatically could be expected to spark heated opposition. To quote Lindblom again: "Policy making in many political systems is typically, though not always, a part of a political process in which the only feasible political change is that which changes social states only by relatively small steps. Hence, decision makers typically consider, among all the alternative policies that they might be imagined to consider, only those relatively few alternatives that represent small or incremental changes from existing policies."[75]

The classic example of a complex, pluralistic policymaking system producing incremental policy outcomes is provided by Aaron Wildavsky's analysis of budgetary politics. Wildavsky found a "near universal practice of incrementalism in budgeting," not only in the United States, but in other developed representative democracies as well.[76] Consistent with Lindblom's analysis, the reasons are both psychological and political: The budget is too complex to permit a comprehensive consideration of all budgetary alternatives, and established interests, agencies, and clienteles make large changes in spending—especially cutbacks—extremely difficult. In Wildavsky's words: "The largest determining factor of the size and content of this year's budget is last year's budget. . . . Long-range spending commitments have been made. . . . There are mandatory programs, such as veterans' pensions, whose expenses must be met. Powerful political support makes the inclusion of other activities inevitable. Budgeting, therefore, is incremental, not comprehensive."[77]

More recent scholarship has largely reinforced Wildavsky's findings. Bryan Jones and Frank Baumgartner examined budgetary changes across sixty-two spending categories over a fifty-two-year period, from 1948 to 2000. They found that a pattern of small spending adjustments, both up and down, characterized the vast majority—though not all—of the cases. Specifically they suggest that hyper-incrementalism might even be the most apt description of their overall findings: "For students of policy change, this distribution has a very important meaning. Many, many programs grew or were cut very modestly—that is, *incrementalism* was the order of the day for most programs most of the time. *Hyperincremental-ism* might be a more accurate description of what happened in the vast majority of cases."[78]

Federal tax policy provides another example of the pluralist-incremental model of policymaking, at least until the 1980s. The federal income tax grew enormously in fiscal importance and complexity after 1913, with the most significant revisions associated with periods of crisis: wartime emergencies and the Great Depression. But these important but relatively brief and infrequent moments set aside, the tax system did not change in basic structure, and proposals to alter it fundamentally seldom advanced very far. John Witte correctly described the standard pattern as beginning with "marginal adjustments to the existing structure. . . . Applicable rates, bracket changes, exemption levels, standard deductions, depreciation percentages, investment credits, depletion allowances—the list of changes that can be accomplished by simply altering a number is very long. . . . Tax laws can also be easily and marginally altered by expanding or contracting eligible groups, actions, industries, commodities, or financial circumstances."[79] Furthermore, the creation and expansion of tax preferences, which is among the more obvious "incremental" additions and changes, has traditionally been attributed to the influence of organized beneficiary groups.[80]

Although incrementalism describes many—perhaps most—policy outcomes, it does not explain all of them.[81] Large, abrupt policy changes are adopted, even in fields such as tax and budget policy that have been held to epitomize incrementalism. The Tax Reform Act of 1986, President George W. Bush's $1.3 trillion tax cut package in 2001, several large budget reconciliation packages adopted in the 1980s and 1990s—all defy the incrementalist label and reflect very different styles of politics. A model that cannot accommodate the most important policy initiatives is clearly inadequate to explain policymaking in general, and the subsequent chapters of this book will examine alternative pathways of federal policymaking. Before doing so, however, this chapter concludes with a brief, illustrative case study of pluralist policymaking in Washington. This capsule explores a case of successful incremental policy change in the pluralist tradition: congressional adoption of the FIRE Act in 2001.

The FIRE Act: A Case Study of Pluralist Policymaking

The enactment of the Firefighter Investment and Response (FIRE) Act of 2000 illustrates many of the characteristics of pluralistic policymaking in the legislative arena.[82] It began as an act of policy entrepreneurship by an interested member of Congress, accumulated support from affected interest groups and other members of Congress, and eventually wound a complex course through the legislative process, launching a new level of federal support for a predominantly local government function.

The immediate precursor of the FIRE Act was introduced by Rep. William J. Pascrell (D-NJ) in 1998.[83] As a former mayor, Pascrell had experienced difficulties funding local fire services, so his bill—the 21st Century Fire and Public Safety Act—called for $5 billion in federal grants to be awarded to local fire departments to provide funding for hiring, equipment, and training. In design it was patterned after the Clinton administration's community policing initiative (the Community Oriented Policing Services program) and thus illustrates one driver of federal program growth: The successful enactment of programs in one area provides a template and justification for comparable programs in other "equally deserving" fields.

Pascrell was a freshman member of the minority party in Congress, and his bill died in committee with little fanfare. But the legislation attracted attention from the major firefighting interest groups, such as the International Association of Fire Fighters (IAFF) and the International Association of Fire Chiefs (IAFC), which helped connect Pascrell to the existing policy network for fire-related issues. They also helped secure a Republican cosponsor for a revised bill in the 106th Congress, Rep. Curt Weldon (R-PA), cochair of the Congressional Fire Caucus.[84] With interest group backing, Weldon and Pascrell introduced the FIRE Act on March 17, 1999. Apart from the new name, this bill was otherwise little changed from the original Pascrell bill, but it now attracted sixty-eight cosponsors and grassroots lobbying support from multiple firefighting organizations.

The new bill stalled in the House Science Committee's Subcommittee on Basic Research—primarily because its conservative chairman, Rep. James Sensenbrenner, opposed the cost and precedent of an expanded federal role in this area. Consequently, Rep. Weldon joined with Rep. Steny Hoyer (D-MD), Democratic cochair of the Congressional Fire Caucus, to offer a smaller ($100 million) proposal for grants to fire departments and funding for research as a floor amendment to the $12.7 billion 2000 Emergency Supplemental Appropriations Act (H.R. 3908) on March 29, 2000. Bolstered by active lobbying by firefighters across the country, the Weldon-Hoyer proposal passed easily by a vote of 386-28, but it was subsequently stripped out in conference committee.[85]

A more successful amendment strategy was also followed in the Senate, where Sen. Chris Dodd (D-CT) succeeded in amending the Defense Authorization Act for Fiscal Year 2001 (S. 2549) with a version of the FIRE Act that would provide $3.1 billion in fire support grants over six years. The amendment received strong backing from the chairman of the Senate Armed Services Committee Sen. John Warner (R-VA), as well as the ranking minority member Sen. Carl Levin (D-MI), and passed by a vote of 97-3.[86] Opposition again arose in conference committee, but Sen. John McCain (R-AZ) succeeded in gaining support within the conference for a two-year, $400 million program of fire department grants ($100 million for fiscal year 2001 and $300 million for FY 2002). Support for the program was enhanced by a provision requiring that no single grant could exceed $750,000—thus solidifying political support by spreading the funds broadly.[87]

Thus, over the course of two years, members from both parties allied with special-interest groups to provide the first major program of federal assistance for fire services. This program was funded alongside other comparable categorical programs aiding first responders, fire research, and fire services—a process that accelerated after the terrorist attacks of September 11, 2001. By 2003, the Government Accountability Office calculated that there were twenty-one categorical grants aiding first responders, funding such activities as training, equipment, planning, and exercises. The funds were funneled to different state and local actors, with some grants passing through states, others targeted to high-priority metropolitan regions, and still others providing assistance directly to local fire or police departments.

Notes

1. Timothy Conlan, *New Federalism: Intergovernmental Reform from Nixon to Reagan* (Washington, DC: Brookings Institution Press, 1988).

2. Julie Kosterlitz, "A Bounty for Business," *National Journal* (October 26, 1996): 2289–92.

3. Ken Godwin, Scott H. Ainsworth, and Erik Godwin, *Lobbying and Policymaking: The Public Pursuit of Private Interests* (Washington, DC: CQ Press, 2013), 60–63.

4. Quoted in *Interest Group Politics*, 3rd ed., Allan J. Cigler and Burdett Loomis, eds. (Washington, DC: CQ Press, 1990), 3.

5. For an extended discussion of this, see Frank Baumgartner and Beth Leech, *Basic Interests: The Importance of Groups in Politics and in Political Science* (Princeton, NJ: Princeton University Press, 1998), chapter 3.

6. Arthur Bentley, *The Process of Government*, cited in James Q. Wilson, *Political Organizations* (New York: Basic Books, 1973), 5–6.

7. David B. Truman, *The Governmental Process: Political Interests and Public Opinion* (New York: Knopf, 1951); Robert A. Dahl, *Who Governs? Democracy and Power in an American City* (New Haven, CT: Yale University Press, 1961); and Charles E. Lindblom, *The Intelligence of Democracy* (New York: Free Press, 1965).

8. Earl Latham, "The Group Basis of Politics: Notes for a Theory," *American Political Science Review* 46 (June 1952): 390.

9. See, for example, Mancur Olson, *The Logic of Collective Action* (Cambridge, MA: Harvard University Press, 1965); William C. Mitchell and Michael C. Munger, "Economic Models of Interest Groups: An Introductory Survey," *American Journal of Political Science* 35 (1991): 512–46; and Kay Lehman Schlozman, "What Accent the Heavenly Chorus? Political Equality and the American Pressure System," *Journal of Politics* 46 (1984): 1006–32. For a more comprehensive review and critique of this literature, see Baumgartner and Leech, *Ba-*

sic Interests, and David Lowery and Virginia Gray, "A Neopluralist Perspective on Research on Organized Interests," *Political Research Quarterly* 57, no. 1 (March 2004): 163–75.

10. Godwin, Ainsworth, and Godwin, *Lobbying and Policymaking*, 30–36.

11. See, for example, Frank Baumgartner, Jeffrey Berry, Marie Hojnacki, David Kimball, and Beth Leech, *Lobbying and Policy Change: Who Wins, Who Loses, and Why* (Chicago: University of Chicago Press, 2009); Andrew S. McFarland, *Neopluralism: The Evolution of Political Process Theory* (Lawrence: University Press of Kansas, 2004); and Virginia Gray and David Lowery, *The Population Ecology of Interest Representation: Lobbying Communities in the American States* (Ann Arbor: University of Michigan Press, 1996).

12. *The Federalist* (New York: Modern Library, 1961), 53–56.

13. V. O. Key Jr., *Politics, Parties, and Pressure Groups*, 5th ed. (New York: Thomas Crowell, 1964), 128.

14. Ibid., 128–29.

15. Theda Skocpol, "How Americans Became Civic," in *Civic Engagement in American Democracy*, Theda Skocpol and Morris P. Fiorina, eds. (Washington, DC: Brookings Institution Press, 1999), 27–47.

16. Alexis de Tocqueville, *Democracy in America*, Richard Heffner, ed. (New York: Mentor Books, 1984), 95.

17. Skocpol, "How Americans Became Civic," 42.

18. See, for example, Robert D. Putnam, *Bowling Alone: The Collapse and Revival of American Community* (New York: Simon & Schuster, 2000), and Marcela Ridlen Ray, *The Changing and Unchanging Face of U.S. Civil Society* (Piscataway, NJ: Transaction, 2002).

19. Seymour Martin Lipset, *American Exceptionalism: A Double-Edged Sword* (New York: Norton, 1996).

20. See Kay Lehman Schlozman and John T. Tierney, *Organized Interests and American Democracy* (New York: Harper & Row, 1986); Jack L. Walker Jr., *Mobilizing Interest Groups in America: Patrons, Professions, and Social Movements* (Ann Arbor: University of Michigan Press, 1991); and Theda Skocpol, "Advocates without Members: The Recent Transformation of American Civic Life," in *Civic Engagement in American Democracy*, Skocpol and Fiorina, eds.

21. Anthony J. Nownes, *Interest Groups in American Politics: Pressure and Power*, 2nd ed. (New York: Routledge, 2013), chapter 2.

22. Cigler and Loomis, *Interest Group Politics*, 6. See also David Truman, *The Governmental Process*, 2nd ed. (New York: Knopf, 1971), 507.

23. Baumgartner et al., *Lobbying and Policy Change*, 267.

24. Robert A. Dahl and Charles E. Lindblom, *Politics, Economics, and Welfare* (New York: Harper & Row, 1953).

25. Ernest S. Griffith, *The Impasse of Democracy: A Study of the Modern Government in Action* (New York: Harrison-Hilton Books, 1939), 182, quoted in Ernest S. Griffith, *Congress: Its Contemporary Role*, 3rd ed. (New York: New York University Press, 1961), 50–51.

26. See, for example, J. Leiper Freeman, *The Political Process: Executive Bureau–Legislative Committee Relations*, 1st ed. (New York: Random House, 1955); Douglass Cater, *Power in Washington: A Critical Look to Today's Struggle to Govern in the Nation's Capital* (New York: Vintage Books, 1964); Harold Seidman, *Politics, Position, and Power: The Dynamics of Federal Organization* (New York: Oxford University Press, 1970); Randall Ripley and Grace Franklin, *Congress, the Bureaucracy, and Public Policy* (Homewood, IL: Dorsey Press, 1976); and Hugh Heclo, "Issue Networks and the Executive Establishment," in *New American Political System*, Anthony King, ed. (Washington, DC: AEI Press, 1978).

27. Baumgartner et al., *Lobbying and Policy Change*, 65.

28. J. Leiper Freeman, *The Political Process: Executive Bureau–Legislative Committee Relations*, rev. ed. (New York: Random House, 1965), 22.

29. Baumgartner et al., *Lobbying and Policy Change*, 33.

30. "Today in Congress," *Washington Post*, May 22, 2003, www.washingtonpost.com /wp-dyn/articles/A23123-2003May21.html, accessed June 3, 2003.

31. Office of the Clerk, US House of Representatives, Résumé of Congressional Activity, http://library.clerk.house.gov/resume.aspx.

32. See Kingdon, *Agendas, Alternatives, and Public Policies*, 2nd ed., and Baumgartner and Jones, *Agendas and Instability in American Politics*.

33. Christopher J. Bosso, *Pesticides and Politics: The Life Cycle of a Public Issue* (Pittsburgh, PA: University of Pittsburgh Press, 1987), 60.

34. John Blodgett, "Pesticides: Regulation of an Evolving Technology," in *The Legislation of Product Safety*, Samuel S. Epstein and Richard D. Grady, eds. (Cambridge, MA: MIT Press, 1974), 3:208, quoted in ibid., 58.

35. Bosso, *Pesticides and Politics*, 59.

36. For an excellent account of this process, see Seidman, *Politics, Position, and Power*.

37. Kenneth A. Shepsle and Barry R. Weingast, "Structure-Induced Equilibrium and Legislative Choice," *Public Choice* 37, no. 3 (1981): 503–19.

38. For a description of this same process within appropriations subcommittees, see E. Scott Adler, "Constituency Characteristics and the 'Guardian' Model of Appropriations Subcommittees, 1959–1998," *American Political Science Review* 44 (January 2000): 104–14.

39. Quoted in Jonathan Cottin, "Wide-Ranging Interests Oppose Administration's Proposals," *National Journal*, April 10, 1971, 773.

40. Ibid.

41. Quoted in Timothy Clark, John Iglehart, and William Lilly III, "Drive to Return Power to Local Governments Faces Hill Struggle over Control of Programs," *National Journal*, December 16, 1972, 1928.

42. Timothy Conlan, *From New Federalism to Devolution: Twenty-Five Years of Intergovernmental Reform* (Washington, DC: Brookings Institution Press, 1998), 39.

43. Ibid., 43.

44. Ibid., 63–64.

45. See Robert A. Dahl, "A Critique of the Ruling Elite Model," *American Political Science Review* 52 (June 1958): 463–69, and John F. Manley, "Neo-Pluralism: A Class Analysis of Pluralism I and Pluralism II," *American Political Science Review* 77 (June 1983): 368–83.

46. Roger H. Davidson, Walter J. Oleszek, and Frances E. Lee, *Congress and Its Members*, 12th ed. (Washington, DC: CQ Press, 2010), 392.

47. Schlozman and Tierney, *Organized Interests and American Democracy*, 75.

48. US Census Bureau, *Statistical Abstract of the United States, 1999* (Washington, DC: Government Printing Office, 1999), 305.

49. Nownes, *Interest Groups in American Politics*, 26–28. Although it is not our focus here, similar trends have been reported at the state level as well. Whereas in the past some state governments were viewed as virtual puppets of a few powerful mining or industrial interests, groups such as teachers, environmentalists, and health care providers now rank among the more effective lobbying groups in many states, although the overall group environment remains weighted toward traditional business and professional groups in most states. See Clive S. Thomas and Ronald J. Hrebenar, "Interest Groups in the States," in *Politics in the American States*, 7th ed., Virginia Gray, Russell Hansen, and Herbert Jacob, eds. (Washington, DC: CQ Press, 1999), 133–36.

50. Schlozman and Tierney, *Organized Interests and American Democracy*, 75.

51. Robert H. Salisbury, "The Paradox of Interest Groups in Washington: More Groups, Less Clout," in *New American Political System*, King, ed., 203–30.

52. Schlozman and Tierney, *Organized Interests and American Democracy*, 87. See also Schattschneider, *Semi-Sovereign People*.

53. Olson, *Logic of Collective Action*.

54. Such small organizations include many business groups and small trade associations, as well as citizen groups and those representing poor clients. See Bob Garfield, "The Sultan of Slag," *Washington Post Magazine*, June 28, 1992, 18–22, 28–30.

55. Quoted in Schlozman and Tierney, *Organized Interests and American Democracy*, 251.

56. See Walker, *Mobilizing Interest Groups in America*.

57. Baumgartner et al., *Lobbying and Policy Change*, chapter 10.

58. Heclo, "Issue Networks and the Executive Establishment," 88.

59. Freeman, *Political Process*, and Arthur Maass, *Muddy Waters: The Armies Engineers and the Nation's Rivers* (Cambridge, MA: Harvard University Press, 1951).

60. Andrew Hacker, "Pressure Politics in Pennsylvania: The Truckers v. the Railroads," in *The Uses of Power*, Alan F. Westin, ed. (New York: Harcourt Brace & World, 1962).

61. For a classic analysis of the relationship between group conflict and congressional policymaking, see David E. Price, "Policy Making in Congressional Committees: The Impact of 'Environmental' Factors," *American Political Science Review* 72 (June 1978): 548–74.

62. James Q. Wilson, "The Politics of Regulation," in *Politics of Regulation*, Wilson, ed., 368.

63. Lowi, "American Business, Public Policy," 777–93.

64. Dahl and Lindblom, *Politics, Economics, and Welfare*, 333.

65. Latham, "Group Basis of Politics," 390.

66. Baumgartner et al., *Lobbying and Policy Change*, 239.

67. Robert Bendiner, *The Obstacle Course on Capitol Hill* (New York: McGraw-Hill, 1964).

68. Stephen Kelman, *Making Public Policy: A Hopeful View of American Government* (New York: Basic Books, 1987), chapter 3.

69. Donald Matthews, "Folkways of the U.S. Senate," *American Political Science Review* 53 (December 1959): 1064–89.

70. Quoted in unit 4, "Congress in Committee," in *Congress: We the People* (Santa Barbara, CA: Annenberg/CPB Project, 1983), videocassette (VHS).

71. Ronald D. Utt, *A Primer on Lobbyists, Earmarks, and Congressional Reform: Backgrounder 1924* (Washington, DC: Heritage Foundation 2006), 1.

72. Sinclair, *Unorthodox Lawmaking*, 104.

73. D. Roderick Kiewiet and Mathew D. McCubbins, "Congressional Appropriations and the Electoral Connection," *The Journal of Politics* 47, no. 1 (February 1985): 59–82.

74. Charles E. Lindblom, *The Intelligence of Democracy: Decision Making through Partisan Mutual Adjustment* (New York: Free Press, 1965), 144.

75. Ibid.

76. Aaron Wildavsky, *The Politics of the Budgetary Process*, 2nd ed. (Boston: Little, Brown, 1974), 216.

77. Ibid.

78. Bryan D. Jones and Frank R. Baumgartner, *The Politics of Attention: How Government Prioritizes Problems* (Chicago: University of Chicago Press, 2005), 111.

79. John F. Witte, *The Politics and Development of the Federal Income Tax* (Madison: University of Wisconsin Press, 1985), 244–45. For a recent analysis of the politics of tax expenditures, see Christopher Howard, *The Hidden Welfare State: Tax Expenditures and Social Policy in the United States* (Princeton, NJ: Princeton University Press, 1997).

80. Stanley S. Surrey, "The Congress and the Tax Lobbyist: How Special Tax Provisions Get Enacted," *Harvard Law Review* 70 (May 1957): 1145–82.

81. Jones and Baumgartner, *Politics of Attention*.

82. Major assistance with this case study was provided by Edward M. Clark.

83. H.R. 4229, 21st Century Fire and Public Safety Act.

84. "What's the Secret?," Bill Manning, *Fire Engineering* 152, no. 1 (January 1999): 4.

85. "Landslide Vote Approves Landmark $100m Step Forward for Fire Service Funding Includes $80 Million Directly to Fire and Rescue Departments in Matching Grants, 'Foot in the Door' for FIRE Bill," Firehouse.Com News, www.firehouse.com, March 29, 2000.

86. Lon Slepicka and Dave J. Iannone, "Senate Moves on $3.1 Billion in Fire Funds: Phased-In Version of FIRE Act Added to Defense Appropriation Still Has High Hurdles to Clear," Firehouse.Com News, www.firehouse.com, July 13, 2000.

87. Lon Slepicka, "Committee Moves on Modified FIRE Act," Firehouse.Com News, www.firehouse.com, August 20, 2000.

CHAPTER THREE

The Partisan Pathway

- In one of the crowning achievements of Lyndon Johnson's Great Society, Congress passed the Elementary and Secondary Education Act (ESEA) in 1965. This act launched a new era in education policy, doubling the federal share of spending for elementary and secondary schooling and shifting the locus of policy innovation from the states to Washington, DC. Programs to aid disadvantaged students, provide instructional materials, promote educational reform, support education research, and modernize state education agencies were all established by ESEA. Most remarkable of all was that this unprecedented program of federal aid to education, which had been debated, fought over, and bottled up in Congress for nearly a hundred years, was passed by the House and Senate in just three months. Such speed reflected the Democrats' landslide victories in the 1964 elections and President Johnson's mastery of the legislative process, which enabled a policy breakthrough that had been thwarted throughout the Truman, Eisenhower, and Kennedy administrations. Enacted along with ESEA in the 89th Congress were other signature features of the Great Society, including Medicare, Medicaid, Model Cities, and the Voting Rights Act.[1]
- In 1981, ESEA and other federal domestic programs were subjected to unprecedented budgetary cutbacks as part of President Ronald Reagan's program to cut federal income taxes and roll back the welfare state. In what the House Republican leader hailed as a partial "repeal . . . of the Great Society," Congress adopted legislation that reduced income taxes by 23 percent, cut corporate taxes by $128 billion in the first two years, decreased federal domestic outlays by $131 billion over four years, terminated sixty-two programs, and consolidated seventy-seven others into block grants. This "budgetary blitzkrieg" was made possible by the Republican Party's 1980 election victories, which wrested control of the White House and Senate away from the Democrats and gave conservatives effective control of the House.[2]
- On March 23, 2010, President Barack Obama signed the Patient Protection and Affordable Care Act, which extended health insurance coverage to millions of uninsured Americans. This law marked the culmination of decades of Democratic efforts, beginning under Harry Truman in the 1940s, to establish

a program of universal national health insurance. Thus President Obama's success at passing the Affordable Care Act was considered a major political victory, particularly in light of Bill Clinton's crushing failure to do so in 1994. However, it was also a highly partisan accomplishment. Every Democratic senator voted for the legislation, while virtually every Republican opposed it in both the House and Senate. Upon passage, provisions of the bill, such as the requirement that all individuals carry health insurance, rallied conservative opposition and contributed to Republican victories in the 2010 midterm elections.

From the perspective of the 112th Congress in 2011 and 2012, partisanship in Congress appeared to be synonymous with gridlock. Ideologically unified political parties, which are prepared to challenge one another aggressively in hopes of gaining electoral advantage, pose special obstacles to enacting legislation in our separation-of-powers system, which by design makes policy change a challenge under the best of circumstances. And yet, as the three vignettes opening this chapter show, parties can also serve as vehicles for overcoming inertia and fragmentation in our political system. They can be the means for building coalitions within Congress and for establishing networks that bridge the barriers between separated institutions sharing governmental powers.

Although the programs of the Great Society, the "Reagan revolution," and "Obamacare" constituted very different sets of public policies under three different presidents in different decades, they shared a common approach to nonincremental policy change. Whereas pluralist policymaking is characterized by low visibility, incremental policy change, or no change at all, these three cases demonstrate that, under certain circumstances, major changes in policy substance and direction are possible in our Madisonian framework of government. These cases illustrate as well the traditional route to nonincremental change in our system of separated powers: the partisan pathway. This chapter examines that pathway in depth, analyzing its origins, dynamics, and patterns of policy outputs.

The Foundations of Partisan Policymaking

Pluralism may represent the single most influential perspective on American politics and policymaking, but an alternative stream of research and interpretation has long emphasized the importance of sharper, deeper, and broader social cleavages as organizing features of American politics.[3] These cleavages—especially region and social class—gain effective expression in politics and policymaking through their intersection with political parties.

Like pluralism, this perspective has had both empirical and normative dimensions. Empirically the partisan perspective has stressed the importance of political parties as actors that enable representation of broad social interests, that nominate candidates and mobilize voters for elections, and that organize the government for consideration and adoption of public policy. During the mid-twentieth century especially, the partisan perspective also conveyed a strong normative dimension, promising an alternative method for organizing politics for those dissatisfied with the inertia and incrementalism of political pluralism.[4] Advocates of the "responsible parties" perspective looked to the tradition of class-based parties in Europe and the progressive tradition in American history and politics and found pluralism wanting.

Political parties in the United States never met the standard of ideologically coherent, class-based, disciplined parties that the reformers sought. American parties traditionally have been broad umbrellas of diverse views and interests, united far more by electoral pragmatism than programmatic purity. They have been, in effect, agents of pluralism as much as or more than they were ever the vanguards of class politics. Accordingly, serious but controversial attempts have been made at times to alter the American party system in the reformers' image. The most notable case occurred in the early 1950s, led by a number of leading political scientists.[5]

Although this formal effort was largely unsuccessful, social and political changes have made American parties more ideologically homogeneous and polarized since the 1980s. Such polarization and homogeneity have provided the foundation for what some political scientists have called "conditional party government."[6] Conditional party government theory holds that Congress can behave—and increasingly has behaved—in ways that approach the responsible parties model when party members in Congress share strong and widespread agreement on major policy issues and empower party leaders to advance that consensus. Long before the contemporary era of partisan polarization, however, the partisan pathway consistently provided an important, if only intermittently successful, technique of nonincremental policymaking.

The Functions of Political Parties

Political parties are prominent features of every modern representative democracy. They appeared with the earliest republican governments of the modern era and are now considered to be indispensable attributes of successful democracy.[7] Various factors appear to be responsible for this strong correlation between political parties and representative democracy.

First, parties often provide the crucial link between public opinion and public policy. Assuring that citizens' views are reflected in the decisions of government is the very foundation of representative government. Accurately transmitting those views is a critical component of this process, and this role falls in large part to parties. There is much scholarly debate about how well parties perform this role in modern American society: whether they give adequate choices to voters, whether citizens are sufficiently aware of the parties' positions on issues to vote accordingly, and so forth.[8] But parties clearly play an important role in the representational system.

In cementing the link between policymakers and the electorate, parties also play an important psychological and social role for citizens in functioning democracies. For inattentive voters and citizens, parties help reduce a range of complex issues and policy positions into a limited number of simple—and often simplistic—guidelines for choices. For example, "Democrats stand for the 'little guy,'" and "Republicans believe in strong defense and smaller government." In developing countries, this simplification role can be so strong that illiterate voters need only recognize their party's symbol on the ballot in order to express a broad policy preference in the electoral process. In the United States, party identification's role as an information-management device was established in some of the earliest empirical research on voting behavior, in the 1950s.[9] At the other end of the participation spectrum, parties also provide an effective tool for communicating with and mobilizing more active and attentive citizens.

While providing choices and a structure for mobilization, political parties also serve a sociological function. Especially in two-party systems, political parties allow for the expression of broad social divisions in society. Whereas the pluralist perspective emphasizes the role of multiple overlapping interest groups in the organization of society, political parties can be viewed as aggregators of interests that can be used to express broader and deeper social cleavages—typically social and economic class divisions but also, potentially, religious, regional, ethnic, and language groupings. If the party system expresses deep economic and cultural divisions too energetically, it may amplify such cleavages in a destructive manner. But in two-party systems especially, the breadth of the parties needed to effectively compete for office can serve to regulate social cleavages, bridging differences between many smaller groups and forcing them into broad alliances for electoral success.

This suggests that institutional rules play an important factor in structuring the role that parties play within a political and policymaking system.[10] Electoral rules can strongly influence whether a country has a one-party, two-party, or multiparty system. For example, "Duverger's law" holds that an electoral system with single-member legislative districts and plurality elections (in which candidates with the most votes win, even if they gain less than a majority) will systematically favor a two-party system, as in the United States. Electoral systems with proportional representation will strongly encourage multiparty political systems.

Finally and most important for public policy, parties organize government following elections. In Congress, majority parties shape legislative rules (especially in the House), structure committee jurisdictions and assign leadership positions, control business on the floor, and set the overall policy agenda. In the executive branch, partisan considerations vie with policy expertise in the appointment of top agency officials.

The Dynamics of Partisan Policymaking in the United States

At the national level, partisan policymaking in the United States has several distinctive characteristics. In contrast to the highly segmented, publicly opaque pattern of pluralistic policymaking, the partisan form of policymaking tends to emerge on a limited number of more visible, often highly conflictual issues, which are capable of uniting the different factions comprising each major party. The lead actors in this style of policymaking are typically the president and party leaders in Congress, who possess the resources needed to build and maintain the large, majoritarian coalitions on which partisan policymaking depends. Such majoritarian coalitions place a high premium on party discipline, especially for the majority party. If the majority party maintains its unity and controls both chambers of Congress, as well as the White House, it may quickly pass a broad policy agenda that has been years in the making. Such unity rarely lasts long, however, so that partisan policymaking historically has been an intermittent approach to public policy formation.

Presidents, Parties, and Congressional Leadership

The partisan pathway is often closely linked with presidential policymaking. Many of the most noteworthy cases of partisan policymaking have been characterized by strong presidents pushing their policy agendas through Congress, often in the wake of an election that strengthened the president's position in Congress and seemed to provide a "mandate" to enact the policies in question. Franklin Roosevelt's New Deal, Lyndon Johnson's Great Society programs, Ronald Reagan's New Federalism, and Barack Obama's economic agenda all fit this pattern of presidential leadership, just as the vignettes highlighted in the opening to this chapter indicated.

The association between presidential leadership and partisan policymaking is so strong that we have sometimes referred to this paradigm as the "presidential-majoritarian" model of policymaking.[11] However, as the Republican Congress demonstrated in the 1990s and as occurred commonly in the late nineteenth century, congressional party leaders are also capable of successfully employing partisan policymaking.[12] This is especially true in the large and more centralized House of Representatives, whose rules and traditions favor disciplined party leadership.

Presidential leadership in partisan policymaking combines the president's dual roles as party leader and "chief legislator." This latter role is a development principally of the twentieth century, as Congress and the public looked increasingly to the president to set the national policy agenda and provide political leadership for the country. In the nineteenth century, presidents often stood formally aloof from both the electoral and legislative processes. Electorally they were expected to maintain the dispassionate appearance of citizens called to office by their sense of civic duty, hoping not to be seen as overly ambitious or soiled by the grubby work of electoral politics. In the ideal, candidates would run "front porch" campaigns, discussing issues publicly with reporters and other visitors while leaving it to surrogates to give speeches and stump for votes across the country.[13] In legislative affairs Congress also expected presidents to keep their distance. Nineteenth-century presidents generally met their annual State of the Union responsibilities by sending a printed message to Capitol Hill, and congressional leaders jealously guarded the legislative process from excessive interference from the executive branch. As David Brady has observed, House leaders "resented attempts by the presidency to become involved in the business of passing legislation."[14]

The president's legislative role changed dramatically during the twentieth century and with it the dynamics of partisan policymaking. Expansion of the president's role began in earnest with the administration of Theodore Roosevelt, who was both an active campaigner and policy promoter. It expanded further under Woodrow Wilson, who believed strongly in executive leadership in policymaking and who brought new Democratic majorities to Congress on the coattails of his election. James Sundquist observes that "Wilson seized the opportunity by presenting his legislative recommendations in person before joint sessions of the Congress. . . . To achieve the legislative objectives a wholly new pattern of intimate congressional-executive relations was developed. The details of the New Freedom—tariff legislation, the Federal Reserve Act, antitrust legislation, and other measures—were worked out in joint meetings, some held at the White House, others on Capitol Hill. The press began to write for the first time about 'administration bills.'"[15]

This role was cemented and institutionalized during the New Deal in the 1930s. Beginning with the proposals of Roosevelt's first "hundred days," the White House and executive agencies took the initiative for developing legislative priorities, strategies, and language. As Sundquist writes, "from that time on, Congress expected and accepted presidential leadership in setting its direction and defining its agenda."[16] This role had become so well established by the 1950s that when President Eisenhower's administration failed to exert sufficient legislative leadership in 1953, administration officials were lectured by a congressional committee chairman: "Don't expect us to start from scratch on what you people want. That's not the way we do things here; *you* draft the bills and *we* work them over."[17] The following year, the administration delivered a package of sixty-five bills, which Richard Neustadt describes as "a comprehensive and co-ordinated inventory of the nation's current legislative needs, reflecting the President's own judgments, choices, and priorities in every major area of Federal action . . . in order to give Congress an agenda, Republicans a platform, and voters a yardstick for 1954."[18]

In the contemporary era, the president's leading role as agenda setter and legislative initiator is taken for granted. The conventional wisdom that "the president proposes and Congress disposes" has been empirically supported in John Kingdon's research on agenda setting. As he found in his interviews with the Washington policymaking community, "the president can single handedly set the agendas, not only of people in the executive branch but also of people in Congress and outside of government. . . . No other single actor in the political system has quite the capability of the president to set agendas in given policy areas for all who deal with those policies."[19]

Modern presidential leadership is especially important for major issues that cut across legislative jurisdictions in Congress and involve broad collective interests. Moreover, to help the president perform this role as "chief legislator," there has been a steady increase in the president's institutional capacity to perform legislative functions, from expansions of White House and Executive Office staff to increased budgetary and legislative clearance authority. The twentieth century saw an almost unbroken expansion of presidential authority and institutional resources for policymaking in order to cope with a much larger government, expanded presidential responsibilities, and the tremendous increases in issue complexity over this period.

Taken alone, presidential involvement is not a sufficient or even necessary condition of partisan policymaking, however. Many presidential and administration initiatives may be relatively uncontroversial, or they may generate bipartisan or cross-partisan coalitions. For example, President Bill Clinton was able to construct a majority coalition in Congress to implement the North American Free Trade Agreement (NAFTA) in 1993 in spite of, not because of, the partisan pathway. Although the measure passed the House of Representatives on a party-line vote, his margin of victory was provided by Republican votes; a majority of House Democrats opposed the president's position. In contrast, partisan presidential policymaking requires the president to use his position as party leader to mobilize a majoritarian coalition in Congress.

Therefore, the president's role as leader of his party is often a critical element in partisan politics. Like the role of chief legislator, this role has also evolved through the twentieth century. The national political parties traditionally served as temporary coalitions of much stronger state and local party organizations. Their function was to come together every four years to nominate and elect a president. But legislatively active presidents discovered that their success as policymakers often depended on their strength as party leader. Bold policy initiatives require strong support from party members in Congress. Although legislative success can sometimes be accomplished on a bipartisan basis—even for major initiatives such as NAFTA or the Marshall Plan after World War II—the most direct path is through a unified party coalition if one's party controls the Congress.

That a president's control over policy direction is often tied to his party's fortunes in Congress was a lesson that Clinton discovered to his dismay after the Republican Party gained control of the House and Senate in the midterm elections of 1994. Suddenly the nation's policy agenda was dramatically altered, and he was forced to publicly protest his continued "relevance" to the policy process.[20] The federal policy agenda shifted just as dramatically for Barack Obama following the 2010 midterm elections. A president who had won adoption of landmark stimulus, health care, and financial reform legislation in the 111th Congress almost entirely on the basis of partisan coalitions confronted an agenda dominated by deficit reduction efforts led by Republican House members.

For their part, members of Congress who belong to the president's party often see their electoral fates tied closely to that of the president and tend to be far more willing to vote with the administration on controversial legislation. One congressman trying to rally support for Franklin Roosevelt's early legislative initiatives put it, "Your president . . . *without whose leadership possibly some of us could not be here*, has called you to arms." Another said, "My people sent me here because they had faith in the President of the United States; and I am here to support that faith."[21]

These members were speaking in the wake of FDR's landslide victory in 1932, in which he brought Democratic majorities to Congress for the first time in twelve years. They held him responsible for their party's victory if not their own election. In many cases, however, Roosevelt ran ahead of many members of Congress in their own districts, illustrating his popularity with the voters. A similar situation—with similar policy consequences—occurred in 1981. In this case, it was a Republican, President Ronald Reagan, who was credited with his party's victory in the 1980 elections. In addition, many southern Democrats were aware that Reagan received more votes in their districts than they did and thus were strongly inclined to support the president's policy agenda in Congress. Only when the president's popularity declined in the face of a steep economic recession in 1982 did conservative Democrats return reliably to their party's fold in the Congress. As will be seen below, this pattern is typical of critical elections, which often are associated with partisan realignments and which tend to produce the most dramatic breakthroughs in public policy. Historically, scholars have found that major, nonincremental breakthroughs in public policy are related most often to a party realignment and the election of a dynamic new president.[22]

Although the twentieth-century pattern has been for presidents to provide effective majority party leadership in Congress, this need not always be the case. As the Republican leadership in Congress in the 1990s demonstrated, and as was also the case one hundred years earlier in the 1890s, party leaders in Congress can construct effective majorities and use the techniques of the partisan pathway without—or even in opposition to—the White House. When Republicans gained control of the House and Senate in 1994, they had many of the attributes of a presidential party following a critical election. The party scored major gains in both chambers, picking up fifty-four new seats in the House and eight in the Senate. House Republicans also had a well-defined party program, the Contract with America, for which it claimed an electoral mandate, and effective party leaders who were capable of building coalitions of unified party loyalists. As a result, congressional Republicans were able to establish a remarkable legislative record in 1995, sending major pieces of legislation to the president's desk largely on the basis of narrow party-line votes. Similarly, large Republican gains in the 2010 midterm elections propelled issues such as deficit reduction to the center of Washington policy debates.

If the United States had a parliamentary system, such dramatic swings in party control over the House of Representatives might have produced the sought after "Republican revolution" in 1995 or enactment of the right-wing "Tea Party" agenda in 2011. But the failure to control the White House and/or the Senate in a separation-of-powers system means that positive use of the partisan pathway—to enact dramatic changes in public policy—is severely limited. In both the 104th and 112th Congresses, many conservative policy initiatives failed to pass the Senate or died at the hands of a presidential veto, including the conversion of Medicaid into a block grant, abolition of the Departments of Education, Energy, and Commerce, the creation of Medicare vouchers, and the termination of Obamacare.

On the other hand, a unified opposition party in control of the House, or even with a sizeable minority in the Senate, can thwart a president's initiatives in the partisan pathway. The end result may be gridlock, or the conflict may prompt cross-partisan negotiations and compromise. Thus while the most audacious House Republican legislation was vetoed by President Clinton in 1995, proposals for welfare reform and farm subsidy reforms became law in 1996 after successful negotiations between the president and Congress. Similarly, in 2011, House Republicans were able to gain administration acceptance of gradually declining caps on discretionary federal spending that would bring such spending to postwar lows by 2022. All told, such cases illustrate the limits, as well as the potential, of the partisan pathway from both directions of Pennsylvania Avenue.

Coalition Building in the Partisan Pathway

Coalition building in the partisan pathway is explicitly majoritarian. Policies favored by the leadership and majority of the largest party in Congress—or party coalition in multiparty systems—are heavily favored in the legislative process.

"All" that is required of the majority in this style of policymaking is to hold to-gether sufficiently to work its will through each stage of the legislative process. In the early 1980s when Republicans had long been in the minority in the House of Representatives, former House minority leader Bob Michel (R-IL) said, "Just once I'd like to wake up in the morning knowing that I had the votes in Committee, in the Rules Committee, and on the floor, that all I had to do was keep my members together and we would win."[23] In fact, Leader Michel was surprisingly successful in 1981 when Democratic failures to hold together allowed Republicans to cobble together a working majority of Republicans and conservative Democrats on key budget and tax legislation. In essence, conservatives had established a working majority in Congress in the early 1980s. In general, however, the partisan pathway is engaged when the majority party uses its numbers to push through major leg-islative adoptions.

This process of majority party coalition building is not as simple as it sounds. Because of the frequent need for supermajorities in the Senate and the risks of defections at any stage of the arduous bicameral process, successful use of the partisan pathway has often relied on large party majorities in both chambers of Congress. As Paul Light found in his study of presidents' legislative success, larger majorities of the president's party in Congress are strongly correlated with presi-dential success in enacting major policy initiatives.[24] Moreover, coalition mainte-nance is complicated by the breadth and diversity of the parties' regional, racial, ethnic, social, and economic factions. By one formulation, there are nine current major political subgroups in United States, from free-market "enterprisers" and social conservatives on the "right" to conservative Democrats and true liberals on the "left."[25] Because we do not have a multiparty parliamentary system, these nine types must be shoehorned together to form two major political parties, leaving much room for internal disagreements.[26]

In recent years both parties have experienced greater cohesion in Congress thanks to the regional sorting of parties in our system. Each party became more ideologically homogeneous as a result. Party unity scores for the two major parties in Congress, which measure the cohesion of party members on contested votes, have risen markedly since the early 1970s.[27] This new cohesiveness has been en-hanced by a variety of developments, including party-building efforts to enhance the recruitment, training, and funding of new members of Congress, strength-ened leadership resources in the House, greater homogeneity of congressional dis-tricts, and erosion of the moderate wing of both political parties. As a result, the conditions required for "conditional party government" have increasingly been met.[28] One of the consequences of greater homogeneity is that parties can achieve victories even when the majority party's margin in Congress is slim. This was evi-dent in the Republican-led House of Representatives from 2001 to 2005 when, despite narrow majorities, major tax cuts, Medicare expansion, and energy legislation were all passed with extraordinary levels of party unity

Thus while political party has long been the single best predictor of congressional roll call votes, its predictive value has increased over time. Research has found greater ideological coherence among members of Congress of the same party, especially on core partisan issues. Indeed, ideological coherence and distinctiveness tends to be much stronger among members of Congress and party activists than among party identifiers among the public at large.[29]

The parties have exerted new forms of control over candidates and members at a time when political campaigning has become more entrepreneurial and sophisticated. Party leadership some sixty years ago was purchased through old-style party organizations that selected candidates and provided armies of party volunteers to support their chosen member's election, solidifying the obligation of the sitting member of Congress to his or her party organization, typically controlled by state and local officials.

Today most members of Congress no longer feel that they owe their election principally to the efforts of party organizations. Contemporary members tend to be self-selected, self-directed, and self-financed (in that they raise the bulk of their own campaign funds). They purchase the electoral services they need, whether they be polling, advertising, consultants, or mailing lists, with their own campaign funds. In turn, modern parties have morphed into superpolitical consulting organizations, assisting candidates with fundraising (including funds raised by "taxing" more senior and bankable members of Congress), training, strategy, and services. Though it no longer equals old-style political "armies," such party and leadership services can help develop and maintain party unity in Congress. Many members of the Republican class of 1994 felt they owed their election in part to the efforts of Rep. Newt Gingrich (GA) and other party leaders. Former Republican House majority leader Rep. Tom DeLay (TX) also inspired member loyalty for his fundraising efforts.

The growth of polarized homogeneous parties in fact has served to elevate the role of leadership as more dominant policymakers and agenda setters for Congress, particularly in the House. Supplanting the time-honored roles of committee chairs, each party is governed by a strong caucus that delegates significant power to its leaders to define and brand the party's positions on the issues of the day. In an era where the president has become ever more visible in using the bully pulpit to appeal to the public, more homogeneous congressional parties need strong leaders to vie with the president in defining the problems and solutions facing the nation.

These and other recent congressional party leaders also possess—and have strengthened—internal congressional leverage for coalition building. House party leaders have exerted greater control over committee assignments, greater control over committee leadership selection (including violating seniority to select more reliable chairmen), expansive use of earmarks and other perks, and very aggressive use of new rules that maximize preferred legislative options. Together these tools can make the difference on close votes, as in the case of the 2004 Medicare prescription drug program. In this instance a major legislative priority of President George W. Bush and the Republican leadership failed on its initial floor vote in the House. However, the bill eventually won passage through a combination of leadership arm-twisting, promises of favorable future action on members' legislative priorities, electoral threats, and manipulation of House rules (including keeping the vote open for three hours rather than the customary fifteen minutes).[30] Together these tactics won just enough Republican votes to pass highly controversial legislation over united Democratic opposition.

Finally, in addition to the tools and tactics mentioned above, party legislative leaders can assume the role of policy and political brokers and assume responsibility for crafting a legislative compromise. In the 1990 reauthorization of the Clean Air Act, for example, Democratic leaders ascertained that the bill crafted in committee was too liberal to pass the Senate. Accordingly, Democratic majority leader George Mitchell (ME) assumed responsibility for crafting a new, compromise bill, spending months meeting with members, interest group representatives, and administration officials in his office off the Senate floor. Eventually a new bill was constructed with enough support to pass the Senate as a whole.[31] Similarly the American Recovery and Reinvestment Act of 2009—aka the $800 billion Obama stimulus program—was crafted with heavy involvement from the office of Speaker Nancy Pelosi (D-CA). Recent budget negotiations with the president have also been led by the leadership of the House and Senate, not by the chairs of budget or tax committees.

Outcomes and Elections

The partisan pathway is the traditional route for adopting large-scale policy changes in the American system in part because of its connection with election politics and results. In fact, most of the major bursts of nonincremental policy change in American history—the Republican nationalism of the 1860s, the New Deal of the 1930s, the Great Society of the 1960s, Reagan's New Federalism in the early 1980s, and the Obama health, stimulus, and financial regulatory reforms of 2009 and 2010—were advanced by employing the partisan pathway.

In each of these cases, the successful use of the partisan pathway was preceded by an important election that altered the partisan balance of power in Congress and changed perceptions of power in Washington and the country at large. Abraham Lincoln's election led southern states to secede and their Democratic representatives to leave Congress. This enabled the remaining Republican majorities to enact their broad agenda of national legislation: the Morrill Land-Grant College Act, the Homestead Act, creation of a federal Department of Agriculture, the transcontinental railroad, the Civil War amendments to the Constitution, the first federal income tax, and more.

Roosevelt's landslide victory in 1932 brought Democrats to power in both the House and Senate. Democratic majorities were subsequently expanded in 1934 and 1936, enabling the adoption of a panoply of New Deal legislation, including Social Security and unemployment insurance, banking and securities regulation, public works programs, the Tennessee Valley Authority, agricultural price supports, and rural electrification. This agenda established Democrats as the majority party for the next forty years.

The seeds of demise for this Democratic coalition were laid, ironically, in the success of the next sweeping partisan agenda—the Great Society of the 1960s. In the wake of President John F. Kennedy's assassination in 1963 and President Johnson's landslide election in 1964, huge new Democratic majorities were elected to Congress in 1964. They promptly set about enacting the liberal legislative agenda bottled up by years of conservative control by southern Democrats and Republicans in Congress. In short order they passed huge new programs in health care (Medicare and Medicaid), a historic program of federal aid to education, higher education loan programs, the Voting Rights Act, and urban and rural antipoverty programs. Republicans complained of being "railroaded" as the large Democratic majorities pushed through programs rapidly and on their own terms.

Such partisan majorities are often short-lived, however. Roosevelt lost his working control of Congress by 1938. Johnson's domination of Congress ended after the 1966 elections when Republicans picked up forty-seven House seats. The Great Society prompted a broader political backlash as well. Republicans won back the White House in 1968, and the civil rights legislation and cultural liberalism of the Great Society began a process of partisan realignment in the South.[32] As a result, the next great political wave carried Reagan into the White House, Republicans into control of the Senate, and conservatives into effective control of the House of Representatives after Republican electoral successes in 1978 and 1980. Again the election results made the partisan pathway an effective legislative option in the 97th Congress as the Reagan administration won passage of major budget and tax reductions pushed through by a political phalanx of Republican unity on key votes in Congress.

After Obama's 2008 election victory, his administration likewise capitalized on his party's control of both houses of Congress to produce historic legislative victories purchased almost exclusively with Democratic votes. The Obama stimulus and health care reform bills received no Republican votes in the House, for instance. Yet the breadth of this legislation, along with continuing economic problems, prompted the countermobilization of Tea Party Republicans in the 2010 term elections, ushering in a Republican House that endured through the 2012 reelection of the president. This divided government era was marked by ever-sharper partisan position-taking and conflict, which undermined progress on major legislation, contributing to delays in raising the debt ceiling that caused the nation to lose its AAA bond rating by Standard & Poor's.

This is the historical pattern of partisan pathway politics: election victories that give one party an effective working majority in Congress, allowing it to push through a broad agenda of policy initiatives that have often built up over years of being stymied in pluralist politics. But such victories do not tend to last, however. Congressional majorities shrink as the political pendulum swings in the opposite direction, and majoritarian strategies lose their appeal as majorities shrink or disappear entirely. Evenly divided parties and weak political attachment by large blocks of independent voters provide ample fuel for rapid countermobilization of the electorate, where major victories achieved by one party bring about their own defeat at the hands of aroused voters on the other side.[33]

Despite the cyclical patterns brought on by partisan mobilization and countermobilization, a trend in recent years toward greater reliance on the partisan pathway has been discernible. As we demonstrate in chapter 6, nearly half (45 percent) of the cases we examine since 2000 have followed the partisan pathway, versus 24 percent of policies in the period from 1981 to 1999. Yet even in this period of seeming hyperpartisanship, a majority of policies examined continued to utilize other pathways, including the newer ideational pathways that are explored in the following two chapters.

Case Study of the Partisan Pathway: The Enactment of National Health Insurance

The Patient Protection and Affordable Care Act, which was signed by President Obama on March 23, 2010, illustrates many of the characteristics of partisan pathway politics. As with other policies adopted through the partisan pathway, party leaders in the White House and Congress played a pivotal role in shaping the policy agenda, building coalitions, and pushing legislation through Congress, and partisan affiliation defined both roll-call votes in Congress and public reactions to the legislation outside Congress.

Since the Truman administration, universal national health insurance had been a major Democratic Party priority, and efforts had been undertaken by a number of presidents to bring it about. However, in almost all cases, these efforts were stymied by a combination of partisan division, issue complexity, and the opposition of powerful health care interest groups. Despite repeated failures, public support remained for the concept of universal health coverage, and health care was a prominent issue during the 2008 presidential primary and general elections. During the fall campaign, Barack Obama differentiated himself from John McCain in part by promising to pursue universal health coverage, and he made this a major administration priority after winning the election.

According to Lawrence Jacobs and Theda Skocpol, President Obama "envisaged 2009 as an extraordinary moment, and he saw health care reform as critical to economic recovery and fiscal responsibility."[34] His broad-based election victory, along with large Democratic majorities in both the House and Senate, had opened a policy window for comprehensive health care reform, and he was committed to using his political capital on its behalf. However, learning from the mistakes of previous efforts, Obama decided to embrace a different set of strategies. In particular, instead of preparing an administration bill for submission to Congress, the Obama administration provided only guidelines for legislation and left it to Congress to craft the details of legislation. As both the House and the Senate were controlled by the Democrats, it was largely left to the congressional Democratic leaders to build and maintain a winning coalition.

At the same time, the Obama administration undertook a number of efforts "to manage and diffuse all-out opposition from health sector stakeholders who in the past had obstructed comprehensive reform."[35] Serious efforts were made by the White House to reach out to the insurance companies, doctors, hospital groups and pharmaceutical companies, and as a result they did not engage in "united and sustained public opposition" of the sort that had doomed earlier reform efforts, although these stakeholders tried hard to advance their interests within the reform legislation. Furthermore, the administration also remained cautious about the "price" of the health care reform, and this is where it played the most active role in ensuring that the reform "combined program expansion with targeted budget cuts."[36] Thus in the case of health care policy, both the president and congressional Democratic leaders played leading roles in policy development, with the Obama administration concentrating on creating a favorable external environment and fiscal strategy for reform and congressional leaders focusing on crafting legislation capable of enactment.

Like the other policies that had been adopted through the partisan pathway, health care reform generated a high degree of conflict. After losing the 2008 election, House and Senate Republicans adopted a strategy of opposing policies developed by the Obama administration. As Senate Republican leader Mitch McConnell (KY) expressed it, his top goal was to make Obama a one-term president.[37] Although Democrats for a time enjoyed a sixty-vote, filibuster-proof majority in the Senate, unanimous Republican opposition would mean that Democrats could not afford even a single defection. At the same time, conservative

"Blue Dog" Democrats were worried that supporting health care legislation in a sluggish economy might hurt their chances of reelection. Developing a winning coalition required significant political maneuvering by both the House and Senate leadership.

In the House three committees had jurisdictions over health policy. To avoid turf fights, Speaker Pelosi asked the three chairmen to "negotiate a single bill that then could be introduced in all their committees."[38] On July 19, 2009, she, House majority leader Steny Hoyer (D-MD), and the chairs of the Ways and Means, Energy and Commerce, and Education and Labor Committees unveiled H.R. 3200, a comprehensive health care reform bill that included a so-called public option, or government-sponsored insurance plan. To help pay for the costs of extending coverage to the uninsured, the House bill included a surtax on high-income taxpayers.[39] The bill was approved by the Ways and Means Committee on a vote of 23-18 and by the Education and Labor Committee 26-22. In both cases all committee Republicans and three Democrats voted against the bill. However, the Blue Dog Democrats held a much stronger position on the Energy and Commerce Committee, and it became very difficult to pass the bill there without their support, given continued unanimous Republican opposition. It took two weeks of intense negotiation and certain concessions to advance the bill out of Commerce by the margin of 31-28. Five Democrats joined with all Republicans in opposing the bill.

In the Senate two committees had jurisdiction over the health care bill, and on July 15, 2009, the Health, Education, Labor and Pensions (HELP) Committee reported the bill on a party-line vote. The chairman of the Finance Committee, Max Baucus (D-MT), however, made an effort to reach a bipartisan deal and announced that there would be no Finance markup before the August recess.

The August recess proved to be a difficult time for the Democrats. Whereas the Democrats lacked a specific proposal to defend, "local networks of conservatives were mobilizing with more intensity . . . to stop any congressional legislative action at all."[40] The Republican leadership endorsed these protests and labeled the entire reform effort an "outrageously expensive big-government power grab." As Democratic members faced sometimes angry crowds in their town hall meetings, congressional leaders pressed the president to play a more decisive role. Accordingly President Obama launched a public relations campaign to build support for health care reform. On September 9, 2009, he delivered a speech to a joint session of Congress and pushed for three key goals: providing security to those who already have health insurance, extending coverage to include those who do not have insurance, and slowing the growth of health care costs. He also stated that the $900 billion plan would "be entirely paid for."[41]

The speech reenergized congressional Democrats, and the Senate Finance Committee, which had failed to reach a bipartisan deal, began its markup. On October 7, the nonpartisan Congressional Budget Office reported that the bill proposed by the Finance Committee would cost $829 billion, which was below the president's $900 billion figure. On October 13, the committee approved the bill 14-9. Only one Republican, Olympia Snowe (ME), joined the Democrats in voting for the bill.

The intense partisan battles in both chambers of Congress, unanimous and unwavering opposition by Republicans, and the electoral concerns of moderate and conservative Democrats made the challenges of coalition building especially difficult. In the House, the Blue Dogs raised concerns about the public insurance plan option, which would tie provider payments to the Medicare rate plus 5 percent. They also wanted strong language within the bill that would prohibit federal funding for elective abortions and bar undocumented workers from receiving health care benefits. Progressive Democrats and the Congressional Hispanic Caucus adamantly opposed these changes. In order to deal with these problems and ensure that they had enough votes to pass this measure, House Democratic leaders were forced to make a number of concessions. Instead of a robust public option, a modified plan that "called for a public insurance plan with rates negotiated by the Secretary of Health and Human Services" was incorporated.[42] In order to solve the abortion dilemma, Rep. Bart Stupak (D-MI) presented an amendment that barred federal funding for elective abortion. At the same time, congressional leaders and the White House heavily lobbied undecided and wavering members. On November 24, 2009, their efforts were rewarded, and the House bill was narrowly passed 220-215.[43] Thirty-nine Democrats voted against the bill, and only one Republican, from a strongly Democratic congressional district, supported it.

Things were even more difficult in the Senate where the Democrats required sixty votes to avoid a filibuster on the floor. In this case too, the incorporation of the public option became a major issue. Although most strongly supported it, and the issue became a cause célèbre among liberal Democrats, a number of Democratic senators stated that they would not support any form of public option, and it was ultimately left out of the Senate bill. At the same time, special deals were made to attract the votes of moderate Democrats from conservative states. The final vote on passage of the bill took place on Christmas Eve, December 24, 2009, and it was adopted on a strict party line vote of 60-39.

By the end of this tortuous process, both chambers had passed versions of health insurance reform that met the basic criteria set forth by President Obama, but the two bills had significant differences that would need to be resolved in conference. The House bill was more liberal in nature, as it included a limited public option, more generous benefits, and higher taxes.[44] The Senate bill lacked a public option and contained special "deals" favoring states such as Nebraska and Louisiana that were anathema to the broader public. Thus merging these two bills into a form that could pass both houses posed a significant challenge—a challenge that became even more difficult when Democrats lost their filibuster-proof majority in the Senate. The death of liberal senator Edward M. Kennedy forced a special election in Massachusetts, and he was replaced by a Republican, Scott Brown, who had campaigned against the health care law.

This Republican win forced the Democrats to seek an alternative to a House-Senate conference. The most attractive option, because it would avoid a Republican Senate filibuster on a new bill, was to have the House simply pass the Senate bill. But Speaker Pelosi lacked the votes to do so because many House Democrats disliked its more conservative provisions. Eventually a path was chosen: The House would take up the Senate bill along with a separate "budget reconciliation" bill that would include compromises between the two chambers. Because special parliamentary rules govern budget reconciliation bills, the Senate would require only fifty votes to pass it.

Adopting this path required exceptionally strong party leadership, forcing compromises on key issues and keeping Democrats in line on key votes. President Obama engaged fully in this exercise in partisan coalition building, holding a health care summit and refocusing the agenda. Meanwhile the House developed its "sidecar" reconciliation bill, which would modify the Senate bill it first would have to pass. This sidecar removed a number of special deals that were proposed to ensure the support of Sen. Ben Nelson (D-NE) and others, and at the same time "reduced and delayed the so-called Cadillac tax on generous employee health plans, increased taxes on health care industries, and imposed taxes on the wealthiest Medicare beneficiaries."[45] On March 21, 2010, the House passed the Senate's version of the bill by a 219-212 vote. At the same time, the sidecar reconciliation bill was passed by a vote of 220-211. Finally, the Senate passed the reconciliation bill 56-43. In all these cases, not one single Republican supported the bill. On March 23, 2010, President Obama signed into law this landmark legislation. The law extended health care coverage to about thirty-two million of the nation's forty-five million uninsured people, expanded Medicaid, provided subsidies to buy insurance, and created state-regulated insurance markets.

The creation of the Patient Protection and Affordable Care Act was a classic example of partisan policymaking. Whereas past efforts to reform health care had often foundered on the shoals of pluralist politics—as labor unions, health care interests, and business groups fought to add or remove specific provisions or opposed reforms outright—President Obama's orchestrated actions neutralized interest group opposition and solidified support from liberal groups. As with any complex piece of public policy, experts were deeply involved in the policy process but mostly in supporting roles to the political leadership. The case of health care reform is one in which the president placed the issue squarely on the policy agenda and intervened periodically to build or bolster support for the legislation, while the congressional Democratic leadership played critical legislative roles in shaping the contours of legislation, directing the process, building winning coalitions, and maintaining high levels of party discipline. In the face of virtually unanimous Republican opposition from start to finish, health care reform was successfully passed because the Democrats maintained high levels of party unity while controlling the White House and both chambers of Congress.

Notes

1. For details about the enactment of ESEA and other Great Society programs, see James L. Sundquist, *Politics and Policy: The Eisenhower, Kennedy, and Johnson Years* (Washington, DC: Brookings Institution Press, 1968); and Eugene Eidenberg and Roy D. Morey, *An Act of Congress: The Legislative Process and the Making of Education Policy* (New York: Norton, 1969).

2. Details of this program can be found in Conlan, *From New Federalism to Devolution*, chapters 7 and 8.

3. See, for example, Samuel P. Huntington, *American Politics: The Promise of Disharmony* (Cambridge, MA: Harvard University Press, 1983), chapter 1.

4. Schattschneider, *Semi-Sovereign People*.

5. Committee on Political Parties, American Political Science Association, "Toward a More Responsible Two Party System," *American Political Science Review* 44, no. 3, part 2 (September 1950), supplement.

6. See David W. Rohde, *Parties and Leaders in the Postreform House* (Chicago: University of Chicago Press, 1991); and John H. Aldrich and David W. Rohde, "The Transition to Republican Rule in the House: Implications for Theories of Congressional Politics," *Political Science Quarterly* 112, no. 4 (Winter 1997–1998): 541–67.

7. See, for example, John Aldrich, *Why Parties? A Second Look* (Chicago: University of Chicago Press, 2011).

8. Angus Campbell et al., *The American Voter* (New York: Wiley, 1964); V. O. Key, *The Responsible Electorate* (Cambridge, MA: Belknap Press, 1955); and Norman Nie et al., *The Changing American Voter* (New York: Twentieth Century Fund, 1999).

9. Campbell, *American Voter*.

10. Anthony Downs, *An Economic Theory of Democracy* (New York: Harper, 1957).

11. Conlan, Wrightson, and Beam, *Taxing Choices*, chapter 9.

12. Barbara Sinclair, *Party Wars: Polarization and the Politics of National Policy Making* (Norman: University of Oklahoma Press, 2006); and David Brady and Phillip Althoff, "Party Voting in the U.S. House of Representatives, 1890–1910: Elements of a Responsible Party System," *The Journal of Politics* 36 (August 1974): 753–75.

13. For examples of such behavior in the 1900 and 1904 presidential elections, see Edmund Morris, *Theodore Rex* (New York: Random House, 2001).

14. Quoted in James L. Sundquist, *The Decline and Resurgence of Congress* (Washington, DC: Brookings Institution Press, 1981), 129–30.

15. Ibid., 131.

16. Ibid., 137.

17. Quoted in Richard E. Neustadt, "Presidency and Legislation: Planning the President's Program," *American Political Science Review* 49 (December 1955): 1015.

18. Ibid., 980.

19. Kingdon, *Agendas, Alternatives, and Public Policies*, 23.

20. "Presidential News Conference: Clinton Lays Down Challenge on Welfare Reform Bill," *CQ Weekly Report* (April 22, 1995): 1138.

21. Quoted in Sundquist, *Decline and Resurgence*, 133–34. Emphasis added.

22. Barbara Deckard Sinclair, "Party Realignment and the Transformation of the Political Agenda: The House of Representatives, 1925–1938," *American Political Science Review* 71, no. 3 (1977).

23. Quoted in *Congress: We the People.*

24. Paul Charles Light, *The President's Agenda: Domestic Policy Choice from Kennedy to Clinton* (Baltimore: Johns Hopkins University Press, 1999).

25. See, for example, Pew Center for the People and the Press, *Beyond Red vs. Blue: Republicans Divided about Role of Government; Democrats by Social and Personal Values* (Washington, DC: Pew Center for People and the Press, 2005).

26. Ibid.

27. See Keith T. Poole and Howard Rosenthal, *Ideology and Congress* (New Brunswick, NJ: Transaction Publishers, 2007); and Barbara Sinclair, "The Dream Fulfilled? Party Development in Congress, 1950–2000," in *Responsible Partisanship? The Evolution of American Political Parties since 1950*, John C. Green and Paul S. Herrnson, eds. (Lawrence: University Press of Kansas, 2002), 129–31.

28. John Aldrich and D. W. Rohde, "Consequences of Electoral and Institutional Change: The Evolution of Conditional Party Government in the U.S. House of Representatives," in *New Directions in American Political Parties*, Jeffrey M. Stonecash, ed. (New York: Routledge, 2010), 234–50.

29. Kara Lindaman and Donald P. Haider-Markel, "Issue Evolution, Political Parties, and the Culture Wars," *Political Research Quarterly* 55 (March 2002): 91–110.

30. Ezra Klein, "Lessons from the Medicare Prescription Drug Benefit Vote," *Washington Post*, March 8, 2010, http://voices.washingtonpost.com/ezra-klein/2010/03/lessons_from_the_medicare_pres.html.

31. Richard E. Cohen, *Washington at Work: Back Rooms and Clean Air* (New York: Macmillan, 1992).

32. Nelson Polsby, *How Congress Evolves: Social Bases of Institutional Change* (New York: Oxford University Press, 2003).

33. M. C. Herron and J. Bafumi, "Leapfrog Representation and Extremism: A Study of American Voters and Their Members in Congress," *American Political Science Review* 104, no. 3 (2010): 519–42.

34. Lawrence R. Jacobs and Theda Skocpol, "Hard-Fought Legacy: Obama, Congressional Democrats, and the Struggle for Comprehensive Health Care Reform," in *Reaching for a New Deal: Ambitious Governance, Economic Meltdown, and Polarized Politics in Obama's First Two Years*, Theda Skocpol and Lawrence R. Jacobs, eds. (New York: Russell Sage Foundation, 2011), 63.

35. Ibid., 64.

36. Ibid., 67.

37. James Fallows, "On Explaining Obama," *The Atlantic*, February 12, 2012, www.theatlantic.com/politics/archive/2012/02/on-explaining-obama/253696/.

38. Barbara Sinclair, *Unorthodox Lawmaking*, 4th ed. (Washington, DC: CQ Press, 2011), 187.

39. Ibid., 189.

40. Ibid., 191.

41. White House, Office of the Press Secretary, Remarks by the President to a Joint Session of Congress on Health Care, September 9, 2009, www.whitehouse.gov/the_press_office/Remarks-by-the-President-to-a-Joint-Session-of-Congress-on-Health-Care.

42. Sinclair, *Unorthodox Lawmaking*, 194.

43. Jan Austin, ed., *CQ Almanac 2009*, 65th ed. (Washington, DC: CQ-Roll Call Group, 2010), H-300.

44. Jacobs and Skocpol, "Hard-Fought Legacy," 73.

45. Ibid., 75.

CHAPTER FOUR

The Expert Pathway

- Farm subsidies have traditionally been viewed as the epitome of pluralist politics. Members of Congress from farm states and assorted interest groups have held sway over the growth of ever more numerous subsidies since the New Deal, to the consternation of economists who railed against the misallocation of national resources such subsidies wrought. In 1995, the reform consensus came to life in the form of the Freedom to Farm Act, endorsed by both congressional Republicans and President Clinton. Prompted by an analytical consensus among economists, the decades-old structure of federal assistance was to be wiped away in favor of declining general-purpose aid to farmers, leading to less federal interference in the farming economy, along with lower federal spending.

- Tax reform has always been viewed as an impossible political dream by the many economists and reformers who occupy think tanks and universities. While the tax code as a whole is disliked by all, the individual subsidies and tax expenditures that constitute the foundation of tax policy are viewed as politically untouchable. Yet surprisingly President Reagan and members of Congress from both parties succeeded in passing comprehensive tax reform legislation in 1986 that bore the imprint of the leading experts and thought leaders in the field. The radical broadening of the base of the income tax achieved by eliminating and trimming numerous important tax subsidies was an outcome that tax policy experts had long sought in order to improve the efficiency of the economy, and their consensus became a powerful driver of the policy process.

- Reforming the federal budget process carries high stakes, for the fiscal rules of decision making profoundly influence the outcomes. In 1985, faced with record peacetime federal deficits, Congress passed the Gramm-Rudman-Hollings Act mandating significant annual spending cuts to achieve fiscal balance over five years. When this reform proved to be unworkable, budget experts put forward a reform that focused not on overall fiscal balance but on control of those items that federal decision makers determined annually: discretionary appropriations and new entitlement and tax cut legislation. Anchored in careful study of the lessons learned from Gramm-Rudman-Hollings, the experts formulated a new budget regime in the Budget Enforcement Act of 1990, which established the discretionary spending caps and the pay-as-you-go (PAYGO) enforcement regime, preventing higher deficits through tax cuts or entitlement spending increases.

The pathways examined in the previous chapters highlighted the roles played by political organizations and interests—the time-honored actors in the public policy process. While narrow or broad-based interests will always serve as a primary source of motivation and allegiance in policy debates, emergent methods of mobilization place the role of ideas and values as key independent factors driving the placement of proposals on the agenda and contributing to enactment. Experts and their professional knowledge have come to play growing roles in policymaking in our system. When issues fall into the *expert pathway*, professional knowledge and technical feasibility become the source of legitimacy against which all proposals are based.

The foregoing examples illustrate that experts in fact can play a formative role in the development of policy agendas and the implementation of complex policy initiatives. While lacking the crucial election certificate that grants elected officials the legal power to make final decisions, experts provide a powerful source of legitimation to new policy ideas and proposals. Vulnerable political leaders from party and pluralist pathways at times find it useful—even compelling—to adopt and embrace expert-based ideas when such proposals are consistent with their primary coalitions and belief systems. As government's role in the economy and affairs of the nation has expanded over the past century, political leaders have become accountable as never before for the success or failure of programs as different as financial regulation, education, health care, and homeland security. Experts have become the new plumbers of the policy process, able to command attention and high prices due to their deep understanding of the ever-more-complex relationships between government programs and public outcomes. Indeed, the growing stakes and complexity of government informed the vision of the early founders of the field of public administration, most notably Woodrow Wilson, who argued for the emergence of a professionalized field of professionals skilled in understanding the "science" of administration.[1]

While the growing force of experts has constituted a new form of mobilization, the expert pathway competes with other pathways for influence and legitimation in policy debates. As the other pathways have become more polarized and mobilized, analysis and evidence is likely to be prized as much for the ammunition it provides for entrenched interest group, partisan, and ideological positions as for its contribution of new and important ideas. Credentialed experts who gained influence by virtue of the credibility of their ideas and their studied detachment from the heat of political battle increasingly find themselves competing with a plethora of more aggressive advocacy analysts eager to become relevant to the policy debates of the moment.[2] Nonetheless, the adoption of expert-based ideas by parties and interest groups confirms by imitation alone the compelling appeal that ideas and research have to the increasingly diverse combatants populating the policy process today.

Foundations for Experts' Role in the Policy Process

Broad changes in the nation's socioeconomic structure have given rise to the growth of the "professional class." This broad category, which includes economists, social scientists, doctors, natural scientists, and policy experts of all persuasions, has increased twelvefold in the postwar period.[3] By one account, associations representing professions tripled their presence in the Washington interest group community between 1960 and 1980 alone.[4] These shifts in the nation's economic and political foundation prompted sociologist Daniel Bell to herald the arrival of a "postindustrial" society where formal knowledge becomes the critical resource for economic growth and social problem solving.[5] While most would agree with his analysis of the shifting nature of economic production, this by no means implies that experts have become a cohesive, unified political force capable of having game-changing influence in political debate. Like other interests, experts at times proved to be every bit as splintered and diverse in their political views and their proclivity to engage in policymaking as other interest groups.

The Shifting Role of Government

Before experts could play a pivotal role in policymaking, they had to be invited in by political leaders and publics to help solve specific substantive and political problems. The growing role of government and the growing complexity of that role all brought demand from political leaders in and out of government for the knowledge and expertise that experts bring. Whether in financial regulation, health care delivery, or homeland security, government became a pivotal player in providing important benefits in critical areas of national life. Total federal spending jumped from 3 percent of the economy in 1930 to 24 percent in 2012.

The nature of the federal role also shifted. Through much of the nation's history, the federal government played a limited role in the economy. Federal programs were typically distributive in nature, featuring the allocation of funds to states and other actors through grants or capital investment projects. As Theodore Lowi would have predicted, such initiatives placed a premium on designing programs to maximize political support—a political rather than a technical challenge, in which legislatures excelled.[6] With the advent of the twentieth century, the federal role expanded in regulatory and redistributive policy areas—arenas that were far more technically demanding.

Over the past fifty years, the expansion of the federal domestic role featured complex interventions that placed a premium on those with technical, not political, expertise to engineer and implement. Health care under Medicare and Medicaid enacted in 1964 called for federal officials to put their foot on both the gas and the brake by expanding benefits while controlling cost inflation that those expansions would invariably promote. This predicament bedevils the nation today, as even experts bemoan the rampant cost growth in health care that so far seems to elude the ability of the nation to reign it in. President Obama's health reform, in fact, delegates responsibility for trimming health care costs to a new expert Independent Payment Advisory Board (IPAB) whose proposals will go into effect unless overridden by a 60 percent congressional supermajority.[7] Education featured first the targeting of enhanced services to neglected groups such as the disadvantaged and disabled but then expanded to promote a newfound federal role in promoting and measuring educational quality under the No Child Left Behind and Race to the Top initiatives spawned by the Bush and Obama administrations. The metrics necessary to track progress across sixteen thousand schools became a cottage industry itself that guaranteed full employment for graduates of public policy and education schools for years to come. Environmental protection was founded on increasingly precise measurement of pollution across different modes and increasingly sophisticated policy tools that featured market-like incentives alongside traditional command-and-control regulation.

Lawrence Brown said many years ago that as the federal policy expansions from the New Deal and Great Society were completed, the opportunities for what he calls "breakthrough policy" diminished as federal programs occupied most areas of domestic policy. Instead he argued that policymakers would increasingly become preoccupied by what he calls "rationalizing policy"—that is, revisions and reforms to the major initiatives of the past. While elected officials may not get as much political credit for rationalizing policies, in fact government programs create their own political and policy momentum by becoming more central to the social and economic well-being of the nation. Accordingly, policymakers become beset with demands to modify, revise, revisit, "fix," and fill gaps in such critical programs as Social Security, Medicare, and education.[8] As Aaron Wildavsky argues, policy was "its own cause" as the "evils that worry us now spring directly from the good things we tried to do before."[9]

Brown states further that the rationalizing agenda catapults policy analysts and technical staff into more prominent roles, since they are the officials who have the greatest understanding of evaluation research and greatest command over the technical terms of program design that are so critical to rationalizing debates.

He argues that the government comes to the table in rationalizing debates armed with its own agenda as government officials increasingly become central in seeking intricate solutions to government-caused problems. Whether it be controlling health care cost, easing transportation congestion, or addressing homeland security or public health threats, parties and interest groups are no longer the exclusive actors. This is not to say that partisan and group positioning does not occur on these issues but that experts have more prominent roles in defining the problem and in mediating and legitimizing policy solutions.

Policy specialists and experts are thus the vital cogs in increasingly complex policy wheels. They are prized by the system for their command of technical issues in designing and managing policy. It is comforting indeed for a subcabinet appointee to be able to turn to policy specialists to tackle the difficult challenges of responding to the crisis of the day or of turning campaign promises into governing realities. These specialists bring more than technical knowledge. They also typically bring what we would call "institutional knowledge" involving deep understanding of the past history of government initiatives in an area, working relationships with other key players in an issue network across many sectors in and out of government, and judgment about integrating technical policy design solutions with overall political agendas of the day.

Political Leaders Need Help

It is these qualities that come to be prized by political leaders who are increasingly on the proverbial hot seat as the stakes involved with government have become broader and more salient to a greater share of the public. Most critically, political leaders are held accountable for outcomes of policies: Did federal education programs achieve better student performance? Did federal drug abuse programs lower teen drug abuse? Did federal welfare reform lower the welfare rolls and improve the lives of lower-income Americans? As Kevin Esterling notes, there is considerable uncertainty surrounding whether and how government initiatives affect these broader indicators. For instance, education outcomes reflect many factors beyond federal programs themselves, including state and local education programs and the investments made by families in their children. Employing experts helps political leaders protect against the risks of policy uncertainty, and evidence suggests that political leaders redouble their search for information the more that issues are conflictual and highly salient.[10]

Regardless of the complex range of factors involved in driving important outcomes, the political environment acts to centralize blame, with particular focus on the president. Thus, for instance, when the response to Hurricane Katrina was viewed as bungled and confused, the public held President George W. Bush primarily responsible, regardless of the fact that many hands were responsible for that tragedy, including those of the mayor of New Orleans and the governor of Louisiana.[11] The fact that the president had appointed a policy novice, Michael Brown, to head the Federal Emergency Management Agency became a magnet for additional criticism, illustrating the key role that expert leadership can play in promoting public confidence in government's responses to problems.

In this high-stakes environment, presidents and other officials alike have incentives to reach out to experts to cover their considerable downside risks. When one surveys the federal landscape, it is clear that the role of experts was first institutionalized in policy arenas where presidents are most centrally responsible for outcomes: national security and economic policy. Interestingly in both cases, the National Security Council and the White House Council of Economic Advisers were both created in the aftermath of World War II. In both cases, presidents needed help in managing sensitive areas where voters were most likely to hold them personally accountable for national outcomes, whether fairly or not. Thus it behooved them to have the best minds on tap to help plan and design policy and budgetary initiatives.

The Growing Supply of Expertise

One of the most important underpinnings for the growth of the expert pathway has been the proliferation of experts in and around government. There has been a marked expansion of first-class policy analysis over the past fifty years that has exceeded anything produced before. This output has been anchored by the institutionalization of analysis in schools of public policy and administration throughout the country, as well as the growth in applied-policy research institutions in and out of government. There are now over 280 schools conferring masters of public administration and policy degrees throughout the nation.[12]

Within government, policy analysis gained its first real foothold in the Department of Defense during the implementation of the Planning, Programming, and Budgeting System (PPBS) by Secretary Robert McNamara in the early 1960s. Armed with analytical "whiz kids," the secretary was able to use policy analysis to gain leverage over the military services in budget conflicts over scarce resources. The introduction of analysis into budgeting and policymaking gained further traction with the formulation and implementation of the Great Society programs under Lyndon Johnson, and it was instrumental in designing such programs as the War on Poverty and education programs for disadvantaged children. The alleged failures and disappointments of these initiatives ironically fueled further expansion of expertise within bureaucracies, as program evaluation gained roots to help policymakers better understand how to design and implement complex programs.[13]

The federal civil service has become more professionalized as well. In 1950, more than half of its employees were in lower-level clerical jobs. By 2000, such jobs made up only 15 percent of positions. The percentage of professional positions exploded during the same period.[14] The percentage of federal workers in professional positions with a graduate degree grew from 26 percent in 1975 to 42 percent in 2005.[15]

In a system of separated institutions sharing powers, other actors could not sit idly by while the federal bureaucracy acquired these highly skilled experts. As analysis became a new high ground for policy debates, Congress, interest groups, and competing agencies realized, in Wildavsky's words, that "it takes one to beat one."[16] Thus the hiring of policy analysts by Defense Secretary McNamara inspired the military services to gain their own analytical capability to contest the secretary's ideas in the new analytical currency for budget debates.

Congress armed itself with its own analytical support institutions. Congressional staff expanded significantly in the wake of the 1970s' congressional reforms empowering committees and subcommittees with new resources to contest the president for policy influence. Already suffering from principal-agency problems in overseeing a bureaucracy of two million federal employees, Congress established and strengthened support agencies that provided ready access to top experts in numerous public policy fields. With the closing of the Watergate era, Congress established the new Congressional Budget Office (CBO), carved out a new home for policy analysts in the Congressional Research Service (CRS) in the Library of Congress, inspired the Government Accountability Office (GAO) to redirect its resources to program evaluations requested by congressional committees, and created an Office of Technology Assessment (OTA) to enable better-informed deliberation of complex policy issues. Although the latter institution was abolished in 1995, the others have become leading producers of primary research on major policy and programmatic issues across the entire range of governmental functions.[17] The concomitant growth of congressional staffs with strong analytical backgrounds has been partly responsible for increasing the demand from these agencies within Congress itself.[18] These trends have been replicated at the state level as well, as many state governments have developed high-level policy analytical and evaluation staffs working in the legislature during this period of renaissance in state governance capacity.[19]

Beyond formal governmental institutions, think tanks emerged at the beginning of the twentieth century as part of the progressive movement's push to introduce greater professionalism and efficiency into public policy. The earliest think tanks—the Russell Sage Foundation and the Institute for Government Research, for example—emphasized the depoliticization of decision making through the introduction of social science research and neutral analysis. The missions of the early think tanks were not ideological, nor were they associated with particular ideologies or interest groups. Donald Abelson has noted that the first generation of think tanks was often funded by philanthropic businessmen, while the second generation was funded by the federal government itself, reflecting the growing interest by policymakers in dealing with more complex policy environments and issues.[20]

The third generation saw a proliferation of think tanks and institutes addressing a wide range of social, economic, national security, and governmental management issues. One study concludes that the number of think tanks at the national level tripled from 1970 to reach 305 by 1996.[21] The new think tanks were different in several respects: They were often issue-specific, and they spurned the neutral policy-oracle role to become advocates of interests and ideologies. Beginning with the emergence of conservative policy institutes in the 1970s such as the Heritage Foundation and the Cato Institute, the new think tanks had a strategy to hire experts who shared both strong advocacy or ideological views and a determination to market those ideas to various target groups. In one survey of Washington journalists, Andrew Rich concludes that the think tanks that were rated as the most credible were no longer viewed as the most influential. While the Brookings Institution was considered to be the most credible organization, it was not viewed as the most influential.[22]

Some of these advocacy think tanks have been organized and supported by interest groups and other advocacy organizations. However, increasingly interest groups themselves house their own research institutes that support in-house experts, as well as consultants from universities and from other think tanks. AARP, one of the largest member-based organizations in the United States, has a research center consisting of a public policy institute, a survey and statistics unit, and an academic affairs group. These units have produced dialogues, papers, and forums with leading experts from all parts of the policy spectrum on such issues as the future outlook for Medicare and Social Security and the implications of fiscal policy on the economy.[23] The American Bankers Association has institutionalized a research capacity, with a center for banking research and an economic policy and research department that develops reports on trends and issues in financial markets.[24]

The foregoing suggests that experts have become more integrated into political and advocacy institutions. The coexistence of experts with political bosses or bureaucratic agencies serves mutual interests. Political leaders gain the shroud of legitimacy for their decisions, while experts gain the opportunity to use ideas to make a difference.

However, even when they are members of broader political organizations, experts gain their foothold because they have different loyalties and accountability from the other actors in the process. They gain their leverage and standing not due to loyalty to political officials or groups but rather due to their adherence to professional norms and values of a professional community. Rather than accountability to political, legal, or hierarchical sources, experts are first and foremost effective and legitimate because they are accountable to a professional community and its norms. Often that community has certifications that authenticate their standing in the community, whether academic degrees or professional certificates. Experts are generally given deference by bureaucratic and political superiors owing to the technical complexity of their field and the significant credibility that expert pronouncements have in policy discussions and bureaucratic implementation. In their classic study of the demise of the space shuttle *Challenger*, Barbara S. Romzek and Melvin J. Dubnick report that the responsibility for technically complex decisions over space launches had gravitated away from experts and toward bureaucratic and political realms. Engineers' recommendation against launching *Challenger* was ignored by their hierarchical superiors, to the ultimate regret of the entire agency and nation.[25]

Experts take root in a number of surprising venues. Of course, we would expect experts and professionals to lead technical agencies. Indeed, the heads of the National Institutes of Health, the National Science Foundation, and the Food and Drug Administration are by tradition scientists and policy experts who often have attained high professional standing, as evidenced by Nobel Prizes or other awards. Nonscientific agencies are also traditionally led by officials who have expertise and credentials of relevance to the agency's mission. The IRS commissioner, for example, has traditionally been a tax lawyer to reflect the technical issues that the agency must rule on, while the director of the CBO is a professional economist respected by the economics community.

However, experts survive and even thrive in political settings as well. The president's budget office, the Office of Management and Budget (OMB), and the CBO make decisions with the highest political stakes imaginable. While the leaders of these organizations are political appointees, the staffs are highly respected professionals who have long viewed themselves as the bastion of "neutral competence," providing the right numbers and facts to support inherently political budget decisions. Unlike health care research, budget experts cannot be left alone to practice their trade without substantial guidance and interference from political leaders, owing to the inherently political nature of budget decisions. However, political leaders have an interest in ensuring that their decisions are anchored in credible numbers and models.[26]

In addition to serving as card-carrying members of political or bureaucratic organizations and agencies, experts can and often do play a more formative and fundamental role in providing the foundation of ideas and terms of debate that animate policy debates and issue networks. Hugh Heclo has called the loosely connected bands of public and private officials "issue networks," a concept that evokes nonstructured interactions among policy specialists in and out of government.[27] The ties that bind these information networks together are a common focus and shared understandings of complex transactions around a policy area, not shared beliefs or positions. Leaders of agencies and programs are no longer the traditional party politicians filling jobs based on patronage, but rather policy politicians skilled at working with and through the many highly specialized professionals needed to design and implement energy conservation, health insurance regulation, or air quality permit trading. In Heclo's concept, expert-based policy concepts and data help frame the questions and the discussion across the issue network. While actors often vigorously disagree, they share common epistemological frameworks and understandings that shape the terms of the debate.

The shared values and references that form the agendas of issue networks have been called "epistemic communities" by other researchers, such as John Ruggie.[28] The epistemic construct has been used to explain the leading role often played by technical experts in developing shared norms and values in policy networks. Although an epistemic community can include professionals with different backgrounds and party affiliations, the experts and other actors in the network come to share a common set of causal beliefs about the problems in their domain and a set of criteria for judging the validity of information and policy claims. Such communities can be instrumental in defining and framing problems, as well as solutions.

The Roles of Experts in the Policy Process

While experts have become a growing presence in government institutions, interest groups, and Washington think tanks, the questions remain: What roles do they actually play in policymaking, and what factors shape these roles? The answers to these complex questions are shaped by a national ambivalence about the normative role that experts should play, as well as by the political contest with other pathways for influence on specific issues and decisions.

The Paradox of Legitimacy

First, the influence and role of experts is shaped by the paradox of legitimacy. On the one hand, expert knowledge provides legitimacy to policy positions when those views are shown to be anchored in research and scientific consensus. In fact, other pathways actively court experts by acquiring their own think tanks and institutes and by funding other researchers who are likely to add compelling support. Party leaders championing reforms such as health reform and tax reform that challenged established groups in the pluralist pathways brought in experts in shaping their initial proposals to capture the policy high ground. Whether it was President Reagan's Treasury I proposal that kicked off the debate on 1986 tax reform or the Clinton health task force, large groups of talented experts were brought together to ensure that reforms reflected established research consensus.

However, the legitimacy of experts themselves is clouded by the nation's long-standing ambivalence about bureaucracy and policy elites in governing the nation. Stephen Skowronek has reminded us that the legitimacy of experts is more tenuous in the United States than in Europe.[29] In those other nations, the legitimacy of bureaucracy was already well established by the time that democracy was ushered in during the nineteenth century. As a new nation, the United States introduced democracy well before it developed a professional bureaucratic state. For much of its early history, the US government was staffed with amateurs who gained their positions through political patronage. Who you knew was more important than what you knew. However, as the state evolved in complexity and scope, Woodrow Wilson was among the early public administrators calling for a professional merit-based bureaucracy to apply expertise to the growing realm of government programs. Wilson's call was among the first in what Brian Cook calls the "arduous search for legitimating arguments to reconcile and thus artificially reattach administration to a regime predicated on popular sovereignty and individual rights."[30]

Indeed, starting with Wilson's classic work, much of public administration has been preoccupied with reconciling the legitimacy of bureaucracies and experts in a democratic system. As Dwight Waldo has said, the romantic vision of democracy has generated deep distrust of unelected officials, as Americans prefer democratic government to efficient public management.[31] Wilson sought to bridge the conflict by articulating the case for a separation of politics and administration, where elected officials would choose goals and administrative experts would be free to implement these goals in the most efficient way possible.[32] Public administration was envisioned as a science of means, not ends. Yet this dichotomy failed to satisfactorily resolve the tension between experts and democratic values. Administrative choices and implementation consisted of another round of policymaking involving political choices between competing claims and goals—a political, not a scientific, enterprise.

Wilson's dichotomy thus failed to carve out a legitimate role for experts and bureaucrats in our system. Experts would have to contest with political actors in other pathways for power and influence on each issue—a prospect that would have consequences for the nature of their influence, as will be discussed shortly.

Experts in the Contest for Policymaking Influence

The actual influence achieved by experts is subject to considerable debate among the experts themselves. One might think that the analysis of the impact of policy analysis by policy analysts would succumb to the cheerleading effect. Far from it. In fact, political scientists, along with other observers, often harbor a largely gloomy outlook for the potential policy contributions of social science. In an influential policy text, James Anderson reflects the dim prospects for policy analysis: "The policymaking process in the United States is an adversarial process, characterized by the clash of competing and conflicting viewpoints and interests, rather than an impartial, disinterested or 'objective' search for 'correct' solutions for policy problems. . . . Given this, policy analyses done by social scientists, for instance, may have little impact except as they provide support for the positions of particular participants in the policy process."[33]

Leading scholars of policy evaluation echo these conclusions. For instance, in her survey of congressional committee staffs, Carol Weiss finds that analysis has very limited prospects in setting the broad direction of public policy.[34] Although the social science community has conducted a prodigious level of research on many leading policy issues, Sheldon Danziger sums up the results by noting, "So much social science, so little impact."[35]

However, the experts' roles in framing and shaping policy debates and outcomes are more robust than the foregoing would suggest. While the uses of research and expert knowledge rarely approximate a Wilsonian ideal, nonetheless research has a palpable, albeit less direct, influence on policymaking. Given the increased political pressures in our system in a media-saturated environment, the continued political viability of policy research as a base for at least some decisions is surprising.

As always, the terms of reference are important when assessing the role of policy analysis in decision making. Some observers have been moved to downplay the impact of policy analysis by noting how infrequently specific studies are used in designing policies either at legislative or executive levels. This is undoubtedly the case; indeed analysts often joke about issuing "Olympic divers"—beautiful reports that make no splash. In fact, proving a link between a specific study and a specific decision is not the most appropriate way to gauge the complex interactions between policy research and decision making.

Rather, there are many other kinds of roles that expert knowledge and studies can play in shaping policy choices and outcomes. Weiss has outlined seven specific models where research gains attention in policymaking.[36] The most direct model is the instrumental model where research provides solutions to policy problems. In this scenario, a linear relationship is posited between research studies and policy decisions. Knowledge itself is assumed to be compelling enough to drive its application in decision making. It is assumed that policymakers agree on the goals and on the gap that research can resolve. While this might have characterized the development of the atom bomb in the Manhattan Project during World War II, examples of this in the social sciences are few and far between. Given all of the influences and factors bearing on any complex policy question, analysts and others who harbor hopes for instrumental influence are destined to be disappointed and disillusioned.

The performance-management arena illustrates the effects that inflated and inappropriate expectations for the role of policy analysis can have. The checkered history of performance reforms at the federal level—from PPBS to zero-based budgeting to management by objective—were all pronounced dead because they seemed to fail to influence federal budgetary decisions. However, this judgment was made based in part on expectations that the performance analysis produced by these reform initiatives would have a direct and mechanical linkage to budget decisions, notwithstanding the numerous other important factors that must necessarily play a role in those decisions.

This view was most powerfully articulated by Sen. William Roth (R-DE) in introducing the 1993 Government Performance and Results Act when he stated that the new performance budgeting process would take politics out of budgeting—that programs that succeed would get more money and programs that fail would get less. But this relationship, of course, is anything but straightforward. Otherwise, if the number of drug abusers went up, we would cut funding for our drug programs! The point is that performance can realistically be expected to be one among several considerations involved in budget decisions, including relative priorities, needs, and equity issues. Performance analysis and measures can realistically be expected to raise new questions on the agenda of decision makers but not necessarily provide the answers.

Weiss has highlighted other roles that analysis from experts can play in the policy process. While less direct, these alternative routes can nonetheless have an impact in their own more circuitous manner:

- Enlightenment: Research most frequently enters the policy arena by shaping and redefining the policy agenda. The body of research in an area can help convert private troubles into public problems. (Obesity is a classic example.) Reorientation of this type is rarely the outcome of a single study. Rather it occurs when experts share a consensus about an entire body of research that is framed in compelling terms to policymakers.
- Interactive: Experts are part of an issue network that is involved and consulted by policymakers. Research alone does not dictate results but is considered in concert with experience, political insight, pressure, and judgments.
- Political: Research serves as ammunition for actors whose positions have hardened. While policymakers are not receptive to research that would cause them to change their view, they are avid users of research that supports their predetermined positions. Weiss argues that as long as the data are not distorted or misinterpreted, research used by partisans constitutes research that makes a difference.

- Tactical. Research can be used as an instrument of agenda denial, as studies are used to deflect pressure by keeping controversial issues off the agenda, among other short-term political purposes.[37]

These models should open us to the multiple ways that ideas can take root in the policy process. Experts have at times played prominent roles through the instrumental use of knowledge by policymakers, as the most demanding of Weiss's models would suggest, but more often experts' influence comes from more indirect routes such as the enlightenment model. Experts can play a role in a wide range of issues, from narrow technical issues where they carry presumptive credibility to broad policy debates where expert-based ideas can reframe and redefine problems in transformative ways. John Kingdon in his garbage-can model suggests that policy arises from the unstructured interplay of three policy streams—the problem stream, the solution stream, and the political stream. He suggests that policy analysts and accountability institutions would have their greatest role in articulating alternatives for the solution stream, flowing from their acknowledged strength in understanding complex interactions between government policies and policy problems.[38] While policy experts have influence over policy alternatives, policy research and audits are also increasingly being marshaled to assess and validate the legitimacy of problems presented in the problem stream for policymakers' attention.

Although conventional wisdom suggests that analysis will only be of tangential importance for high-stakes policy issues, in fact the input of experts was critical in setting the agenda and defining alternatives for such major reforms as airline deregulation, welfare reform, the 1983 Social Security reform, the 1986 tax reform, and the 1996 farm reforms. Beyond these higher-level cases, analytical input has been critical in setting the agenda and in developing policy alternatives across a range of issues that Brown would characterize as rationalizing in nature. Whether the issue was Medicare reimbursement formulas, formulas allocating billions in grant dollars, or financial reforms of federal deposit and pension insurance programs, analysts from the GAO, the CBO, federal agencies, and think tanks have played vital roles in problem definition and solution development.

Student loan reform provides an excellent example of this dynamic. As loan defaults rose to exceed 20 percent in the mid-1990s, the student loan program earned the dubious distinction as a "high-risk area" by the GAO, prompting attention from the administration and Congress. With the assistance of staff from the GAO and the Education Department, Congress developed a wide-ranging set of reforms targeted at reversing the incentives facing the key actors in this elaborate system of third-party government: the banks, the state guarantee agencies, the trade schools generating many of the defaulting students, and the former students themselves. As a result, the default rate was lowered to less than 10 percent. Here experts were influential in both problem and solution streams, using the garbage-can model.[39]

Our research suggests that the expert pathway is characterized by distinctive modes of problem definition and conflict when compared to other policy pathways. While feedback from clients and monitoring by interest groups constitute principal ways that problems were defined in the pluralist pathway, problems in the expert pathway, by contrast, were defined based on indicators and data and policy research. For instance, the need for farm reform, ultimately passed in 1996, was informed by economic studies showing the impacts of the web of federal subsidies on consumer prices and the federal budget. Bills on the expert and symbolic pathways largely steered clear of high levels of conflict as well. Once the expert frame became the primary frame for addressing the issue, both parties steered clear of outright opposition to expert-driven proposals. Once reaching the agenda on the expert pathway, both parties sought to either endorse the proposal or work out differences in bargaining among experts from different factions, parties, and branches.

While policies on the partisan pathway prompted the most extensive policy changes, expert-based policies also showed the potential to yield nonincremental reforms to major areas thought at one time to be locked down in pluralistic pathway. The 1986 Tax Reform Act, the 1996 farm reform, and the 1983 Social Security reform are cases in point. Daniel Béland and Alex Waddan conclude that ideas often form the basis for policy reforms by offering new ways to construct social problems and credible alternatives to existing policies, overcoming political resistance, institutional constraints, and path-dependent policy coalitions. However, they are careful to note that ideas achieve their most significant roles when working in tandem with other parallel institutional and political forces. For instance, the welfare reform of 1996 was a product of conservatives' successful reframing of the old Aid to Families with Dependent Children (AFDC) program as the problem, as well as the decline of Democratic influence in the 104th Congress and the rise of budget deficits, which sparked interest in reforms yielding savings.[40]

The formative influence of pathways on the terms of debate can best be seen by the accommodations that various actors must make to recast their claims when pathways shift. When issues take an expert turn, groups formerly skilled in the pluralistic pathway have to begin to develop research capabilities to mount effective expert-based arguments for their claims. Industries such as the tobacco industry, for instance, had to commission their own scientists to attempt to at least neutralize the increasingly compelling case made by antismoking groups on the expert pathway.

Conditions Affecting the Emergence of the Expert Pathway

As the foregoing suggests, experts play wide-ranging roles that elude our ability to predict or categorize their impact. Those who conclude that experts play only a limited role in policy except for narrow technical issues may be right most of the time but nonetheless fail to capture those episodes when experts can suddenly break open established iron triangles and policy images by reframing the problem underlying political coalitions.[41]

Nonetheless it is possible to suggest areas where experts are likely to have the greatest role in public policy. Their roles will tend to be most significant under the following circumstances:

- Rationalizing policy: Experts are likely to have more influence in adjusting established policy to account for performance shortfalls or redundancies where technically complex program-design questions have the highest salience. Conversely, breakthrough policies where policymakers make a great leap forward to address new problems are likely to be informed more by ideas, ideologies, and party positioning than expert ideas and data.

- Low visibility: It is likely that experts will play more vital roles on low-conflict issues where other actors perceive minimal political stakes to their own vital interests. R. Schwartz and B. Rosen find that differences among problems in the extent to which data are used in the policymaking process are largely explained by their political salience. Policy decisions with jurisdictional turf or macrobudgetary implications have high political salience and tend toward data immunity despite the conscious effort to rationalize decision making. More technical and professional policy decisions with low political salience tend to be more data-driven.[42]

- Complexity and uncertainty: Experts are likely to play greater roles when policy is viewed as being too complex for ordinary laymen to understand the risks entailed by adopting changes. Overburdened public decision makers are often likely to delegate complex specialized issues to expert committees or agencies to resolve to reduce their own culpability and legitimize policy outcomes. The use of the National Academy of Sciences by Congress to resolve technically vexing issues is an example of delegation at work. The Base Realignment and Closure Commission is another case where Congress mandated a presidentially appointed commission to develop a comprehensive downsizing proposal based on expert-based reviews supported by the Pentagon. Important, delegating such contentious issues to experts transfers potential political blame from Congress to nonpolitical agents.

- Limited engagement of other actors from other pathways: This frees up the experts to play a major role. As the foregoing suggests, other actors may perceive certain issues to be too technical and complex or too politically charged to warrant their involvement. In these cases, deference is given to experts to step in but with a short leash should problems and stakes escalate. At times, the disengagement of other actors occurs at the onset of problem definition where interest groups and party officials may be insufficiently organized or aware of the stakes associated with the issue. In these cases, expert institutions can occupy the field. The emergence of health problems such as cigarette smoking or obesity often occurs first in expert research institutions and journals, which get a clear path to frame the problem in compelling ways that eventually become difficult for other pathways to ignore.

- Enlightenment and problem definition: When considering the roles played by experts across all stages of the policy process—agenda formation, decision making, and implementation—ideas and analysis play a more formative role in agenda-formation and problem-definition stages than the drafting of specific legislation where positions have often become firmly established. Andrew Rich argues that experts and ideas play their greatest role in reframing issues or defining problems through new research and data, while their prospects become dimmer as political actors solidify positions and engage in mobilization. In Weiss's terms, the role of experts shifts over the stages of policymaking from the enlightenment model to the political model, as experts recede from independent shapers of dialogue to supportive ammunition for entrenched political actors.[43]

Conversely, other forces diminish experts' prospects. The high salience and mobilization of other pathways limit the degree of deference to experts in policymaking. In some issues, ideology, interests, and party positions are perceived to be of greater importance than ideas. The passage of the Bush tax cuts in 2001 is one example where a conservative president mobilized to deliver this policy plank to the conservative base that had come to define the Republican Party. In contrast to the 1986 tax reform, where an expert consensus fueled this major initiative to broaden the income tax base through elimination of various tax expenditures, in 2001 tax cuts became a political line in the sand that gathered various and often conflicting policy justifications.[44]

The failure of experts to establish and sustain a research consensus is a critical factor that mediates the influence of the expert pathway. Whether it be policy enlightenment or instrumental models, the role of experts is premised on a clear agreement about the meaning of data and research by people who are viewed as the most credible experts in a field. Thus the freedom-to-farm reforms in 1996 and the Tax Reform Act of 1986 were premised on the broad consensus among economists that the old farm subsidies and tax expenditures alike constituted an unjustified drag on the economy that ended up costing the entire nation in the form of reduced economic growth and higher costs. Conversely, conflict among experts dissipates their collective influence and enables actors in other pathways to divide and conquer by recruiting those experts who happen to agree with their particular policy prescriptions. The failure of experts to speak with one voice on health care reform has served to empower interest groups and partisan advocates with greater influence to offer alternatives that cannot be assessed against a comprehensive expert-based benchmark or criterion.

The failure of expert-based knowledge to solve policy problems can erode the influence of experts and lead to dissensus among experts themselves. When the economy of the 1970s was plagued by stagflation, political leaders and some economists lost faith in standard macroeconomic theory, which had failed to anticipate the concurrence of both high inflation and high unemployment. This policy disillusionment prompted the search for new theories and policy reforms that prompted the rise to prominence of supply-side economics. Unlike conventional Keynesian economics, this line of thinking shifted policy attention from influencing demand to promoting greater incentives for work, capital formation, and savings to improve productivity and long-term growth prospects. This in turn lent itself to more conservative policy prescriptions including reduction of tax rates, which allegedly discouraged labor supply, savings, and investment. Taken to extremes, this theory paved the way for the articulation of the "Laffer curve," which predicted that lower tax rates would bring higher revenues in their wake— a conclusion unsupported by data or informed opinion. The demoralization of economic experts paved the way for the emergence of new ideas cast to serve officials on the partisan and pluralist pathways. The 1981 tax cuts of the Reagan administration and the tax cuts of the Bush administration in 2001 and 2003 were premised on dissolution of the old economic consensus.[45]

When thinking about what specific roles expert knowledge will play in individual policy areas, two dimensions are critical: the degree of consensus or conflict among experts themselves and among relevant political actors. Table 4.1 illustrates that cohesion or dissensus among the suppliers and consumers of expert information may go a long way in determining what role experts play in the policy process.

In this model, cohesion by both experts and political leaders encourages the instrumental use of research knowledge. As Weiss suggests, this is the most demanding form of research utilization and one that can only be expected when strong agreement occurs on both sides of the information equation. Conversely, political and expert polarization provides the least propitious environment for expert influence. Weiss suggests that such an environment lends itself to the political model where contrasting groups of experts are employed by partisan combatants as political ammunition.

An enlightenment role might be expected to emerge when there is a research consensus but when political leaders are insufficiently cohesive to agree on specific

Table 4.1
Conditions for Differential Roles of Experts

EXPERTS/POLITICAL ACTORS	EXPERT CONSENSUS	EXPERT POLARIZATION
POLITICAL CONSENSUS	INSTRUMENTAL	SPECULATIVE AUGMENTATION
POLITICAL POLARIZATION	ENLIGHTENMENT	POLITICAL

applications to solve specific policy questions. Instead the research consensus works through issue networks to reframe and refocus the questions facing divided political leaders. Finally, unified political leaders can be expected to pursue public policy solutions even in the face of disagreement among experts when policies deliver electoral advantages, as will be discussed below. When experts are divided, leaders could either demur and avoid incurring potential risks from acting without the benefit of expert guidance, or they could take action through "speculative augmentation." In his study of air pollution, Charles Jones notes that anxious and ambitious policymakers legislated air pollution goals knowing that the technology was not yet available to meet those standards. Anxious to demonstrate their fealty to symbolic cleanup goals, they nonetheless ventured forth, which caused them to have to revise timetables and strategies when the original plans proved to be infeasible, costly, and politically ruinous.[46]

The Demand for Experts: The Mixed Incentives of Political Leaders

The variable prospects for experts rest in part on the uncertain receptivity of expert information by political leaders in the White House and Congress. On the one hand, many studies presume that political leaders have little reason to pay attention to expert theories or research. Leading treatments of Congress have been premised on rational choice perspectives where members are assumed to respond to the median voter. Classics in congressional analysis such as works by David Mayhew and R. Douglas Arnold assume that the primary goal of members of Congress is to appeal to their constituents through a range of policy positions, both real and symbolic, as well as localized benefits and constituency service.[47] Anxious members of Congress have their hands full in these frameworks, satisfying attentive publics and keeping latent inattentive publics from becoming mobilized against them in their districts. Anchored as delegates of their districts, members of Congress have little incentive to reach for policy optimization defined by policy analysts. Bureaucracies also have been regarded as resistant to policy analysis that disturbs their prevailing policy networks and images.[48]

There is strong evidence, moreover, to suggest that these negative incentives have intensified in recent decades.[49] When contrasted with that of the 1950s and 1960s, our policymaking process has become less consensual, more polarized along partisan lines, more contestable by increasingly well-organized interests, and more transparent thanks to the proliferation of media coverage. Walter Williams's classic work chronicles the decline of influence of policy analytical offices in federal agencies in recent years, stemming from the eclipse of neutral competence as a central value in executive agencies.[50] The Office of Management and Budget is a good case in point. While OMB budget analysts traditionally viewed themselves as the practitioners of neutral competence, this has become increasingly more tenuous as the number of political appointees increased from one—the director—to numerous officials in charge of major divisions on the budget, regulatory, and management of the agenda.[51]

The climate shift on Capitol Hill has been equally stark. The centralization of power in leadership and the polarization of politics have been responsible for a decline in deliberation. This is particularly the case for authorizing legislation, as much legislation skips potentially contentious authorization cycles to become attached to omnibus bills that bear the stamp of political leadership.[52] The amount of time members spend in Washington has declined precipitously in recent years; the number of legislative days for voting is scheduled for seventy-one days, the lowest in sixty years according to Norman Ornstein. Moreover, Ornstein chronicles a similar decline in the number of committee and subcommittee meetings, from an average of 5,300 in the 1960s and 1970s to 2,100 in the 2003–4 Congress. These trends partly reflect growing anxiety faced by members increasingly responsible for running their own campaign organizations and fundraising, with greater time spent in districts and less time spent in Washington governing.[53]

The flowering of more ideologically polarized parties has prompted less serious attention to policy research. As parties become increasingly captured by primary constituencies, elected officials become more preoccupied with appearing to support the hard-core ideas animating their extreme wings. Indeed, many members may perceive themselves to be at political risk by endorsing expert-based ideas and problems if these are at odds with their base. The political embrace of fundamentalist assaults on the teaching of evolution and the willful disavowal of expert opinion on global warming are two manifestations of these trends.

Susan Jacoby observes that these political trends are coupled with broader social and media factors, including the rise of a free-for-all internet environment, that are undermining the crucial role played by scientists and other experts in mediating what we know about our world.[54] Her book, published in 2009, echoes the pathbreaking work by Richard Hofstadter in the 1960s, which pointed to the recurrent strain of anti-intellectualism that penetrates public debates in our nation.[55] He notes that historically we idolize the self-made man and despise intellectual elites, believing that common sense is a more reliable guide to decisions in private and public life than formal knowledge and expertise.

Notwithstanding these trends, experts' political prospects are more mixed than might be expected. First, although members of Congress must remain focused on their home district coalitions and the needs of the median voter, members are also driven by the desire to create good policy.[56] Recent work on Congress has discovered that at times members of Congress go to extraordinary lengths to promote general benefits, even delegating its power to extralegislative commissions and the executive in specific cases.[57]

Given the goal of achieving good policy, Congress has an interest in understanding the potential for particular legislative proposals and designing alternatives to achieve the outcomes promised. As Keith Krehbiel's pioneering work on information theory suggests, congressional institutions are designed to equip Congress with the necessary specialization to address the uncertainties associated with legislative policymaking.[58] Central to information theory is the reconceptualization of the goals of members of Congress. Far from merely being interested in asserting positions on legislation in order to claim credit as Mayhew suggests, legislators are portrayed by Krehbiel and others in this tradition as focused on achieving policy success.[59] While always interested in the electoral connection, members are also vitally interested in the connections between their policy position and actual policy outcomes. New work has shown that the public's view of overall congressional performance has real electoral consequences for members. Incumbents in fact are held accountable not only for taking positions and delivering earmarked benefits to their districts, but also for the general performance of Congress in solving national problems.[60]

Esterling's important work follows in this tradition.[61] In his view Congress has significant incentives to use policy expertise to identify socially efficient policies. The considerable uncertainty that surrounds any major legislative proposal is a source of political risk to members of Congress interested in good policy and concerned that they may be identified with policy failures. Fortunately for Congress, Esterling argues that it can resolve uncertainties about policy outcomes by paying attention to interest group arguments that are focused on the pursuit of efficient policies. In this theory, advocates become the harbinger of analysis, as members of Congress can look for consensus or conflict among interest groups to identify the degree of uncertainty and disagreement over the prospective outcomes of policy proposals.

Other work suggests that Congress relies on its own independent policy-analysis capacity for policy development and oversight, whether through its own staff or through its support agencies—the CBO, the GAO, and the CRS. David Whiteman's study of congressional information shows that policy analyses and information produced by these offices played a surprisingly central role in the substantive development of legislative policy proposals and in policy argumentation.[62] Although congressional staff and members use information strategically to support positions they have already arrived at through other means, Whiteman finds a striking level of analytical utilization both to shape the concrete details of policy proposals and to set the overall conceptual frame for the policy debate. For instance, over the four major policy cases he examined, most committee staff reported using analytical reports from congressional support agencies and other think tanks to actually formulate legislation.

If elected officials are indeed interested in good policy, we need to understand more carefully the political incentives and conditions under which such incentives might become activated. The following factors are among those that help bring together the electoral connection with the expert pathway:

- Shame: At times expert ideas gain compelling political status, rising to the level of a valence issue. As will be noted in the next section, ideas grounded in a consensus by mainstream experts can gain credibility that can move agendas and prompt their embrace by members in the face of opposition by interest groups. Whether they are free trade, second-hand smoking bans, or trans fat prohibition initiatives, expert-based policies can enable leaders to more easily blunt opposition by narrow interests that heretofore had hegemonic influence over these areas.

- Competition: Political actors in Congress and the bureaucracy can be motivated to adopt recommendations or initiate their own expert-based ideas to compete with expert claims by other actors. The movement to create report cards assessing agencies and programs in an open, public process constitutes a strategy to jump-start competition among actors for public approbation and the high ground.[63] The foregoing suggests that multiple actors in competitive policymaking environments can inspire a "race to the top" among other actors to ratchet up attention to expert-based ideas.

- Conflict management: Reliance on policy research also can help policymakers channel and contain conflict by providing a credible base of information that is considered by all contestants as setting the parameters for agreement on a set of underlying empirical or analytical assumptions helps limit conflicts. The independence and respect accorded the CBO is an example of how much legislators need an independent referee to resolve fact-based questions, thereby controlling the scope of conflicts. Although there have been calls from some conservatives to open up CBO's "black box" to deploy dynamic scoring for tax policy changes, the validity and assumptions about specific CBO cost estimates are rarely challenged openly. It is conceivable that political actors observe norms of reciprocity, knowing that a challenge by one side would precipitate corresponding challenges by competing actors on other estimates, thereby throwing the entire process into disarray.

- Blame avoidance: Political leaders often turn to auditors and analysts to insulate themselves from political heat. Cloaking themselves in the legitimacy of analytical institutions can help leaders make hard choices. In the United Kingdom, the political establishment turned to the National Audit Office to certify the national budget numbers prior to elections, thereby legitimizing these politically charged data with the imprimatur of a disinterested party.

Concluding Observations

Expert-based policymaking is alive in our system, if not always well. It has become a competing avenue to achieve policy change in our system. Although they provide compelling appeal and advantages to policymakers, it is equally clear that expert policies compete with other pathways for influence and possible hegemony. The policy achievements of experts are hard fought and also vulnerable to countermobilization by actors in other pathways.

We are fortunate indeed that experts have become institutionalized in the policy process. Unlike the officials in other pathways, experts are responsible to a profession, not to the electorate or media markets. While undercutting their political legitimacy, this professional accountability helps ensure that they can make independent contributions to help national leaders chart a course toward more informed and effective policy in increasingly uncertain and challenging times. They have left a legacy of major policy reform that gained legitimacy and political appeal as a result of expert-based ideas and mobilization.

Ultimately the fate of the expert pathway will be a function of trends in the broader political system. Many of these trends do not auger well for the influence of credible analysis. Short-term political perspectives, partisan polarization, and media-driven policymaking are on the rise. However, as noted above, there are continued sustainable incentives on the part of political leaders to use and support traditional consensus-based research and research institutions.

As experts gain greater currency, their gains inspire actors in other pathways to redouble their efforts to contest their influence. The proliferation of scientists, economists, and policy analysts employed by contending interests is an ironic tribute to the growing appeal of the expert pathway. Although reflecting the new-found power of professional ideas and knowledge, this development threatens to ultimately undermine the credibility of expert communities by eroding professional consensus, which is so vital to their impact on policymaking.

Certainly the use of expert-based arguments by advocacy groups has the potential to elevate the dialogue. At the very least, policy arguments may be conducted on analytical grounds susceptible to validation and legitimation. However, on balance these trends are worrisome, for they portend the erosion of informed decision making anchored in consensus-based research ideas, to be replaced by a more opportunistic advocacy "analysis" where ideas become props to advance particular interests and preformed positions.

The Troubled Asset Relief Program (TARP): A Case Study

The year 2008 was a troubled time for the nation's economy. The US economy had slipped into a financial crisis that brought about the most serious recession experienced since World War II. The seeds of the crisis were laid in the previous twenty-five years of innovative financing and borrowing that sent the nation's housing and stock markets to record heights. Borrowing served as the shaky foundation undergirding corporate investment, government debt, and personal consumption.

Nowhere were these trends as strong as in housing. Advanced financing strategies vacuumed more money into housing thanks to the securitization of mortgages, the use of credit scoring that extended housing credits to larger numbers of lower-income families, and low interest rates that encouraged a speculative spike in housing prices. Questionable housing loans were securitized and sold to investors throughout the world, appearing on the balance sheets of many financial institutions. As the underlying value of the loans themselves became more suspect, these instruments contaminated balance sheets and eroded the confidence of counterparties and investors. By early 2007, experts working at different institutions of the federal government, including the Department of the Treasury, the Federal Reserve Board, and the Federal Deposit Insurance Corporation, were well aware of the housing crisis and predicted that the situation was getting worse and would have important implications for the financial system. By early 2008, it became evident that their predictions were correct, and the mortgage crisis started to hurt Wall Street's largest financial institutions. On March 14, 2008, the investment firm Bear Stearns collapsed. The experts pointed out that the government should take necessary steps as soon as possible or risk the entire financial system. Consequently, with the help of the Treasury, a deal was reached whereby the Fed provided JPMorgan Chase with financing to purchase Bear Stearns.

The experts in the Treasury took steps to devise a future plan in case of financial emergency. Based on inputs from market participants, they concluded that a government fund of $500 billion would be necessary to avert the expected losses in case of a future emergency. One such expert, Phillip Swagel, pointed out that given the political and economic conditions of 2008, it was highly unlikely that Congress would allow this, and in fact the proposal went nowhere.[64]

The crisis, however, reached a more intense phase by the early summer of 2008, when the effects of the housing crisis were realized through the collapse of the Independent National Mortgage Corporation (IndyMac) and severe pressure was placed on government-sponsored enterprises the Federal Home Loan Mortgage Corporation (Freddie Mac) and the Federal National Mortgage Association (Fannie Mae)—all large institutions critical to the functioning of the housing market and implicitly backed by federal guarantees. By August it became clear to the Treasury that both Fannie and Freddie were "deeply insolvent," and on September 7, 2008, the federal government in effect took over both firms, a commitment costing $200 billion. Overnight the federal government became the largest holder of home mortgages in the country, thanks to the takeover of these housing finance agencies.

The final phase of the crisis took place on September 15, 2008, when Lehman Brothers—another large Wall Street investment bank—collapsed. The Treasury tried but failed to find a private-sector buyer, and Lehman was allowed to fail. In response the Dow Jones average lost an extraordinary five hundred points in one day. Foreign investors also reacted sharply to this event and began withdrawing money from the US stock market and financial firms. On the very next day, American International Group (AIG), the insurance giant, collapsed. Faced with a mounting financial crisis, this time the Treasury and the Fed decided to intervene, as analysts in those agencies agreed that these events would have far-reaching and disruptive effects on the entire financial system and the US economy. Consequently, the government extended an initial $85 billion line of credit to AIG. Despite this, the news of these disasters created panic as investors began pulling out funds, and bank lending ground to a halt. The Dow dropped another 449 points with no end in sight.

In order to deal with this financial crisis, Henry Paulson, secretary of the Treasury, and Ben Bernanke, chairman of the Federal Reserve's board of governors, went to Congress on September 18, 2008. They informed congressional leaders that the financial crisis posed a serious threat to the economy. In order to deal with this, they wanted authority to buy the illiquid assets that were creating uncertainty about the viability of firms at the core of financial system. The Treasury sent a three-page proposal to the Congress which would give the secretary "unprecedented, one time authority" to spend $700 billion to purchase mortgage-related assets over the next two years under a Troubled Asset Relief Program (TARP). The proposal sought maximum flexibility and did not offer any information about the nature or value of the troubled assets. Furthermore, the proposal also included a controversial section stating that "decisions by the Secretary pursuant to the authority of this Act are non-reviewable and committed to agency discretion and may not be reviewed by any court of law or administrative agency." Thus the initial proposal contained very limited legislative oversight and judicial review over the actions taken by the Treasury Department.

Members of Congress, though acknowledging that something should be done, were not happy about the blank check. Under considerable pressure from the market and the White House, this original three-page proposal was rapidly expanded to a 110-page bill, with new sections added providing for congressional oversight, regulatory reform, and bans on financial executives using TARP funds to pay themselves bonuses and inflated salaries. However, as Congress was approaching the November election and opinion polls showed a strong public opposition to the bailout, the House rejected the initial proposal (228-205) on September 29, 2008. Members of both parties defied their leadership by voting against it. World markets reacted sharply, dropping the Dow by another 777 points. This reaction compelled congressional leaders to reconsider the bill. Ultimately it was expanded to 451 pages, ensuring further oversight mechanisms, and adding an additional $150 billion in unrelated tax sweeteners. The inclusion of these provisions swung the balance in favor of the bailout. On October 3, the House passed the act, and on that same day the president signed the Emergency Economic Stabilization Act of 2008 into law.

If we look at the process through which the bill came onto the agenda, it becomes evident that two factors played the most important roles: the presence of a crisis and the role played by the experts. From the very beginning the issue was dominated by the experts working in different government agencies, including the Department of the Treasury and the Federal Reserve Board. These experts actually predicted the economic crisis, recommended solutions, and took different actions to deal with it. The interest groups and political parties rarely intervened in the working of the experts. However, if there had been no crisis at hand, it is unlikely that the experts would have played such a dominant role in setting the agenda. As Swagel argued, "a massive intervention in financial markets could be proposed only if Secretary Paulson and Chairman Bernanke went to Congress and announced that the financial system and the economy were on the verge of collapse."[65] This is precisely what happened on September 18, 2008.

Similarly, the symbolic pathway was also at play when the House rejected the initial proposal. By rejecting the proposal, it had reacted to broad public distaste for federal bailouts in general, anticipating the potential fallout in the elections less than two months away. As of September 25, the offices of Sen. Dianne Feinstein (D-CA) had received a total of 39,180 e-mails, calls, and letters on the bailout, with the overwhelming majority against it. However, the prevalence of the crisis and agreement among the experts about the proposed solution forced the House leaders to change their position, and the expert pathway dominated the final passage of the bill as the Treasury got what it demanded—a $700 billion TARP fund. In the House a majority of Democrats supported the legislation, while Republicans were nearly evenly divided. President George W. Bush signed the bill within hours of its passage.

As often happens with broad-based and expert-based reform legislation, majorities favoring the bailout quickly eroded, recaptured by actors in the symbolic and pluralist pathways. Financial institutions complained about regulations and salary restrictions that were attached to placate liberal Democrats. Broader segments of the Republican Party reframed the bailout as part of the Tea Party movement against activist government, toppling such Republicans as Sen. Bob Bennett from Utah, who had voted for the legislation. In the final analysis, the bailout was sustained, even though some of the members who voted for it were ousted for their support.

Notes

1. Woodrow Wilson, "The Study of Administration," *Political Science Quarterly* 55: 481–506.

2. Andrew Rich, *Think Tanks, Public Policy and the Politics of Expertise* (New York: Cambridge University Press, 2004).

3. Steven Brint, *In an Age of Experts: The Changing Role of Professionals in Politics and Public Life* (Princeton, NJ: Princeton University Press, 1994), 3.

4. Kay Schlozman and John Tierney, *Organized Interests in American Democracy* (New York: Harper & Row, 1986), 77.

5. Daniel Bell, *The Coming of Post-Industrial Society* (New York: Basic Books, 1973).

6. Lowi, "American Business, Public Policy."

7. Robert Blendon, Sara Abiola, and John Benson, "Evidence-Based Policymaking in a Polarized Environment: Can the IPAD Bridge the Gap?," Health Affairs Blog, August 16, 2012, http://healthaffairs.org/blog/2012/06/15/evidence-based-policymaking-in-a-polar ized-environment-can-the-ipab-bridge-the-gap/.

8. Lawrence Brown, *New Policies, New Politics* (Washington, DC: Brookings Institution Press, 1981).

9. Aaron Wildavsky, "Policy as Its Own Cause," in *Speaking Truth to Power: The Art and Craft of Policy Analysis*, Aaron Wildavsky, ed. (Boston: Little, Brown, 1979), 63.

10. Kevin Esterling, *The Political Economy of Expertise* (Ann Arbor: University of Michigan Press, 2004).

11. Brad T. Gomez and T. Matthew Wilson, "Political Sophistication and Attribution of Blame in the Wake of Hurricane Katrina," *Publius* 38, no. 4 (September 2008).

12. Network of Schools of Public Policy, Affairs, and Administration website, www .naspaa.org/about_naspaa/about/overview.asp.

13. See Beryl A. Radin, *Beyond Machiavelli: Policy Analysis Comes of Age* (Washington, DC: Georgetown University Press, 2000).

14. Patricia W. Ingraham, "The Federal Public Service: The People and the Challenge," in *The Executive Branch*, Joel D. Aberbach and Mark A. Peterson, eds. (New York: Oxford Press, 2005).

15. Congressional Budget Office, *Characteristics and Pay of Federal Civilian Employees* (Washington, DC: Congressional Budget Office, 2007).

16. Quoted in Radin, *Beyond Machiavelli*, 37.

17. For analysis of the saga of the Office of Technology Assessment, see Bruce Bimber, *The Politics of Expertise in Congress: The Rise and Fall of the Office of Technology Assessment* (Albany: State University of New York Press, 1996).

18. David Whiteman, *Communication in Congress* (Lawrence: University Press of Kansas, 1995).

19. John A. Hird, *Power, Knowledge and Politics: Policy Analysis in the States* (Washington, DC: Georgetown University Press, 2005).

20. Donald Abelson, *Do Think Tanks Matter? Assessing the Impact of Public Policy Institutes* (Montreal: McGill-Queens University Press, 2002).

21. Andrew Rich and R. Kent Weaver, "Advocates and Analysts: Think Tanks and the Politicization of Expertise," in *Interest Group Politics*, Cigler and Loomis, eds., 243.

22. Rich, *Think Tanks*.

23. AARP website, www.aarp.org/research/.

24. American Bankers Association website, www.aba.com/tools/economic/pages/default.aspx.

25. Barbara S. Romzek and Melvin J. Dubnick, "Accountability in the Public Sector: Lessons from the Challenger Tragedy," *Public Administration Review* 47, no. 3 (May–June 1987).

26. Joseph White, "The Two-Faced Profession," *Public Budgeting and Finance* (Fall 1990): 92–102.

27. Heclo, "Issue Networks and the Executive Establishment."

28. John R. Ruggie, "International Responses to Technology: Concepts and Trends," *International Organization* 29 (1975): 560–70.

29. Stephen Skowronek, *Building a New American State: The Expansion of National Administrative Capacities, 1877-1920* (New York: Cambridge University Press, 1982).

30. Brian Cook, *Bureaucracy and Self-Government: Reconsidering the Role of Public Administration in American Politics* (Baltimore: Johns Hopkins University Press, 1996), 137–38.

31. Dwight Waldo, *The Enterprise of Public Administration: A Summary View* (Novato, CA: Chandler & Sharp, 1980).

32. Wilson, "Study of Administration."

33. Anderson, *Public Policymaking*, 163.

34. Carol Weiss, "Congressional Committees as Users of Analysis," *Journal of Policy Analysis and Management* 8, no. 3: 411–31.

35. Cited in Hird, *Power, Knowledge and Politics*, 12.

36. Carol Weiss, "The Many Meanings of Research Utilization," *Public Administration Review* 5 (1979): 426–31.

37. Ibid.

38. Kingdon, *Agendas, Alternatives, and Public Policies*, 1st ed.

39. Paul L. Posner, "Accountability Challenges of Third Party Government," in *The Tools of Government*, Lester Salamon, ed. (New York: Oxford University Press, 2002).

40. Béland and Waddan, *Politics of Policy Change*, 175.

41. Brint, *In an Age of Experts*, 136.

42. R. Schwartz and B. Rosen, "Bringing Data to Bear: The Politics of Evidence-Based Health Policymaking," *Public Money and Management* 24, no. 2 (2004): 121–28.

43. Rich, *Think Tanks*, 139.

44. See Timothy J. Conlan and Paul L. Posner, "A Solution for All Seasons: The Politics of Tax Reduction in the Bush Administration," in *Building Coalitions, Making Policy*, Martin A. Levin, Daniel DiSalvo, and Martin M. Shapiro, eds. (Baltimore: Johns Hopkins University Press, 2012).

45. Bryan Jones and Walter Williams, *The Politics of Bad Ideas: The Great Tax Cut Delusion and the Decline of Good Government in America* (New York: Pearson-Longman, 2008).

46. Charles O. Jones, *Clean Air: Policies and Politics of Pollution Control* (Pittsburgh, PA: University of Pittsburgh Press, 1975).

47. David Mayhew, *Congress: The Electoral Connection* (New Haven, CT: Yale University Press, 1974), and R. Douglas Arnold, *The Logic of Congressional Action* (New Haven, CT: Yale University Press, 1991).

48. James Q. Wilson, *Bureaucracy: What Government Agencies Do and Why They Do It* (New York: Basic Books, 1991).

49. David R. Beam, "If Public Ideas Are So Important Now, Why Are Policy Analysts So Depressed?," *Journal of Policy Analysis and Management* 15, no. 3 (1996): 430–37.

50. Walter Williams, *Honest Numbers and Democracy* (Washington, DC: Georgetown University Press, 1998).

51. Shelly Tompkins, *Inside OMB* (New York: M. E. Sharpe, 1998).

52. Paul Quirk, "Deliberation and Decision-making," in *The Legislative Branch*, Paul J. Quirk and Sarah A. Binder, eds. (New York: Oxford Press, 2005), 314–48.

53. Norman Ornstein, "Part-Time Congress," *Washington Post*, March 7, 2006.

54. Susan Jacoby, *The Age of American Unreason* (New York, Vintage, 2009).

55. Richard Hofstadter, *Anti-Intellectualism in American Life* (New York: Vintage, 1966).

56. Richard E. Fenno Jr., *Home Style: House Members in Their Districts* (Boston: Little, Brown, 1978), 137.

57. Lawrence Becker, *Doing the Right Thing: Collective Action and Procedural Choice in the New Legislative Process* (Columbus: Ohio State University Press, 2005).

58. Keith Krehbiel, *Information and Legislative Organization* (Ann Arbor: University of Michigan Press, 1992).

59. Mayhew, *Congress*.

60. E. Scott Adler and John D. Wilkerson, *Congress and the Politics of Problem Solving* (New York: Cambridge University Press, 2012).

61. Esterling, *Political Economy of Expertise*.

62. Whiteman, *Communications in Congress*, 170.

63. William T. Gormley and David L. Weimer, *Organizational Report Cards* (Cambridge, MA: Harvard University Press, 1999).

64. Philip Swagel, "The Financial Crisis: An Inside View," *Brookings Economic Papers*, Spring 2009.

65. Ibid., 33.

CHAPTER FIVE

The Symbolic Pathway

- In 1974, following an article in *Parade* magazine, a national Sunday newspaper supplement, Sen. James Buckley (R-NY) introduced a bill to protect the privacy of students' school records. In order to move the legislation quickly and avoid "hearing the bill to death," Buckley subsequently offered it instead as an amendment to an upcoming education reauthorization bill. A few senators raised concerns about the lack of hearings on the issue, but even skeptics agreed that "everyone is for protecting privacy." The full Senate quickly adopted the measure on a voice vote, and the "Buckley Amendment" went directly to conference with the House, where the Family Educational Rights and Privacy Act was enacted as part of an omnibus education bill.[1]

- In 1986, federal legislation mandating the removal of asbestos from the nation's schools (the Asbestos Hazard Emergency Response Act, or AHERA) raced through Congress, winning unanimous approval by both the House and Senate before being signed by a conservative president. Although the science supporting this legislation was incomplete—and the costs it imposed on school districts ran into billions of dollars—little opposition arose, even from the state and local governments that would have to pick up the tab. Because the measure was perceived as saving schoolchildren from a deadly menace, few legislators or lobbyists dared to publicly challenge or oppose it.[2]

- In 1999, federal budget policy became focused on the concept of a Social Security "lockbox." Although the notion was widely derided as a ploy distorting rational budget making, both parties quickly began competing for ownership of the popular idea. Republicans had invented the concept as a way to protect themselves from charges that their tax cut proposals would sap the Social Security trust fund. After their version of the lockbox passed the House by an overwhelming margin, President Clinton was prompted to propose his own variation in October 1999. By the following year, Vice President Al Gore had extended the concept even further, championing a new lockbox for Medicare as well.

These three policies might seem to have little in common. Each dealt with a different substantive issue, in a different decade, within a different political climate. Yet they all share an important characteristic: Each is difficult to explain in terms of commonly accepted perspectives on the policy process.

Neither the pluralist nor partisan pathways can explain the adoption of these programs. Interest groups were largely invisible in the process, and to the extent that "pressure groups" were pressuring Congress in these cases, they tended to be in opposition. The major education interest groups were caught off guard by the suddenness with which the Buckley Amendment appeared and moved forward. Although they sought to water down the measure in conference committee—their first and last real opportunity to do so—they had bigger fish to fry in a large and complex education bill and failed to win changes in the privacy provisions. Likewise, in the case of school asbestos removal, the National School Boards Association and other state and local groups were generally opposed to what became a multibillion-dollar federal mandate, but they were too "ambivalent and crosspressured" to be effective players in the process.[3] Nor was the Social Security lockbox idea developed and promoted by groups representing elderly citizens. Many of these groups were surprised by the political appeal of this notion, and they were forced to scramble to work with the White House on a version that they could support.

Political parties also failed to play the leading role that one might expect in these legislative dramas. They lacked so much as a walk-on part in the politics of the Buckley Amendment and AHERA. When it began, the lockbox issue did appear to be a good old-fashioned partisan battle in Congress—with Democrats on one side and Republicans on the other. But it evolved into an elaborate dance of bipartisan blame avoidance instead. The concept was invented by Republican strategists looking for a way to inoculate their party against Democratic charges that they were raiding Social Security to fund Republican tax-cut proposals. Although Democrats attempted and failed to table the proposal on a party-line vote in the House, they were afraid to be seen opposing this appealing notion, and all but twelve voted for the lockbox on final passage. Democrats were more successful at stalling action in the Senate, but open opposition was considered dangerous, and President Clinton subsequently felt compelled to offer his own version of a lockbox later in the year.

If not the politics of organization, what about the expert pathway? As chapter 4 makes clear, some of the most important initiatives in contemporary policymaking—airline deregulation, tax reform, and TARP—can only be understood by taking the independent role of *ideas* seriously, and not just any ideas but *serious ideas*.[4] The outlines and details of such policies were crafted by cadres of policy experts and professionals in government, academia, and Washington think tanks, whose influence derived from the persuasive power of ideas that have been refined, refereed, and perfected within specialized policy communities. Such cases all demonstrate that policy experts can serve as effective reference points for the media, decision makers, and other nonspecialists in the policymaking arena, especially when they have achieved a broad degree of consensus among themselves.

Yet, again, none of the cases raised at the beginning of this chapter can be explained by the politics of expert ideas. The idea for the Buckley Amendment came out of a celebrity magazine, not a peer-reviewed journal in education or the social sciences. AHERA had stronger scientific foundations, but even here there was no expert consensus on the dangers posed by asbestos or the appropriate policy response. And many budgetary experts thought the lockbox idea was a worthless charade—or worse. Journalist David Broder wrote: "A longtime Republican budget writer describes this legislation as 'a piece of trash' . . . cheap symbolism that is doomed to fail if put to the test."[5]

Symbolism is the key word here. There is another form of the politics of ideas that has grown increasingly important in recent decades but whose role is less appreciated than the politics of expertise. Like Broder's expert source suggests, this form of idea-based politics is highly "symbolic," a term that highlights the less rigorous but often powerfully emotive character of the ideas that power the symbolic pathway.

The Nature, Origins, and Dynamics of Symbolic Politics

A symbol is "something that stands for another thing, especially an object used to represent something abstract."[6] By the same token, symbolic policymaking is based on representations and appearances. Its appeal derives from favorable association with the abstract goals expressed in legislative purpose or policy pronouncements, rather than support for the policy alternative, instruments, or program structure employed. An example from environmental policy can serve to illustrate the point. In 1969, Congress passed the National Environmental Policy Act (NEPA), which required that potential environmental impacts be studied and identified in all federally supported construction projects. The legislation proved to have far-reaching effects on federal, state, and local highway and infrastructure projects, often causing long delays and changes in approach. Passage of the act was described this way by Richard Liroff: "NEPA was enacted when public interest in the environment was rising. . . . Clearly a gesture of Congressional concern was in order. For many legislators, undoubtedly, a vote for NEPA was symbolic—akin to a vote for motherhood and apple pie."[7]

Reliance on symbolic goals to generate support for legislation in Congress, with little consideration of how the goals will actually be achieved, is a distinctive approach to coalition building. It contrasts with more traditional means of fashioning support for legislation, such as compromising over the provisions of an act in order to gain majority support, logrolling many different benefits and programs into one bill, bowing to the imperatives of party unity, or deferring to the expertise of policy specialists. Compared with these methods, symbolic politics is typically a less expensive, faster means to win support. To be successful, it must strike a rich vein of preexisting sympathy, but it does not presuppose that advocates possess a reservoir of power or resources for bargaining with a broad array of interests. So long as Congress's attention can be focused on some widely held *goal* of legislation rather than on more complex questions of which program approach is most appropriate to address the goal, coalition building can be greatly simplified.

This focus on symbolism as a coalition-building device is different from the perspective on symbolic politics that has been previously discussed in political science literature. Influential research in the past has emphasized the role of symbolism as a policy *output*: actions that purport to address a problem but that are designed to accomplish little. This is what David Mayhew meant when he equated political symbolism with the term "position taking": "The term symbolic can . . . usefully be applied where Congress prescribes policy effects but does not act so as to achieve them. . . . Position-taking politics may produce statutes that are long on goals but short on means to achieve them."[8] This is comparable to the meaning that Murray Edelman attached to the concept in his well-known work on "the symbolic uses of politics."[9] An example might be the Civil Rights Act of 1957, which among other things established the US Commission on Civil Rights. Passed over the strenuous objections of Southern conservatives in the Senate, the act was widely disparaged by civil rights advocates as a "pitiful remnant of a civil rights bill" after its major enforcement provisions were removed to ensure passage.[10]

In contrast to the politics of position taking, we are emphasizing symbolic politics as a *means*—a method of generating support for what may be highly consequential but poorly understood public policies. And, as in the case of NEPA, the policies adopted by these means may have far-reaching substantive effects even if these are not considered at the time of passage. NEPA, for example, generated much more controversy and political recriminations *after* it was adopted than before. Potential implementation problems were not anticipated in the legislative process because careful scrutiny and understanding of the substantive provisions of the policy were sacrificed in the focus on goals and intentions. As Liroff notes in his study of NEPA, "little did [legislators] realize . . . that in voting to enact NEPA, they were placing a potent weapon in the hands of citizen activists."[11] A congressional staff member even asserted that "if Congress had known what it was doing, it would not have passed the law."[12]

Key Features of Symbolic Policymaking

What sorts of ideas can become the basis for symbolic politics? One feature of symbolic ideas is that they tend to be evocative and metaphorical rather than precise and analytical. Such ideas tend to elicit emotional and visceral responses from people rather than reflection and deliberation. In addition, symbolic ideas tend to be simple rather than complex. They must be easy to grasp by a large and often inattentive public, which, if suddenly awakened to the issue, may become very attentive indeed. Because of their emotive and simplistic framing, symbolic policies also tend to be considered and adopted rapidly by Congress, with relatively little deliberation. A single focusing event or political spark may set off a race to legislative enactment, regardless of the size or complexity of the legislation. Finally, symbolic policies tend to generate significant unanticipated consequences. Serious debate about the costs and benefits of legislative action and the most appropriate tools of policy response often occurs during implementation rather than enactment. Each of these features warrants some elaboration.

First, symbolic politics tend to be evocative rather than rational. Whereas expert ideas draw persuasive power from the strength of their logic, reasoning, and evidence, symbolic ideas derive power from metaphors and/or their ability to evoke widely shared values and broadly accepted folk wisdom. Mark Moore observes in his essay "What Makes Public Ideas Powerful?": "It is not clear reasoning or carefully developed and interpreted facts that make ideas convincing. Rather, ideas seem to become anchored in people's minds through illustrative anecdotes, simple diagrams and pictures, or connections with broad commonsense ideologies that define human nature and social responsibilities."[13] Consequently, if a policy under consideration can become so closely and inextricably linked to some widely accepted value or idea so that the decision becomes viewed as one of support for the value or idea itself rather than the particular approach to achieving it, then a favorable outcome is often a foregone conclusion.

An example is provided by former New York City mayor Ed Koch, who penned a widely cited essay denouncing the costs and administrative restrictions imposed by federal regulations on local governments. Washington was placing a "mandate millstone" around the necks of mayors and governors, Koch declared. Ironically, however, as a member of Congress prior to becoming mayor, he had supported many of the regulations he later denounced. Underscoring the dynamics of symbolic politics, he claimed that he had had little choice in doing so: "I do not for a moment claim immunity from the mandate fever of the 1970s. As a member of Congress, I voted for many [mandates]. . . . The bills I voted for in Washington came to the House floor in a form that compelled approval. After all, who can vote against clean air and water, or better access and education for the handicapped?"[14] Thus one of the chief tactical decisions in symbolic coalition building is portraying an issue in such a way that it becomes identified with the symbolic goal itself. The growing prominence of symbolic politics helps explain why we hear so much about "spin" and "issue framing" in politics today.

A second and related characteristic of symbolic ideas is that they tend to be visceral and emotive rather than deliberative and reflective. Philip Heymann has observed that "frequently, perhaps generally, unproven and perhaps unprovable assumptions about human behavior are crucial to government choices. These assumptions are grounded more in our personal psychologies and histories, in our group memberships and accepted mythologies, than in any scientific evidence."[15] Emotional responses allow for snap judgments and quick decisions. Policy advocates often seek to take advantage of this and move quickly; opponents may seek to slow the process and hope that the outcome will change as emotions cool and reflection sets in.

A late 1980s proposal to adopt a constitutional amendment outlawing "flag burning" provides a good example. Few symbols in American politics carry greater emotional attachment than the national flag. So long as proponents of the amendment could focus on visceral images of long-haired, flag-burning demonstrators, they had a clear political advantage, and congressional enactment of the amendment seemed quite likely for a time. Outnumbered opponents were able to stem the tide, however, by slowing down the legislative process and allowing passions to cool. As the public lost interest and other issues gained more prominence, the political advantage shifted their way.

Welfare "reform" provides another example of visceral symbolic politics. Historically few issues have incorporated more emotional and symbolic baggage in American politics than welfare. For example, polls of public opinion have produced dramatically different results depending on whether people were asked about their support for "welfare" or for "aid to needy citizens," because each phrase elicits very different images in the minds of respondents.[16] This is what lent such power to Bill Clinton's 1992 promise to make work-and-time limits the cornerstones of his welfare reform policy. Experts who had spent years conducting studies to investigate work disincentives in welfare programs suddenly found that "values trump analysis" once issues were moved to a broader public arena where "two years and you're off" was all it took to capture the public's imagination.[17]

The "two years" slogan illustrates a third important characteristic of symbolic ideas: simplicity. To be effective, symbolic ideas do not have to be, and indeed ought not to be, complex and comprehensive. Short slogans that express the public mood, tap an emotional current, or capture the conventional wisdom are the best candidates for symbolic success. To quote Mark Moore again: "Many ideas that become powerful lack the intellectual properties that policy analysts hold dear. Most . . . are not very complex or differentiated. There is no clear separation of ends from means, of diagnosis from interventions, or assumptions from demonstrated facts, or of blame from causal effect. All are run together in a simple gestalt that indicates the nature of the problem, whose fault it is, and how it will be solved."[18]

Examples of this process in modern politics seem almost too numerous to list. Slogans such as "three strikes and you're out," " two years and you're off," and ending the "marriage penalty" or the "death tax" have not only littered the realm of political rhetoric in recent decades—they have also proceeded to shape and constrain the actual policies adopted in ways that most substantive experts found nonsensical or repugnant. Nor are symbolic ideas confined to sloganeering. Even powerful concepts that have shaped long-term economic policy, such as the crusade against deficit spending, have been rooted more in "commonsense" extensions from family budgeting practices than in sophisticated economic theory.

From Obstacle Course to Legislative Race Track

Congress is often portrayed as an obstacle course or a place where innovative policy solutions go to die. With its complex structure of two chambers, dozens of committees and subcommittees holding virtual ex ante and ex post vetoes, Senate filibusters, polarized parties, and so forth, it is no wonder that the large majority of bills introduced in any given session of Congress fail to be considered, much less passed.[19] The legislative process is often compared to a series of potential choke points, with each successive stage acting to slow down consideration of legislation if not to kill it outright.[20] Yet it is also the case that some pieces of legislation—including very complex and consequential pieces of legislation—race through Congress, making the process look more like a sprint than a series of high hurdles. Often such policies are advanced along the symbolic pathway.

For example, the USA PATRIOT Act passed just six weeks after draft legislation was first sent to Congress by the George W. Bush administration in 2001. This complex and important piece of legislation expanded procedures for tracking and gathering the personal communications of persons suspected of terrorism-related activities, eased restrictions on foreign intelligence gathering within the United States, afforded the US intelligence community greater access to information unearthed during criminal investigations, eased the rules for conducting surveillance under the Foreign Intelligence Surveillance Act (FISA), expanded the authority of the secretary of the Treasury to regulate the activities of American financial institutions, required securities brokers and advisers and commodity dealers to file suspicious-activity reports, defined a series of new terrorism-related crimes, authorized "sneak-and-peek" search warrants, permitted nationwide execution of warrants in terrorism cases, lengthened the statute of limitations applicable to cases of terrorism, and increased the reward for information in terrorism cases, counterfeiting, cybercrime, and charity fraud.[21]

Many of these provisions had been considered, debated, opposed, or consigned to limbo by Congress or executive branch officials in the past. Yet, combined into the wide-ranging USA PATRIOT Act, formerly controversial provisions rushed through Congress with overwhelming bipartisan support in both the House and the Senate. The final version of the bill was introduced in the House on October

23. It passed the House the following day on a vote of 357-66, and the House bill was passed intact by the Senate the very next day on a vote of 98-1.

What made the difference? Passage of the PATRIOT Act was viewed as an urgent response to the terrorist attacks of September 11, 2001. In the context of what President Bush portrayed as a battle between good and evil, and backed by strong popular support to "do something," members of Congress from both parties overcame prior misgivings and came together to quickly pass the bill. House minority leader Dick Gephardt (D-MO) said at the time: "We are shoulder to shoulder. We are in complete agreement and we will act together as one. There is no division between the parties, between the Congress and the President."[22] Nor was the PATRIOT Act the only rapid legislative response to 9/11. By the time that Congress adjourned in December 2001, it had passed nine bills and three joint resolutions related to the attacks. This included legislation designed to bail out the airline industry, combat terrorism, provide an emergency supplemental appropriation, and authorize the use of military force in Afghanistan. Many passed unanimously or virtually so, including the resolution for military action in Afghanistan that still governed military involvement there more than a decade later.

Thus 9/11 epitomized what Kingdon called a "focusing event"—a dramatic event or crisis that dominates attention, resets the policy agenda, and opens a policy window for rapid and often ambitious policy response.[23] Such focusing events often provide the context for symbolic policymaking behavior.

The role of a perceived crisis or focusing event can be seen in another contemporary piece of complex and important legislation, the so-called Sarbanes-Oxley Act of 2002 (P.L. 107-204). The law, which President Bush called "the most far-reaching reforms of American business practices since the time of Franklin Delano Roosevelt," established stronger standards for corporate governance and management, strengthened the Securities and Exchange Commission (SEC), created a new regulatory agency—the Public Accounting Oversight Board—and strengthened rules for public accounting practices, auditor independence, and financial disclosure.[24]

The legislation emerged in the wake of a series of financial scandals in the late 1990s and early 2000s that highlighted weaknesses in corporate accounting and financial reporting, the most significant of which involved the giant Enron Corporation and Arthur Andersen LLP, Enron's auditors. These scandals appeared sufficient to force a legislative response by Congress, but heavy lobbying by the financial and accounting industries watered down legislation in the House and appeared to stymie action in the Senate.[25] This situation was abruptly altered when Arthur Andersen was found guilty in federal court of obstruction of justice charges in the Enron case.[26] In the shock that followed, the Senate Banking Committee passed a strong reform bill by a vote of 17-4 on June 18, 2002. Within weeks, the entire Senate followed suit after yet another accounting scandal led to the fall of WorldCom. Feverish public concern about the integrity of the financial reporting system led the full Senate to pass the Sarbanes accounting reform bill unanimously, by a vote of 97-0, on July 15, 2002.[27] Senators who just weeks earlier had publicly opposed the legislation suddenly switched sides and voted for it. After a hurried conference committee took just three days to iron out differences between the two chambers' bills, both houses overwhelmingly passed final landmark legislation on July 25, 2002. The House passed what became known as the Sarbanes-Oxley Act by a vote of 423-3, and the Senate followed the same day with a vote of 99-0 in favor.[28] What normally would have been an arcane, complex, and, to the general public, nearly invisible piece of legislation had been transformed by financial crisis into the lodestar of reform, which suddenly propelled it through Congress along the symbolic pathway.

The Consequences of Symbolic Policymaking

Apart from the tactics used and the actors involved, what difference does it make if symbolism is the major coalition-building device relied upon in policymaking? The cases outlined above suggest that symbolic policymaking tends to have several important consequences: It is difficult to control, it is highly prone to producing unexpected outcomes, and it tends to defer key policy choices and debate until after policy passage or adoption.

Symbolic politics are difficult to control. Once a powerful idea is let loose in the political arena, it can morph into unintended forms and open a Pandora's box of problems for the initiator, as well as the intended political targets. Clinton's experience with welfare reform is an excellent example. As noted earlier, his election promise to "end welfare as we know it" was one of the signature slogans of his campaign and the chief symbol of his political identity as a "New Democrat." His own administration's efforts to devise a reform bill fulfilling his pledge of time-limited welfare with enhanced work requirements, while still appeasing the liberal wing of the Democratic Party, largely failed. But Republicans were emboldened to include a much more sweeping and punitive version of welfare reform in the Contract with America, which they succeeded in passing in the 104th Congress. Clinton was faced with the painful dilemma of either signing a conservative version of reform, over the strident opposition of many welfare policy experts in his own administration and many Democrats in Congress, or seeming to violate a major promise of his election. At the mercy of his own symbolism, Clinton signed welfare reform into law and saw several of his political appointees resign in disgust.

A second important consequence of symbolic policymaking is that it appears particularly prone to producing unintended effects. This is a danger, of course, for any type of policy designed for a complex environment, but the speed and superficiality with which symbolic ideas can be adopted heighten the threat.

FERPA provides a good example. Having been adopted without hearings or serious debate, it was quickly found to contain significant defects, especially as it applied to postsecondary education. For example, as originally passed, the Buckley Amendment prevented schools from disclosing grades and other information to the parents of students over eighteen years old without the student's consent. Naturally, parents who were paying thousands of dollars to support their sons and daughters in college objected strongly to not being able to learn if they were flunking courses. Even more controversial was the amendment's provision concerning confidential letters of recommendation. The law enlarged student access to previously confidential student evaluations, and it appeared to jeopardize the future usefulness of recommendations. Colleges reported purging files of confidential letters prior to the act's effective date. Finally, higher education institutions complained that FERPA interfered unnecessarily in their administrative processes and recordkeeping and imposed substantial costs of compliance. Such consequences led to rapid realization that the act was "badly drafted" and "did not sufficiently account for the difficulty of legislating in this area."[29] "Higher education was an afterthought" in FERPA, said an official of the Department of Health, Education, and Welfare (HEW), and the department found itself unable to issue regulations until Congress modified the law.[30]

Another example of unintended consequences in symbolic legislation is Title IX of the Education Amendments of 1972, which prohibits sex discrimination by educational institutions receiving federal funds. Title IX received more legislative scrutiny preceding its enactment than the Buckley Amendment, but this prior consideration was dwarfed by the debate that followed its enactment. Jeffrey Fishel and Janice Pottker, the authors of a study of its passage and implementation, emphasize that Title IX shared many of the traits of symbolic policymaking: "When Congress passed Title IX in 1972, it was voting for a general principle of equality, and the specific implications of the law were understood by few members of Congress. . . . Congress made no attempt to provide a clear and complete definition of what constituted sex discrimination in education. As a result, the real public debate on the issues involved in eliminating sex discrimination followed, rather than preceded, the passage of the law."[31]

In fact, legislative intent regarding Title IX was so unclear that HEW was granted great flexibility in promulgating regulations. To quote Fishel and Pottker again: "Because of the absence of any kind of consensus, DHEW policymakers felt free to decide issues as they thought best from legal and policy perspectives."[32] Once the regulations were developed, the chief House author of the statute, Rep. Edith Green (D-OR), disassociated herself from the result, stating: "If I or others in the House had argued that [Title IX] was designed to do some of the things which HEW now says . . . I believe the legislation would have been defeated. I myself would not have voted for it, even though I feel very strongly about ending [sex] discrimination."[33]

Congresswoman Green's remarks draw attention to a related characteristic of symbolic policymaking: the tendency to make key policy decisions *after* formal adoption of the policy rather than before. This was true of the USA PATRIOT Act as well, particularly the bill's provisions dealing with library-use information and warrantless searches. As former congressman Bill Frenzel (R-MN) acknowledged, "in periods of crisis, legislation that is less than perfect tends to move quickly. As a lawmaker, when you pass bills in an emergency, you know you're going to make mistakes."[34] Absent an emergency, there would have been heated debate, multiple amendments, and an uncertain outcome involving these and other features of the legislation. Rather, under the circumstances, it was passed with little reflection and deliberation.

The Institutionalization of Symbolic Politics

Symbolic politics is clearly not the only process responsible for creating sloppy public policy, nor is the use of symbolic politics entirely new. Symbolism has been a potent element of politics from the beginning of organized political activity. American history is replete with examples of symbolic policymaking, from Andrew Jackson's war against the Second National Bank to various reforms of the Progressive Era. But symbolic politics appear to have become more prevalent and increasingly institutionalized in recent decades.

Historically, symbolic politics have been the favorite strategy of political outsiders and independent political entrepreneurs. With the right issue and the right political talents, entrepreneurs have found that they don't necessarily need a strong power base in Congress or the executive branch in order to exert an important influence on the policy process. Indeed, some well-known policy entrepreneurs, such as Ralph Nader and Rachel Carson, never held any formal position of authority. Others who did, such as Sen. Bill Bradley (D-NJ) and Rep. Jack Kemp (R-NY) on the issue of tax reform and Rep. Charles Vanik (D-OH) on accessibility rights for the disabled, were relatively junior members of Congress at the time, or they lacked a position of power within the House or Senate from which to push forward and negotiate for their favored policy position.[35] They were able to build coalitions and political momentum through skillful development and manipulation of symbols rather than through negotiation and bargaining. The ability to identify issues that can appeal to a broad public audience in their living rooms and effectively market those ideas through the mass media is of far greater value in symbolic politics than the ability to close deals with other legislators in committee rooms.

Both the "inside game" and the "outside game" are widely used in coalition building today. Both have important roles to play in modern policymaking. We would argue, however, that American politics has changed in ways that have encouraged the growth of symbolic politics, enhancing its appeal even to established political leaders who have alternative resources and options for coalition building. This has led to an institutionalization of symbolic policymaking, moving it from the predominant domain of political outsiders in the 1960s, into the halls of Congress in the 1970s, and into the arena of leadership politics by the 1990s and 2000s.

It is widely recognized that the traditional organizational foundations of American politics have eroded, while new communication structures in politics have proliferated and gained importance. For example, the "foot soldiers" who traditionally were provided by political parties to work out in the precincts have become less important than before, while money for campaign consultants, social media, and television and online advertising matters more. Increasingly, both election and policy battles are fought out more "over the air" or in "cyberspace" than, as in days past, "on the ground."

Concurrently, the media have become ever more central to both electoral and policy politics, as have political entertainment values: contests for power, the drama of debate and conflict, financial scandals and moral improprieties. Consequently, politicians—young ones bred on them and their seniors bowing to the new realities—have discarded traditions of deference and courtesy that once were commonplace in legislative operations and become more aggressively offensive and warily defensive in campaigning and policy positioning.

As a result, even political organizations have begun to rely increasingly on idea-based politics, in both its expert and symbolic forms. Old policy dogs, in a sense, have been learning new tricks. For example, interest groups, attempting to maintain control over issues that are important to them, have been going beyond traditional methods of interest representation and adopting techniques borrowed from political parties and expert and symbolic politics.[36] Thus the big growth areas of interest group activity in recent years have been grassroots organizing, coalition formation, and media marketing.[37] Although many groups have a long history of participation in party politics, they have become increasingly sophisticated actors in the electoral arena. On the ideational tracks, groups hire their own experts, create their own think tanks or mobilize counter-elites, and they seek to play in the realm of symbolic politics by mounting independent media campaigns and issue advocacy drives. In this way, the health insurance industry enjoyed considerable success in taking to the airwaves to scuttle Clinton's health care reform proposals. More recently, soft drink companies and the sweetener industry successfully fought off recent attempts to tax or regulate high-calorie, low-value drinks with a major advertising campaign that focused on the negative symbols of government interference and excessive new taxes, quickly killing prospects for legislation in the area.

Political parties have also gone the ideational route, building links to sympathetic or affiliated think tanks and using the techniques of symbolic manipulation, as exemplified by the Contract with America. For example, focus groups and market testing were used to help frame the issues and select titles for the items included in the Republicans' Contract with America. The result was a "sales pitch" comprising items such as the Taking Back Our Streets Act, the Personal Responsibility Act, and the American Dream Restoration Act. A summary of these popular titles was then advertised in *TV Guide* before the 1994 election. Similarly, the lockbox became a device central to the politics of budgeting in 1999, illustrating again how even party leaders in Congress have come to depend on symbolic devices in their coalition-building efforts. Symbolic politics, in other words, have moved in from the periphery of politics since the 1960s, becoming thoroughly institutionalized by the 1990s.

Symbolic Politics and the Defense of Marriage Act

The Defense of Marriage Act of 1996 (DOMA) was drafted by and introduced into Congress by Rep. Bob Barr (R-GA), a freshman Republican, on May 7, 1996. The legislation was designed to address concerns that the recognition of same-sex marriage in one state would require reciprocal recognition of such marriages by other states, pursuant to the "full faith and credit" clause of the US Constitution. The legislation held that "no State, territory, or possession of the United States, or Indian tribe, shall be required to give effect to any public act, record, or judicial proceeding of any other State . . . respecting a relationship between persons of the same sex that is treated as a marriage under the laws of such other State . . . or a right or claim arising from such relationship."[38]

Stimulus for the proposed legislation was a 1993 decision by the Supreme Court of Hawaii in *Baehr v. Lewin*, which held that denying the rights and benefits of marriage to same-sex couples constituted gender discrimination.[39] The plaintiffs in the case had argued that the denial of marriage licenses to same-sex couples was a violation of their right to privacy, as well as a violation of the due process and equal protection clause of the Hawaii state constitution.[40] Although this was not the first lawsuit of its kind, it was the first to show a significant potential for success and as such greatly elevated the national salience of gay marriage.[41] In particular, conservative opponents of same-sex marriage were concerned that if the practice was legalized in Hawaii, other states would be required to recognize such marriages.

In response to this potential for legal recognition of same-sex marriages, conservative activists moved swiftly to capitalize on public discomfort with the concept. During the 1996 election cycle, all of the candidates for the Republican presidential nomination publicly endorsed policies that would prohibit the recognition of same-sex marriage.[42] Moreover, states across the country began passing "mini-DOMAs" as early as 1995, and some amended their state constitutions to define marriage as the relationship between one man and one woman.[43]

Barr's proposed Defense of Marriage Act was a congressional response to this same situation. Once introduced, it was placed on a legislative fast track through Congress, as is typical of symbolic legislation. The bill was introduced on May 7, 1996, and hearings were held by the House Judiciary Committee's Subcommittee on the Constitution the very next week.[44] The bill was marked up and passed out of subcommittee on May 30, less than a month after it was introduced. The full Judiciary Committee held hearings on the bill on June 11 and 12, passed the legislation by a two-to-one margin, and reported it to the full House on July 9. There it was placed almost immediately on the House calendar. DOMA was debated and passed without change by the full House on July 12 by a lopsided vote of 342-67.[45] Only a single Republican opposed the bill—Rep. Steve Gunderson (R-WI), the only openly gay Republican member of Congress at the time. Democrats too voted overwhelmingly in favor of the legislation, by a vote of 118-65.

The Senate received H.R. 3396 on July 16, and it was placed directly on the Senate calendar the following day, bypassing consideration by the Senate Judiciary Committee. After parliamentary steps were taken in early September to speed consideration of DOMA, the House-passed bill was brought to the floor on September 10. After only three hours of debate, it passed overwhelmingly and without amendment, with eighty-five senators voting in favor, including a sizeable majority of Democrats. Only fourteen Democrats voted against it. On September 21, 1996, President Bill Clinton signed the bill as Public Law 104-199.[46]

DOMA thus typifies the tendency for symbolic legislation to be rushed through the legislative process. It raced through the House in a little over two months, skipped hearings and committee consideration in the Senate, avoided filibuster and extended debate on the Senate floor, and passed the Senate in the identical form as the House's version in order to avoid the need for a conference committee. Yet, substantively, there was no need for such rushed consideration. At the time of DOMA's enactment, no state had legally recognized same-sex marriage or civil union, so the full-faith-and-credit issue had not yet been tested. The Supreme Court of Hawaii, whose decision set off the concerns of gay marriage opponents, had sent the case back for rehearing in the lower courts, so the issue even in Hawaii had not yet been settled. In fact, DOMA did not directly impact any state government or individual until 2003, when the Supreme Court of Massachusetts ruled that banning same-sex marriage was unconstitutional in *Goodridge v. Department of Public Health.*

Rather than legal necessity, the politics of DOMA were driven by symbolic politics. Gay marriage was a contentious and emotional social issue for both proponents and opponents of DOMA. Proponents of the law viewed gay marriage in terms of religious morality, and they saw it as a direct threat to the traditional family. Opponents viewed this as a fundamental issue of civil rights. There was little room between the two views for negotiation and compromise. What made the difference politically was that public opinion polls at the time of DOMA's passage showed opponents of gay marriage outnumbering proponents by more than two to one, with 65 percent opposed and only 26 percent of the public in favor.[47] Given such one-sided—and intensely held—views among much of the public, Republicans used their majority in Congress to push the legislation through quickly, in hopes of using it as a wedge issue in the fall elections. Democrats, however, sidetracked the partisan strategy by voting overwhelmingly in favor of DOMA themselves. In the end, the "defense of marriage" was treated as a valence issue with bipartisan support and pushed rapidly along the symbolic pathway.

Notes

1. Timothy J. Conlan and Steven L. Abrams, "Federal Intergovernmental Regulation: Symbolic Politics in the New Congress," *Intergovernmental Perspective* 70, no. 3 (1981).

2. Paul L. Posner, *The Politics of Unfunded Mandates: Whither Federalism?* (Washington, DC: Georgetown University Press, 1998), chapter 6.

3. Ibid., 112.

4. See, for example, Derthick and Quirk, *Politics of Deregulation*; Mark Moore et al., *Dangerous Offenders: Elusive Targets of Justice* (Cambridge, MA: Harvard University Press, 1984); and Conlan, Wrightson, and Beam, *Taxing Choices*.

5. David S. Broder, "Look Who's in the Driver's Seat," *Washington Post*, June 8, 1999.

6. *Webster's New World Dictionary* (Cleveland: World Publishing, 1962).

7. Richard Liroff, *A National Policy for the Environment: NEPA and Its Aftermath* (Bloomington: Indiana University Press, 1978), 5.

8. Mayhew, *Congress*, 134.

9. Murray Edelman, *The Symbolic Uses of Politics* (Urbana: University of Illinois Press, 1964).

10. James L. Sundquist quoting Sen. Clifford Case (R-NJ) in *Politics and Policy*, 237. Sundquist argues that the commission actually achieved a substantial policy impact by investigating and documenting the effects of segregation and the extent of racial discrimination in the South, thus contributing to the passage of subsequent and much stronger civil rights laws. Be that as it may, the 1957 act was widely believed to have only symbolic effects by both supporters and opponents at the time.

11. Ibid., 5.

12. Ibid., 35.

13. Mark Moore, "What Makes Public Ideas Powerful?," in *The Power of Public Ideas*, Robert B. Reich, ed. (Cambridge, MA: Ballinger, 1988), 79.

14. Edward Koch. "The Mandate Millstone," *The Public Interest* (Fall 1960): 44.

15. Philip B. Heymann, "How Government Expresses Public Ideas," in *Power of Public Ideas*, Reich, ed., 89.

16. R. Kent Weaver, Robert Y. Shapiro, and Lawrence R. Jacobs, "Poll Trends: Welfare," *Public Opinion Quarterly* 59, no. 4 (Winter 1995): 606–27.

17. For an insider's account of this process in the case of welfare reform legislation, see David T. Ellwood, "Welfare Reform as I Knew It: When Bad Things Happen to Good Policies," *American Prospect* 26 (May–June 1996).

18. Moore, "What Makes Public Ideas Powerful?," 79.

19. On committee powers, see Kenneth A. Shepsle and Barry R. Weingast, "The Institutional Foundations of Committee Power," *American Political Science Review* 81, no. 1 (March 1987): 85–104. For data on legislative productivity, see Michael J. Malbin, Norman J. Ornstein, and Thomas E. Mann, *Vital Statistics on Congress 2008* (Washington, DC: Brookings Institution Press, 2008).

20. Bendiner, *Obstacle Course on Capitol Hill*, and Sarah Binder, *Stalemate: Causes and Consequences of Legislative Gridlock* (Washington, DC: Brookings Institution Press, 2003).

21. USA PATRIOT Act, H.R. 3162, 107th Congress, 2001.

22. Quoted in *CQ Weekly* (September 15, 2001), 2116.

23. Kingdon, *Agendas, Alternatives, and Public Policies*, 2nd ed., 94–100.

24. Michael A. Perino, "Enron's Legislative Aftermath: Some Reflections on the Deterrence Aspects of the Sarbanes-Oxley Act of 2002," *St. John's Law Review* 76, no. 4 (Fall 2002): 671.

25. Alexander Bolton, "Accounting Reform Plans Endangered by Senate Banking Committee Democrats," *The Hill*, June 5, 2002, 6.

26. Marilyn Geewax, "Andersen Verdict Bolsters Senate Bill on Eve of Key Vote," Cox News Service, June 17, 2002.

27. Susan Milligan, "Senate Backs Corporate Reform Bill," *Knight-Ridder/Tribune Business News*, July 16, 2002, 1.

28. Keith Perine, "Regulation Is Back in Vogue," *CQ Weekly*, July 27, 2002, 2018.

29. Merle Steven McClung, "Student Records: The Family Educational Rights and Privacy Act of 1974," *Inequality in Education* 22 (July 1977): 10.

30. Interview with Edward Glieman, former director, Fair Information Practices, HEW, quoted in Conlan and Abrams, "Federal Intergovernmental Regulation," 24.

31. Andrew Fishel and Janice Pottker, *National Politics and Sex Discrimination in Education* (Lexington, MA: Lexington Books, 1977), 132. Joseph A. Califano Jr. also stressed the symbolic character of the issue in *Governing America: An Insider's Report from the White House and the Cabinet* (New York: Simon & Schuster, 2007), 264.

32. Fishel and Pottker, *National Politics and Sex Discrimination in Education*, 115.

33. Former Rep. Edith Green, quoted in Ralph Kinney Bennett, "Colleges under the Federal Gun," reprinted in *Congressional Record*, June 6, 1976, E3596.

34. Sarah Binder and Bill Frenzel, "The Business of Congress after September 11," *Brookings Institution Policy Dialogue*, no. 1 (February 2002), www.brookings.edu/~/media/research/files/papers/2002/1/01politics%20binder/pd01.pdf.

35. For more on these examples, see Conlan and Abrams, "Federal Intergovernmental Regulation"; Timothy Conlan, Margaret T. Wrightson, and David R. Beam, *Taxing Choices: The Politics of Tax Reform* (Washington, DC: CQ Press, 1990); and Robert Katzmann, *Institutional Disability* (Washington, DC: Brookings Institution Press, 1986).

36. Concerning the counterattack by business, see David Vogel, *Fluctuating Fortunes: The Political Power of Business in America* (New York: Basic Books, 1989), especially chapter 8.

37. Schlozman and Tierney, *Organized Interests and American Democracy*, 155–57.

38. US House of Representatives, 104th Congress, H.R. 3396, sec. 2a.

39. Bob Barr, "No Defending the Defense of Marriage Act," *Los Angeles Times*, January 5, 2009, online edition.

40. Marty K. Courson, "Baehr v. Lewin: Hawaii Takes a Tentative Step to Legalize Same Sex Marriage," *Golden Gate University Law Review* 24, no. 1 (1994): 2.

41. Gregory B. Lewis and Jonathan L. Edelson, "DOMA and ENDA: Congress Votes on Gay Rights," in *The Politics of Gay Rights*, Kenneth Wald, Craig Rimmerman, and Clyde Wilcox, eds. (Chicago: University of Chicago Press, 2000), 198.

42. *A Short History of the Defense of Marriage Act* (Washington, DC: Gay and Lesbian Advocates and Defenders, 2009), www.glad.org.

43. Barry D. Adam, "The Defense of Marriage Act and American Exceptionalism: The 'Gay Marriage' Panic in the United States," *Journal of the History of Sexuality* 12, no. 2 (2003): 259.

44. Congressional Research Service, *Bill Summary and Status, H.R. 3396*, 104th Congress, 1995–96, http://thomas.loc.gov/cgi-bin/bdquery/z?d104:h.r.03396, accessed September 8, 2013.

45. Final Vote Results for Roll Call 316, http://clerk.house.gov/evs/1996/roll316.xml, accessed September 6, 2013.

46. Congressional Research Service, *Bill Summary and Status, H.R. 3396*, 104th Congress, 1995–96.

47. See the *Time*/CNN poll, September 1, 1996, in Joshua K. Baker, "Summary of Opinion Research on Same-Sex Marriage," *iMAPP Policy Brief*, December 5, 2003.

CHAPTER SIX

Pathways and Policy Change

As in any democratic society, the receptivity of our system to new ideas and policy change is a central concern. In a nation that is all too critical of its political process, it is no surprise that pessimistic beliefs about policy change easily take root. The policy process literature had tended to reflect a similar view. Major change in a Madisonian system is considered difficult, and the changes that do occur are thought to be largely incremental in nature. Add to that the potential for institutional gridlock in periods of partisan polarization, and the prospects for legislative action can seem daunting.

Yet our work assessing the politics of federal mandates, taxation, and budgeting over a number of years has found that public policy in these fields has been anything but stable. In fact, federal revenue and spending enactments over the past thirty years have careened about in dramatically different directions with decidedly nonincremental results. Between 1981 and 2012, an astonishing number of major tax and budgetary laws were enacted, suggesting that even in this era of oft-divided government, Congress's output can be impressive in both scope and volume, if not consistency.

In explaining the underlying political processes giving rise to this volatile flux of policy enactments, this book argues that traditional incremental and party mobilization models are incomplete. They fail to capture fast-changing and often unpredictable policy actions in many areas. We believe that the fourfold typology of "pathways of power" more successfully captures the diverse ways that new issues reach the agenda and take policy form, as each pathway draws upon different political resources, appeals to different actors, and elicits its own unique strategies, language, and styles of coalition building.

In this chapter we seek to go beyond the discussion of individual pathways to consider how the four pathways together help us to better understand policy change within and across eight discrete policy areas. Using a longitudinal perspective, we identify significant legislative changes and proposals in these eight areas over the past thirty years. We seek to use the pathways framework to assess the underlying political mobilization approaches and styles giving rise to policy change and also attempt to gauge how shifts in the pathways at work help us to understand shifts in policy outcomes.

Recognizing that limitations are inherent in any rigid typology, we also seek to use a more fluid and dynamic approach to emphasize how pathways interact in various ways that serve to either expand or contract issue formation and policy action possibilities. Because different pathways tend to favor different actors and values, we suggest that policy actors attempt to steer the framing of issues, coalition building, and institutional design in ways that capitalize on the pathways that best promote their goals and interests. The pathways framework can be useful to understand the secular shifts under way in the types of mobilization strategies deployed by actors in our system.

Models of Policy Change: A Brief Overview

Traditional models of policymaking are generally based on the twin principles of incrementalism and negative feedback.[1] Leading political scientists such as Aaron Wildavsky and Charles Lindblom conclude that the policy process has a conserving bias stemming from political interests, as well as institutional routines structuring and channeling change. The Madisonian system's checks and balances reinforce a perception of a system where major change must overcome numerous hurdles, which at times are so severe that they have been dubbed "veto points." Economists, moreover, have argued that the representation of broader interests is constrained by free-rider problems, limiting the range of interests that could gain effective voices in national policymaking processes.[2]

Major changes that did occur were viewed as principally orchestrated by strong presidents with cohesive party support. Even then, strong presidents required some kind of paradigmatic crisis to reinforce their leadership. In this traditional view, real reform required mobilization of mass political support sufficient to overcome the entrenched interests associated with current policies.[3]

More recently, the policy process literature has recognized a greater volatility and potential for major change than had heretofore been the case. Widely noted shifts in our political institutions created greater opportunities for new issues and interests to take root. At least for a time, Congress became a more open and decentralized body by maximizing credit-claiming opportunities for members to take the lead on a variety of issues, both old and new. Interest group systems became more diverse and competitive as new broader-based interests showed an inclination and capacity to organize, leading some scholars to spurn iron triangle metaphors for more open concepts such as networks or advocacy coalition frameworks.[4] The media presence in policymaking expanded and exploded, with more outlets combing official Washington, as well as other regions of the nation for new issues and problems.

These trends bore fruit, with major new policy innovations in the past thirty to forty years that many would have thought impossible under traditional models.

Whether it was environmental protection, deregulation, tax reform, farm reform, or welfare reform, major policy changes were indeed enacted in ways that at the time seemed idiosyncratic or remarkable.

John Kingdon was one of the first scholars to attempt to model this evolving and more dynamic policy process. He applies garbage-can theory to describe an open and fluid process where ideas and interests are joined on the public and governmental agendas through an opportunistic combination of problems, solutions, and entrepreneurial political leaders searching for new issues to gain attention and electoral advantage.[5] Frank Baumgartner and Bryan Jones also portray a dynamic process where long periods of issue stability were punctuated by spikes of major policy change and reformulation. The agenda-formation process they describe is quite prone to nonincremental changes that can literally take the system by surprise.

Although the system's potential for change may be greater than once thought, considerable uncertainty exists over how to account for and explain the changes that do and don't occur. For instance, Edella Schlager argues that although major change may appear to occur overnight, it is in fact often preceded by several decades' worth of events and factors setting the stage. And whether such buildup of forces actually precipitates major policy reform is largely viewed in the literature as a serendipitous process.[6] Baumgartner and Jones similarly acknowledge that policy punctuations can be precipitated by major blows or minor events, leaving the realm of predictions to those less informed of their own limitations.

Although both Baumgartner/Jones and Kingdon suggest processes and factors associated with the surfacing of nonincremental change, understanding is still a work in progress. In a perceptive study of issue evolution, Edward G. Carmines and James A. Stimson conclude that

> chance is the fundamental driving force in producing change. That does not imply that change is either chaotic or knowable but, most explicitly, that it is neither determined nor inevitable. . . . We do not assume that any particular issue evolution could only have happened as it did. Instead, scenarios of issue evolutions are more akin to Tolstoy's battle scenes, where calculation, force, confusion, and chance commingle to produce an outcome, the appearance of which is orderly only after the fact.[7]

Nonetheless, social science can help us develop insights into patterns that govern seemingly random processes. As William Riker says, "to admit that disequilibrium is the characteristic state of politics and that the rise and decline of issues is a random process does not mean that it is impossible to generalize about regularities in the process."[8] Such a project was less complex when examining incremental changes to existing policies where policies and change were structured, limited, and regulated by known institutions and actors. The process of idea generation and agenda formation is less deterministic and more vulnerable to uncertainty. Even though every policy regime has the potential to generate major policy reforms, it is quite a research challenge to understand systematically why major reforms and policy breakthroughs occur at particular times and to particular policy areas.

Pathways and Policy Change

In this book we argue that the clusters of actors, behaviors, and outcomes that we term "pathways of power" can help with this explanatory task. Applying this framework across eight policy arenas, we seek to explore the degree to which it can help us shed light on the complex process of policy change.

Specifically, in this chapter we use comparative analysis of cases across eight discrete policy areas to look for patterns across different policy domains. This approach has several advantages when compared with traditional approaches used to assess policy change. Case studies of individual issues do portray the dynamics of change, but these are limited in their capacity for generalization.[9] Large-N quantitative studies can provide some useful measures of the correlates of change, but their focus on a limited number of quantitative variables, often with a heavy emphasis on socioeconomic measures, limits their utility in assessing the critical role played by ideas, perception, and information in shifting focus and attention in agenda setting and policy formation.[10] In addition, the longitudinal dimension in our analysis allows us to explore policy changes over time, strengthening our capacity to draw inferences about both the patterns of changes in pathways and their consequences for the politics of policymaking. The eight policy areas we have chosen each have experienced at least one, if not several, notable policy shifts over the past ten to twenty years.

Table 6.1 displays each of the forty-two cases within the eight areas and shows the primary path(s) involved in putting the issue on the agenda and gaining passage or defeat in each case. The cases and the eight policy domains represent some of the most important issues facing the nation in recent times, covering such areas as health care, tax policy, welfare reform, budget-process reform, and gun control. We understand that these areas are not representative of all policy outputs and decisions during this period. Many, such as veterans' benefits, have undergone little change, and others may have shifted in limited ways contained within a single pathway. However, our objective here is not to classify the universe of policy outputs by pathway but to better understand the dynamics of policymaking and policy change using the pathways model as a basis for insight.

Our review of the forty-two cases confirms the important role pathways play in framing issues and shaping policy outcomes. The cases show that both the scope

Table 6.1
Cases and Pathways

AREA/CASE	PATHWAY
HEALTH CARE	
1988 Medicare Catastrophic	EXPERT
1989 Catastrophic Repeal	PLURALISTIC
1994 Clinton Health Plan	PARTISAN
1997 Children's Health Program	PLURALISTIC
1997 Balanced Budget Act Medicare Cuts	EXPERT
2000 Medicare Restoration	PLURALISTIC
2003 Medicare Part D	PARTISAN
2010 Affordable Care Act	PARTISAN
GUN CONTROL	
1986 Firearm Owners Protection	PLURALISTIC
1993 Brady Bill	PARTISAN
1994 Assault Weapons Ban	PARTISAN
1999 Gun Show Controls	SYMBOLIC
FARM POLICY	
1990 Farm Bill	PLURALISTIC
1995 Freedom to Farm	EXPERT
2002 Farm Bill	PLURALISTIC
2008 Farm Bill	PLURALISTIC
TAX LEGISLATION	
1981 ERTA Tax Cut	PARTISAN
1982 TEFRA	EXPERT
1986 Tax Reform	EXPERT
1993 OBRA Tax Increases	PARTISAN
1997 TRA Tax Cuts	SYMBOLIC
1998 IRS Restoration	SYMBOLIC
2001 Tax Cuts	PARTISAN
WELFARE POLICY	
1998 Family Support Act	EXPERT
1996 TANF Welfare Reform	SYMBOLIC
2006 TANF Extension	PARTISAN
FINANCIAL REGULATION	
1999 Gramm-Leach-Bliley Act	PLURALISTIC
2002 Sarbanes-Oxley Reform	SYMBOLIC
2008 TARP	EXPERT
2010 Dodd-Frank Act	PARTISAN

Table 6.1 (*cont.*)

AREA/CASE	PATHWAY
FEDERAL MANDATES	
1986 Safe Drinking Water Amendment	SYMBOLIC
1986 School Asbestos Mandate	SYMBOLIC
1990 Clean Air Act Amendments	EXPERT
1996 Drinking Water Changes	PLURALISTIC
1996 Defense of Marriage Act	SYMBOLIC
2002 No Child Left Behind	EXPERT
2005 REAL ID Act	SYMBOLIC
BUDGET POLICY AND REFORM	
1985 Gramm-Rudman Act	SYMBOLIC
1990 Budget Enforcement Act	EXPERT
1999 Lockbox	SYMBOLIC
2010 Pay-As-You-Go Act	PARTISAN
2011 Budget Control Act	SYMBOLIC

and the method of political mobilization for an issue play a formative role in shaping and explaining policy decisions. The particular pathway that primarily shapes an issue's fortunes powerfully affects both the types of actors that are empowered to play roles in agenda formation and decision making as well as the kinds of questions that are viewed as legitimate to raise. Because certain frames, interests, and outcomes are promoted by different pathways, significant policy change is to be expected when the primary pathway driving an issue shifts. It is not surprising that not only are the pathways useful analytical categories in explaining policy change, but they also serve as strategies for mobilization pursued by various actors and interests. Whether explicitly or implicitly, actors in the process understand their own stakes in the pathways that govern policy issues in our system.

Issue Framing and Reinforcement

Issue framing and reframing are critical predicates to major policy change. When the underlying policy image supporting the existing policy shifts, the prospects for policy reform brighten. Issue definitions are critical in shaping the pathways in play. The legitimacy of certain language and styles of debate and political organization are influenced by the unique properties of each pathway. Terms of debate that might be legitimate for one arena may not be when the issue switches paths. Different kinds of claims and arguments are appropriate for different pathways.

A shift in policy image thus often drives a shift in the underlying pathway driving the policy debate. Indeed, political leaders and policy actors alike are quite opportunistic in reshaping the definition of issues and institutions to manipulate the pathways to favor their position. On health care reform, leaders such as presidents Clinton and Obama use public appeals to attempt to redefine the issue as a coverage crisis, which is calculated to mobilize the party faithful and broader publics, thereby triggering the engagement of both partisan and symbolic pathways. During the 1990s, health insurers succeeded in steering the issue back to the confines of the pluralistic pathway by redefining the issue from redistributive to regulatory terms, triggering concerns about the potential impact of reform on existing benefits and costs enjoyed by most Americans.[11] Their defensive campaign, most notoriously reflected in the "Harry and Louise" commercials featuring a family worried about the effects of health care reform, succeeded in defeating President Clinton's initiative. Their inability to do so in 2010 contributed to passage of the Patient Protection and Affordable Care Act, although positioning the issue securely in the partisan pathway made it vulnerable to challenge as Democrats' strength in Congress diminished.

Groups that succeed in one pathway can be disarmed and outflanked when the issue shifts to other pathways with different forms of mobilization and appeals. Gary Mucciaroni's research suggests that producer groups that have succeeded in the pluralist track may not thrive in the expert or symbolic realms unless they can recast their arguments to address the broader issues and publics engaged in these pathways.[12] For example, the National Rifle Association (NRA) achieved considerable success as long as the gun-regulation issues stayed in the pluralistic path. Notwithstanding the consistently strong public opposition to their policies, they have been able to forestall broader reforms by defeating these claimants in the arena where their arguments and resources were unparalleled. However, when the issue was shifted to a symbolic and partisan realm, as in the mid-1990s, they lost considerable leverage as pro-gun-control interests emerged to shift the terms of debate, engaging President Clinton in gaining approval of the Brady Handgun Violence Prevention Act (aka the Brady Bill) and a temporary ban on the sale of assault weapons. A similar process has worked more recently to place gun violence at the top of the policy agenda in the wake of the 2012 Newtown school shootings. In the years following the assault weapons ban, the NRA regained its footing as the organization learned to work in the partisan path by rallying its members to turn out in congressional and presidential elections and by using symbolic politics to reach its clientele through a series of infomercials.[13]

Similarly, when environmentalists succeeded in shifting drinking water regulation to the symbolic and expert pathways in the 1970s and 1980s, it became less legitimate for local governments to raise concerns over the cost of safe drinking water legislation. In the new frame, public safety became the overriding concern. Consequently, Congress passed one of the most expensive unfunded federal mandates in this area in 1986. However, as the EPA's regulations were unveiled over the ensuing six years, the costs of the new standards to local communities became more salient, reviving the pluralist pathway where local cost claims had greater legitimacy. Ultimately, the reemergence of pluralist group politics and interest-based arguments convinced Congress to modify its earlier regulatory handiwork to accommodate some of the most significant local concerns.[14]

The rise and fall of pathways fundamentally condition which arguments and positions are considered legitimate in a given period of time. As budget surpluses accumulated in the late 1990s, for instance, economists found their standards and criteria were ignored as politicians rushed to embrace the symbolic goal of "saving Social Security." Both parties adopted lockbox proposals promising to save at least the portion of the budget surplus corresponding to the surplus of Social Security payroll taxes over current benefit payments. Seasoned budget experts and Washington economists were dismayed by the terms of this debate. The new target, they argued, had not been selected based on economic criteria and therefore had little or no legitimacy in their expert eyes. Eugene Steurle, a prominent Washington economist, argued for a surplus target grounded in a professional consensus on the amount of savings needed to improve the levels of long-term growth and productivity for the economy.[15] Arguments such as Steurle's might well have proved compelling if the expert pathway held sway, but political leaders were in the grips of the symbolic pathway and determined to show the public that they were addressing a salient issue in dramatic and symbolic terms that could be readily grasped by media and inattentive publics alike.

The formative influence of pathways on the terms of debate can best be seen by the accommodations that various actors must make to recast their claims when pathways shift. For instance, interest groups representing accounting firms had to recast their arguments as being relevant to the symbolic turn that the financial reporting issue took after the collapse of WorldCom in 2002. Following the Columbine shootings in 1999 and the Newtown shootings, a number of Republican congressional allies of the NRA felt that they had to develop a legislative proposal for regulating gun sales at gun shows. When issues take an expert turn, groups skilled in the pluralistic pathway may further develop their research capabilities to challenge expert-based arguments against their claims. Industries such as the tobacco industry, for instance, had to commission their own scientists to attempt to neutralize the increasingly compelling case made by opposition groups on the expert pathway.

Exploring whether the form of problem definition across the forty-two cases varies systematically by the principal pathway, table 6.2 utilizes the threefold typology developed by John Kingdon: crisis, indicators, and feedback.[16] It shows that for the cases in our study, the modes of problem definition do in fact tend to vary by pathway in expected ways.

As expected, the pluralist path generally emphasized feedback as the principal modality for defining problems. Complaints by program clientele and monitoring

Table 6.2
Principal Mode of Problem Definition

	Crisis	*Indicator*	*Feedback*
PLURALIST			100%
			(9)
EXPERT	20%	80%	
	(2)	(8)	
PARTISAN	18%	54%	27%
	(2)	(6)	(3)
SYMBOLIC	50%	25%	25%
	(6)	(3)	(3)

by their interest group representatives and federal agency overseers constituted the principal ways that problems were defined and legitimized in pluralistic settings. Thus when the shoe pinched and seniors organized to protest the Medicare Catastrophic Coverage Act of 1988, Congress quickly repealed the law a year later. Similarly, when health care providers organized to protest the cuts in reimbursable fees ushered in by the Balanced Budget Act of 1997 (BBA), Congress responded by adjusting and rolling back some of these earlier constraints.

The expert path, by contrast, would be expected to legitimize problems based on indicators and data, and that is what we have found in our cases. Indicators of inappropriate reimbursements enjoyed by such providers as health maintenance organizations and home care providers were provided in data and reports by such federal entities as the Health Care Financing Administration and the General Accounting Office. These studies were sufficiently compelling to define fees as a problem that needed to be addressed, leading to the 1997 BBA changes. And TARP was rapidly developed by the Bush administration in 2008 as financial indicators pointed to a freezing of credit markets, well before the wide-scale effects of the Great Recession were felt by average citizens.

The role of crisis—often considered pivotal for many issues to attain agenda status—in fact played the principal role in problem definition in only ten of the forty-two cases. As expected, however, this form of alarmed discovery was the most prevalent way that symbolic pathways were activated. A classic example is the accounting reform debate in the summer of 2002, when the spectacular failures of a number of major corporations created a perceived crisis prompting major policy reform of financial reporting and auditing.

Institutional frameworks also help determine and reinforce the pathways for particular issues. As Muccciaroni notes, different institutional frameworks provide differential prospects for political mobilization.[17] Similarly, Baumgartner and Jones suggest that policy change can occur through issue reframing discussed above or through venue change, where policy actors succeed in changing the institutions responsible for driving policy formulation and implementation.[18]

Modern trade policy, for example, has been able to resist the traditional blandishments of pluralism partly because decisions have been delegated to administrative processes where expert paths predominate. Proposals for closure commissions for Amtrak routes and veterans' health facilities similarly have the expectation that transferring institutional focal points and processes will shift the path from pluralist to expert with major consequences for decisions.[19] In a perceptive study explaining the sustainability of major policy reforms, Eric Patashnik concludes that permanent changes in institutional underpinnings for policy regimes is a critical factor explaining the success of airline deregulation over twenty-five years in contrast to the erosion of reform experienced in tax and farm policy.[20]

Much of the federal budget debate in recent years has entailed shifting congressional rules to strengthen the role of party leaders in developing comprehensive packages to address deficits and presidents alike. The budget reconciliation process and discretionary spending caps, for instance, were tailor-made to reinforce the partisan pathway by giving leaders a mechanism to develop omnibus budget packages and enforce budget discipline that might not survive in the pluralist realm of the individual committees and their interest group allies.[21]

Conflict in Policy Formulation

Pathways constitute distinct ways to organize conflict and consensus around issues. We would expect that pathways would, accordingly, engender discrete patterns of party conflict and consensus. The results in table 6.3 use three categories to chart levels of policymaking conflict in contemporary era: high, medium, and low.

As expected, the issues in the partisan track prompted the greatest levels of political conflict. All eleven cases that followed the partisan pathway in our analysis were characterized by high levels of political conflict. These included such high-stakes issues as the Clinton and Obama health plans, the 2001 Bush tax cuts, and the 2009 economic stimulus plan. In several cases, however, partisan issues triggered bipartisan bargaining as both parties sought to claim some credit for climbing aboard a moving train. The tax cuts of 1981 and tax reform in 1986 are prime examples of how competition in divided government settings can in fact promote policy action and agreement.

Not surprisingly, the pluralist pathway for the most part engendered low conflict—and typically bipartisan—policy formulation patterns. Whether it was doctors pressing for relief from Medicare cuts or seniors seeking to overturn fees for expanded coverage or farmers seeking greater subsidies, both parties rushed to respond to these mainstream and electorally important groups in fits of consensual

Table 6.3
Level of Conflict

	High	*Medium*	*Low*
PLURALISTIC	—	22%	77%
		(2)	(7)
PARTISAN	100%	—	—
	(11)		
EXPERT	—	60%	40%
		(6)	(4)
SYMBOLIC	8%	25%	66%
	(1)	(3)	(8)

policymaking. The 2002 farm bill is a good illustration of the pressures faced by members of both parties. The Agriculture Committee chairman listed fifty-two groups, ranging from the National Milk Producers to the Farm Bureau Federation to Ducks Unlimited, that were heard from in a single day in support of the bill.[22]

Bills on the expert and symbolic pathways largely avoided high levels of conflict as well. Once the expert frame became the primary frame for addressing the issue, both parties steered clear of outright opposition to expert-driven proposals. Once reaching the agenda on the expert pathway, both parties sought to either endorse the proposal or work out differences in bargaining among experts from different factions, parties, and branches. Policies framed on the symbolic pathway generally prompted widespread support. Once the issue was defined on the agenda in a compelling symbolic manner, both parties typically scrambled to endorse the idea to either claim credit or avoid blame. The Bush administration and congressional Republicans championed the USA PATRIOT Act of 2002 as a symbol of the domestic war on terrorism. The bill's implications for First and Fourth Amendment rights prompted many in the civil liberties community to question or oppose it, but congressional Democrats felt compelled by the way the issue was framed to endorse the bill, which was quickly passed and signed by President Bush.

Patterns of Change

We might expect that the issues engendering the most conflict among the parties would also be those carrying the greatest potential for nonincremental change. We have classified the policy outcomes for each of the forty-two cases, even those not enacted, by the magnitude of change entailed when viewed in the context of the issue area.

As table 6.4 shows, the partisan pathway prompted the greatest rate of nonincremental change. Such issues as the Obama and Clinton health plans and the 2001 tax cuts met our expectations of nonincremental changes that prompted

Table 6.4
Magnitude of Policy Change

	Nonincremental	*Incremental*
PLURALISTIC	12%	88%
	(1)	(8)
PARTISAN	91%	9%
	(10)	(1)
EXPERT	70%	30%
	(7)	(3)
SYMBOLIC	58%	42%
	(7)	(5)

high-stakes partisan conflicts. Also as expected, issues in the pluralistic pathway were generally of an incremental character, with relatively low levels of conflict among the parties. The two ideational pathways fell in between and were capable of producing both incremental and nonincremental changes. The finding that idea-based pathways provide a widely used alternative to partisan, majoritarian coalitions for ushering in major nonincremental changes remains an important one. The tax reforms of 1986, farm subsidy reform in 1995, and TARP were among those expert-driven major policy reforms that did not inspire gridlock between the parties but rather commanded a level of support and even competition across party lines that attests to the compelling role ideas have come to play in our contemporary policy process.

When examining our eight policy areas in depth, one is impressed with the degree of policy volatility occurring across individual policy decisions in those areas. A policy area such as health care may veer from nonincremental, dramatic policy expansions to incremental tinkering in a few short years. Path switching helps explain these shifts over time in the nature and rate of policy change in specific policy arenas.

As the information in table 6.5 illustrates, most of the major areas underwent considerable ferment in policy development in recent years. Health care and tax policy experienced the most prolific outpouring of important policy actions, and with the exception of Clinton's health care plan, most of the cases led to enactments. Traditional pluralist theory would lead us to expect considerable stability over time, with most issues nesting comfortably within the stable confines of the pluralist pathway. Even punctuated equilibrium frameworks advise us to look for major change over a period of many decades. What is surprising here is the prevalence of important changes over a relatively short period of time.

Reflecting this volatility over time, most of the cases migrated through different paths from one decision point to the next. Far from a continuous process of change, each of the eight areas showed a pronounced tendency to jump pathways.

Table 6.5
Change across Eight Policy Areas

HEALTH POLICY

	1988 Medicare Catastrophic	1989 Medicare Catastrophic Repeal	1994 Clinton Health Care Reform	1997 Childrens' Health	1997 Balanced Budget Act Medicare Savings	2000 Medicare Restoration	2003 Medicare Part D	2010 Affordable Care Act
PLURALIST		•		•		•		
PARTISAN			•				•	
EXPERT	•							•
SYMBOLIC					•			
INITIATIVE	1988 Medicare Catastrophic	1989 Medicare Catastrophic Repeal	1994 Clinton Health Care Reform	1997 Childrens' Health	1997 Balanced Budget Act Medicare Savings	2000 Medicare Restoration	2003 Medicare Part D	2010 Affordable Care Act

GUN CONTROL

	1986 Firearms Protection	1993 Brady Bill	1994 Assault Weapons	1999 Gun Show Registration
PLURALIST	•			
PARTISAN		•	•	
EXPERT				•
SYMBOLIC				
INITIATIVE	1986 Firearms Protection	1993 Brady Bill	1994 Assault Weapons	1999 Gun Show Registration

FARM POLICY

	1990 Farm Bill	1995 Freedom to Farm	2002 Farm Bill	2008 Farm Bill
PLURALIST	•		•	•
PARTISAN				
EXPERT		•		
SYMBOLIC				
INITIATIVE	1990 Farm Bill	1995 Freedom to Farm	2002 Farm Bill	2008 Farm Bill

TAX POLICY

	1981 ERTA	1982 TEFRA	1986 TRA	1993 OBRA	1997 TRA	1998 IRS	2001 Tax Cuts
PLURALIST	•			•			•
PARTISAN		•					
EXPERT			•				
SYMBOLIC					•	•	
INITIATIVE	1981 ERTA	1982 TEFRA	1986 TRA	1993 OBRA	1997 TRA	1998 IRS	2001 Tax Cuts

Table 6.5 (*cont.*)

FEDERAL MANDATES

	1986 Safe Drinking Water Act	1986 School Asbestos	1990 Clean Air Act	1996 Drinking Water Act	1996 DOMA	2002 NCLB	2005 REAL ID
PLURALIST				•			
PARTISAN							
EXPERT			•			•	
SYMBOLIC	•	•			•		•
INITIATIVE	1986 Safe Drinking Water Act	1986 School Asbestos	1990 Clean Air Act	1996 Drinking Water Act	1996 DOMA	2002 NCLB	2005 REAL ID

WELFARE REFORM

	1988 FSA	1996 Welfare Reform	2006 Reauthorization
PLURALIST			
PARTISAN			•
EXPERT	•		
SYMBOLIC		•	
INITIATIVE	1988 FSA	1996 Welfare Reform	2006 Reauthorization

FINANCIAL REGULATION

	1999 Gramm-Leach-Bliley	2002 Sarbanes-Oxley	2008 TARP	2010 Dodd-Frank
PLURALIST	•			
PARTISAN				•
EXPERT			•	
SYMBOLIC		•		
INITIATIVE	1999 Gramm-Leach-Bliley	2002 Sarbanes-Oxley	2008 TARP	2010 Dodd-Frank

BUDGET PROCESS & POLICY

	1985 Gramm-Rudman	1990 BEA	1999 Social Security Lockbox	2010 PAYGO Act	2011 Budget Control Act
PLURALIST					
PARTISAN				•	
EXPERT		•			
SYMBOLIC	•		•		•
INITIATIVE	1985 Gramm-Rudman	1990 BEA	1999 Social Security Lockbox	2010 PAYGO Act	2011 Budget Control Act

For instance, pluralistic forces might drive change in one year only to be supplanted by symbolic or expert forces the next time. Of the forty-two policy cases, all but twelve—or 67 percent—jumped pathways from one decision to the next.

Table 6.5 documents this pattern of considerable flux over time. In some cases pathway shifts occurred within a year. The Medicare catastrophic health insurance legislation of 1988 was largely placed on the agenda by experts who designed the provision to ensure that drug coverage would be paid for by wealthier seniors. However, within a year, the proposal jumped to the pluralist path as a group of wealthier seniors, led by James Roosevelt, engineered a stunning turnaround. Congress unanimously voted to renounce the protections it had endorsed nearly unanimously only a year before.[23] Similarly, the 1981 tax cut championed by President Reagan exemplified the power of a popular president acting through the partisan path to achieve major nonincremental change. However, only a year later, budget and tax experts, worried about the growing budget deficit, took charge of the debate and were able to achieve a partial reversal of the tax cuts through the Tax Equity and Fiscal Responsibility Act of 1982.

Even after the sudden collapse of Enron and legal action against Arthur Andersen in 2001, reforms to corporate accounting and auditing were written off as late as April 2002, as pundits saw the pluralistic path working to defeat reforms proposed in the wake of the scandal.[24] In their book on agenda denial, Roger W. Cobb and Marc Howard Ross include a chapter by John F. Mahon and Richard A. McGowan on accounting reform to illustrate how a profession succeeded in using what we call the pluralistic pathway to keep reforms from reaching serious agenda status. The chapter, "Making Professional Accounting Accountable: An Issue Doomed to Fail," concludes that the only chance for reform was to move to what we call the symbolic track by simplifying the issue, gaining strong media attention, and ultimately heightening the interest of broader publics.[25] Although considered extremely unlikely at the time of their writing, the roadmap for change they prescribed did occur thanks to the combination of a perceived crisis, induced by a falling stock market and corporate reporting failures, and opportunistic political leaders such as Sen. Paul Sarbanes (D-MD), who adroitly capitalized on the crisis to achieve passage of new legislation. His bill passed with all the hallmarks of the symbolic pathway. Republicans Rep. John Boehner (R-OH) and Sen. Phil Gramm (R-TX) both decried what they called a stampede by politicians seeking to pass something, yet both voted for the final bill as did nearly all of their colleagues. The Sarbanes-Oxley Bill was the perfect vehicle for lawmakers desperate to reassure voters they were doing something about the market crisis.[26]

Pathways sometimes switch during the course of the movement of the issue from agenda status to legislative decisions, and these switches can be instrumental in shifting the nature and prospects of the issue in the policymaking process. Most notably, the Clinton health plan was introduced with a fanfare and compelling framing that galvanized support, or at least neutrality, from all four pathways. Although primarily on the partisan pathway, this proposal tapped deep wellsprings of symbolic support in the media and broader publics and drew heavily on the expertise of health economists. At least some interest groups, such as large businesses, saw the proposal as an opportunity to reduce soaring health care costs for their employees. As noted before, the health insurance and small business interest groups succeeded, along with congressional Republican allies, in shifting the issue definition from a redistributive to a regulatory focus as the proposal worked its way through Congress. Aided by a more congenial framing, these groups were able to bring the pluralistic pathway into play as their members became mobilized to apply pressure to leading congressional actors positioned to block the wide-ranging reforms. As one observer noted, the health reform experience illustrates how high political stakes and actively engaged interests eclipsed the technical experts who played a large role in framing the original proposal.[27] Other proposals migrated across pathways in their journey to successful passage. Both the Tax Reform Act of 1986 and the Freedom to Farm Act of 1996 were inspired and framed by experts, but as the issues moved into active legislative debate, the partisan pathway became engaged to fully mobilize majorities needed to adopt these nonincremental changes. For instance, the Treasury 1 proposal was developed by the Department of the Treasury's tax policy experts but then modified and reissued as Treasury 2, shorn of some its most controversial provisions. The switching of pathways was reflected in the change of the department's leadership from the blunt Donald Regan, who had nurtured the development of Treasury 1, to James Baker, who applied his political leadership skills to the management of the bill through the congressional process.[28]

Several pathways were often at work promoting a single issue. Although we made a determination about which pathway was the principal force behind the framing of the issue on the governmental agenda, these determinations were sometimes difficult to make because of the intertwining of several other pathways. The support of multiple pathways can help ensure success, as was the case with welfare reform when symbolic and partisan pathways were both instrumental to passage of this important reform. The coupling of idea- and interest-oriented mobilizations can be a powerful combination indeed.

However, the involvement of multiple pathways is a mixed blessing, particularly when those pathways are either conflicted or opposed to the proposal. For instance, the Columbine shootings prompted the introduction of legislation to extend handgun controls to the sale of guns at gun shows, as well as mandating gun locks among other controls. If the issue had stayed on this symbolic pathway, it seemed assured of the kind of alarmed response and rush-to-judgment characteristic of symbolically defined issues. However, the opposition of the NRA mobilized the pluralist pathway against a quick response, which also enabled the engagement of congressional Republicans. As the issue migrated from a symbolic to a partisan one, its fate was sealed as both parties sought to define their differences by resisting compromises necessary to pass this bill in a form necessary to gain the support of both a Republican Congress and a Democratic president.[29]

Does this suggest that the involvement of multiple pathways will defeat a proposal? Not necessarily. Political scientists rightly have assigned significance to the role of intensity in determining outcomes, giving rise to the expectation that the pluralist pathway will govern policy choice due to the presumption that narrower interests will have greater potential to mobilize support or opposition when compared to broader publics. However, in several cases, the intense opposition emanating from one pathway, usually the pluralist path, was neutralized when an alternative pathway was successfully engaged in support of the legislation. Corporate accounting reform, the 1996 farm reform, and the Brady Bill are three cases where intense opposition within the pluralist sector—which once ruled the roost on these issues—was outflanked when other pathways were engaged to frame the issue in politically compelling terms. As these cases illustrate, the rise of competing pathways can be quite productive of policy change, unseating established pathways from years of dominance.

The Direction of Change

Does pathway change occur in predictable directions? Is there an underlying dialectic of pathway change? This is not an unfamiliar topic in political science. E. E. Schattschneider argued years ago that interests losing in the pluralist pathway will seek to expand the scope of conflict to broader venues, typified in his day by the partisan pathway.[30] Anthony Downs highlighted another direction of change when he wrote about the issue-attention cycle. In this scenario, he argues that issues will ultimately contract from broad- to narrower-scoped conflicts. In Downs's view, issues quickly become elevated through a cycle of alarmed discovery that typifies the symbolic path in our model. He suggests that symbolically defined issues are ultimately destined for the pluralist track as the implicit costs of these policies become revealed to mainstream groups and publics. The foregoing discussion of the evolution of the safe drinking water issue from symbolic to pluralistic paths illustrates the issue-attention cycle at work.

Yet our cases illustrate a far more diversified course than these two models would suggest. When viewing the prospects for movement from the pluralist pathway, Schattschneider envisions a process where party leaders and other advocates succeed in expanding the range of publics paying attention, transforming the policy agenda as a result. However, the pathways model enables us to show that conflict expansion and issue transformation can occur through three types of change: partisan, symbolic and expert. For instance, the Clinton health plan illustrated a traditional migration of health care from pluralist to partisan, while the 2002 corporate accounting reform illustrates a mobilization from pluralistic to symbolic, and the 1996 Freedom to Farm Act highlights the switching of farm policy from a pluralistic to an expert pathway. In all cases, the switch generated nonincremental change proposals. All told, in twelve of the thirty-four opportunities for path switching in our data, movement was from a narrow path (pluralist or expert) in the former incarnation to a broader path (partisan or symbolic). Most of these were associated with nonincremental reforms.

Another eight of our thirty-four change opportunities moved from broad pathways—partisan or symbolic—to narrow pathways—pluralist or expert. Typically these shifts were associated with incremental policy outcomes. The 1995 amendments to the Safe Drinking Water Act and the 1982 TEFRA tax changes are examples of cases where major policy initiatives formerly driven by broad pathways were recaptured by narrower venues of experts and groups.

Changes across time in the evolution of our cases cannot be captured solely by the broad-versus-narrow dimension. Indeed, as noted above, this only characterizes about one-third of our cases. For the remainder of the cases, other dimensions better reflect the shifts in policymaking. The shift from interests to ideas characterized changes in pathways in eight of our cases; five of these consisted of shifts from interest-based pathways to the expert pathway. Experts gained new prominence for such cases as the 1997 Medicare reimbursement cuts, the 1996 Freedom to Farm Act, and the 1986 tax reform legislation. Conversely, seven cases shifted from ideational pathways to interest-based mobilization, with such cases as the Medicare Catastrophic Coverage Repeal Act of 1989 and the 2002 farm bill epitomizing the successful revolt of interest groups against expert reforms, as contemplated by Downs's issue-attention cycle.

The overturning of policy actions was a familiar story across the eight policy domains. In fact, about 42 percent of our individual policy actions were not fully sustained and were either fully or partially overturned or modified subsequently (not including post-2008 actions for which sustainability is still in question). In each case the reversal of fortune was prompted by the switching of paths from the one responsible for the initial action. Paths grounded in interests and organization—pluralist and parties—produced policies that were more sustainable, as only about a third of the policies here were overturned or rejected. However, the idea-based paths—expert and symbolic—proved to be most vulnerable to reversal. Of the twelve policy actions in the symbolic track, six failed to be fully sustained. Of the nine expert policies, five were not fully sustained.

These developments suggest certain inherent political vulnerabilities associated with particular paths that may serve to lay the ground for subsequent regeneration of other paths. Symbolic policies are prone to what some might call a rush to judgment, as decisions are taken to respond to values framed in valence terms.

Table 6.6
Policy Sustainability (pre-2008 enacted measures only)

	Percent sustained
PLURALIST	77 (7)
PARTISAN	66 (4)
EXPERT	44 (4)
SYMBOLIC	50 (6)

It is not surprising, then, that policies enacted through the symbolic route may not fully or adequately consider all relevant interests and information, thereby increasing the chances for latent conflicts and interests to raise their heads in policy implementation. An example is the Safe Drinking Water Act amendments of 1986, where new standards were embraced by Congress in nearly unanimous votes framed in environmental terms, notwithstanding EPA's cost estimate of $10 billion for compliance by local water systems. Once the regulations were issued and the costs became more apparent, particularly to many smaller communities, the reaction prompted Congress to revise the program to ease the regulatory burden.

In his study of the politics of air pollution, Charles Jones shows how policymakers were pressured to respond to a compelling issue framed in valence terms by enacting legislation that was known to be technically infeasible at the time it was enacted—a process he calls the politics of speculative augmentation. The sponsors, such as Sen. Edmund Muskie (D-ME), expected that such standards would be "action forcing" by prompting automobile manufacturers and other major polluters to invest the requisite resources to achieve compliance over time. In fact, the standards and timetables have been repeatedly amended to account for the economic and technical concerns raised by the business community.[31] The replacement of the Gramm-Rudman deficit-reduction strategy with the Budget Enforcement Act is another illustration of the unwinding of a highly symbolic and compelling reform that experts warned, and many supporters even acknowledged at the time, would be unworkable and politically unsustainable.

Expert policies were often undone by the lack of political support to sustain these reforms over time. The Freedom to Farm Act is a good example of a reform in farm subsidies long endorsed by economists and embraced by congressional Republican leadership that was in essence overturned in 2002. A weakening farm economy and several natural disasters helped undermine, and perhaps revealed, the lack of sustainable support for the free-market concepts undergirding the 1996 reform legislation. The unraveling of income-based fees for new Medicare benefits also illustrates how an expert-based proposal failed to gain the requisite political support to sustain itself even for a period of one year.

Concluding Observations

We began this chapter with two general questions. First, is the pathways framework useful in helping us understand the dynamics of policy change? Second, does the pathways framework provide insights into the characteristics of policies—their origins, their durability, their appeal—across a range of different policy domains? Based on the data in this chapter, the answer to both questions appears to be yes.

Our analysis of forty-two different policy initiatives in eight policy domains confirms the utility of the pathways framework. Across policy areas over a thirty-year period, we found systematic differences in the scope of policy outputs and in the politics of formulation and design that conform to the characteristics of the four pathways of power. Systematic differences in problem-definition strategies, rates and direction of policy change, and policy sustainability were observed for differing pathways.

Indeed our cases suggest that policy actors engage in deliberate strategies to steer issues into pathways most congenial to their interests and ideas. Shifts in institutions, policy framing, and policy design are principal strategies used to shift the pathways involved with particular issues. Policy actors recognize that pathways are not simply an academic concept but a vital and high-stakes strategy that carries clear potential to shift the potential winners and losers from policy debates.

The evolution of policy across the cases in this study shows the volatility and diversity of policy change in our system. The switching of pathways played a formative role in driving shifts of policy dimensions in agenda formation and policy formulation. These forces have produced a set of policy outcomes that are both more volatile and less predictable because policies are more prone to jump tracks more often. The switching of policy pathways had the result of transforming policy from narrow pathways to broader ones, leading to nonincremental reforms, but also serving to permit narrower interests to recapture policy from broader publics, as we saw with farm reform in 2002. These developments have wide-ranging consequences for the pathways themselves, as well as for the rate and direction of policy change. We explore these developments in more depth in the next three chapters on the role of pathways in the budget, tax, and intergovernmental policy domains.

Notes

1. Baumgartner and Jones, *Agendas and Instability in American Politics,* 9.
2. Olson, *Logic of Collective Action.*
3. See Michael T. Hayes, *The Limits of Policy Change* (Washington, DC: Georgetown University Press), 115.

4. Jeffrey Berry, *The New Liberalism* (Washington, DC: Brookings Institution Press, 1999); and Sabatier and Jenkins-Smith, *Policy Change and Learning.*

5. Kingdon, *Agendas, Alternatives, and Public Policies*, 1st ed.

6. Edella Schlager, "A Comparison of Frameworks, Theories, and Models of Policy Processes" in *Theories of the Policy Process*, Paul A. Sabatier, ed. (Boulder, CO: Westview, 1999), 252.

7. Edward G. Carmines and James A. Stimson, "On the Evolution of Political Issues," in *Agenda Formation*, William H. Riker, ed. (Ann Arbor: University of Michigan Press, 1993), 151–68.

8. William K. Riker, *Liberalism against Populism* (Prospect Heights, IL: Waveland, 1988).

9. Baumgartner and Jones, *Agendas and Instability in American Politics*, 42.

10. William Blomquist, "The Policy Process and Large-N Comparative Studies," in *Theories of the Policy Process*, Sabatier, ed., 201–32.

11. Cathie Jo Martin, "Dead on Arrival? New Politics, Old Politics, and the Case of National Health Reform," in *Seeking the Center: Politics and Policymaking at the New Century*, Martin A. Levin, Marc K. Landy, and Martin Shapiro, eds. (Washington, DC: Georgetown University Press, 2001), 264–91.

12. Gary Mucciaroni, *Reversals of Fortune: Public Policy and Private Needs* (Washington, DC: Brookings Institution Press, 1995).

13. See Peter H. Stone, "Gun Control: In the NRA's Sights," *National Journal*, July 22, 2000.

14. Posner, *Politics of Unfunded Mandates*, 234.

15. Eugene Steurle, "Spending the Budget 'Surplus' on Social Security, *Tax Notes*, January 29, 1999.

16. Kingdon, *Agendas, Alternatives, and Public Policies*, 2nd ed., chapter 5.

17. Mucciaroni, *Reversals of Fortune.*

18. Baumgartner and Jones, *Agendas and Instability in American Politics*, chapter 12.

19. David M. Walker, *Government Management: Observations on the President's Proposed Freedom to Manage Act*. No. GAO-02-241T (Washington, DC: General Accounting Office, 2001).

20. Eric M. Patashnik, "After the Public Interest Prevails: The Political Sustainability of Policy Reform," paper presented at the annual meeting of the American Political Science Association, San Francisco, 2001.

21. Allen Schick, *The Federal Budget: Politics, Process, Policy* (Washington, DC: Brookings Institution Press, 2000).

22. Jonathan Rauch, "Social Studies: The Farm Bill Is a Bad Joke with a Good Punch Line," *National Journal*, May 18, 2002.

23. Ibid.

24. Keith Perine, "Accounting Overhaul Looks Doubtful as Other Matters Capture Spotlight," *CQ Weekly*, April 20, 2002, 1026.

25. John F. Mahon and Richard A. McGowan, "Making Professional Accounting Accountable: An Issue Doomed to Fail," in *Cultural Strategies of Agenda Denial: Avoidance, Attack, and Redefinition*, Roger W. Cobb and Marc Howard Ross, eds. (Lawrence: University Press of Kansas, 1997), 84.

26. Perine, "Regulation Is Back in Vogue."

27. Martin, "Dead on Arrival?," 265–66.

28. Conlan, Wrightson, and Beam, *Taxing Choices.*

29. Peter H. Stone, "Gun Control: Shoot-Out on Gun Laws Could End in Standoff," *National Journal,* January 22, 2000.

30. Schattschneider, *Semi-Sovereign People.*

31. Jones, *Clean Air.*

CHAPTER SEVEN

Pathways and Budgeting

In this and the following three chapters, the pathways framework will be applied in three different policy fields—the federal budget process, federal tax policy, and intergovernmental policy—to ascertain its value for assessing policy change and variation within specific policy niches. The key question to be explored is whether the dynamics of policy pathways discussed in earlier chapters can help us understand political behavior and policy evolution in fiscal and federalism-related policy. One common theme across all three areas is that policymaking has evolved from historical roots anchoring decisions in pluralist pathways. Policy decisions were largely incremental, reflecting a relatively stable balance of power among organized interests. Over time each area—budget, tax, and intergovernmental—slipped these traditional pluralist moorings thanks to the emergence and stronger institutionalization of the other three pathways—partisan, expert, and symbolic. Policy change, as a result, became more unpredictable as different pathways served as a platform for the mobilization and countermobilization of competing ideas and interests. The old predictable world of incrementalism was supplanted by a policy process that was more dynamic, with greater potential for major policy change. However, as Eric Patashnik notes in *Reforms at Risk*, major policy reforms were often just as easily overturned by what we would call the countermobilization from other pathways.[1]

In this chapter the focus will be primarily on understanding shifts in the federal budget process itself and in the decision rules applying to federal budgetary decisions at both macro and micro levels. Does understanding the pathways associated with budget process regimes help better explain the political dynamics and institutions giving rise to and sustaining these regimes? Have the processes, rules, and models driving federal budgetary decisions experienced the kind of volatility and pathway switching that have occurred in other policy areas? To what extent can shifting across pathways help one understand the source of those shifts?

Budgeting on the Pluralist Pathway

For most of our history, federal budgeting was exhibit A of the pluralist pathway in action. During the time when federal spending rarely breeched 2 percent of the economy, budget decisions largely reflected congressional appropriations actions taken by a Congress that was the primary budgetary "decider" until the 1920s, when the president first got authority to propose his own budget. During this period the relevant interest groups and other specialized actors in appropriations committees and agencies exercised hegemonic influence and control over discrete budgetary areas, ranging from veterans to public health to transportation.

Until relatively recently, the federal budget process was characterized as predominantly incremental, both among practitioners and within the scholarly literature. In the traditional works by Aaron Wildavsky and Richard Fenno, budgeting at the federal level primarily focused on shifts in resources at the margin from the base. Incrementalism was justified both as an empirical observation and a normative framework, and studies revealed that it played out against a backdrop of consensus on the overall budgetary base in the political system more broadly and in budgetary institutions more particularly.[2] The federal budget process was characterized as decentralized, fragmented, and insulated from broad political crosscurrents by strong institutional norms and rules prevailing in the appropriations process.

The pluralist pathway continues to be sustained by institutional features of the budget process. While discretionary appropriations have diminished as a share of the overall budget, the appropriations committees still maintain control over annual decisions in this arena. While party leaders intervene from time to time on macrobudgetary issues, the appropriations committees and other card-carrying members of the pluralist pathway have the great advantage of persistence and longevity, which enables them to wait out and circumvent the initiatives of their leaders.[3]

Other budgetary institutions have served to reinforce the control of interest groups over sectors of the budget. While appropriations committees still rule the roost for discretionary appropriations, these funds make up only a third of the budget, leaving control of the mandatory entitlements to authorizing committees. Whether they focus on agriculture subsidies or student loans, organized interests become major players shaping decisions for these programs as well. For instance, transportation interest groups and their congressional authorizing allies succeeded in insulating transportation trust funds from the control of other actors in the process. Instituting a budgetary concept known as "revenue-aligned budget authority," these interests succeeded in ensuring that all dedicated revenues deposited into trust funds would be allocated for highways and other transportation programs and not available to reduce the deficit as was the case in the past.

The pluralist pathway still fills a critical representational role in federal budgeting. Indeed, its influence over spending priorities has been viewed as being excessive, since it encourages Congress and the president to focus on microdecisions benefiting particular constituencies, to the exclusion of the broader economy and publics that have to pay for these programs with tax dollars. The epitome of this dynamic involves what James Q. Wilson called "client politics," whereby an asymmetry of influence exists between those reaping the narrow benefits and those paying the costs. As he has observed, "clientele" politics promotes the expansion of government benefits because those enjoying concentrated benefits have a greater incentive to mobilize than do the broad publics paying for these programs. Moreover, efforts to unwind these programs are undermined because those bearing the concentrated costs of cutbacks have greater incentive to voice their concerns than do broad publics who stand to realize diffuse gains.[4] This asymmetry of interests causes a deficit bias. The most intense interests with the greatest incentives to mobilize are the narrow groups benefiting from higher spending or lower revenues, not the broader publics who have to finance the costs in one way or the other.

The interest group system institutionalizes this bias enjoyed by narrow interests. Economists such as Mancur Olson argued that interest group coalitions come to dominate policy areas in advanced nations and have incentives to impose inefficient policies on broader-based populations that don't have sufficient incentives to mobilize as interest groups. Ultimately, he theorized, advanced nations will experience economic decline in the grips of these self-interested cartels.[5]

The interest group bias is further accentuated by the politically self-reinforcing dynamics triggered by existing public policy programs and commitments. As framed by Paul Pierson, social welfare programs breed "path dependency," which serves to mobilize political action by recipients supporting current benefits and opposing reforms and reductions to those programs. He concludes that the political mobilization and organization of beneficiaries and providers makes a frontal assault on the welfare state "politically suicidal" in most nations.[6]

Pluralist systems are notoriously crippled in bringing about deficit reduction. From the narrow perspective of each group, accepting fiscal sacrifice is fraught with risks. The classic prisoner's dilemma game describes the situation faced by groups asked to give up benefits in deficit-reduction initiatives. This game acquires its name from the dilemma facing two prisoners who conspire to commit a crime. When apprehended and questioned separately, they may wish initially to cooperate with each other—all they have to do to escape punishment is cooperate in a story covering up their involvement in the crime. Cooperation by both with each other in the cover-up would free them from serving any jail time. But while there are rewards in cooperation, there are risks. Each would face the highest penalty of two years in jail if they continued the false story while the other confessed. As a result, they both confess, and each spends one year in jail due to their mutual fear of being exploited by one another.

This same logic applies to budgeting. Groups and agencies that may support the overall goal of fiscal balance will be reluctant to sacrifice out of fear of being exploited by other groups that may fail to reciprocate. As in other areas of life, so in budgeting no good deed goes unpunished.

The Partisan Pathway

The partisan pathway has traditionally been conceived as the major way in which broad-based change is ushered into our system; party leaders have episodically been able to mobilize broad publics to outflank and shift the framing of issues away from the narrow confines of pluralistic bastions. Reforms in executive budgeting giving the president a budget office and the congressional budget process helped ensure that party leaders would play a more significant role in both macro- and microbudgeting. The congressional budget process was part of a general emergence of stronger congressional parties in the "post-reform Congress." Armed with a process for holding Congress accountable for voting on budgetary totals, along with a process for cascading macro fiscal policy downward to the micro level through committee allocations and points of order, congressional party leaders emerged with a far stronger role in the process.[7] The congressional budget process has also arguably given the president greater leverage over congressional decisions, as the process can be used by his allies to impose macroconstraints on the microbudgetary decisions of congressional spending and revenue committees. Votes on the congressional budget resolution and the numerous amendments in the Senate give party leaders tools to frame issues and establish voting records useful for electoral strategies. Much of the federal budget debate in recent years has entailed shifting congressional rules to strengthen the role of party leaders in developing comprehensive packages to address deficits and presidents alike. The budget reconciliation process and discretionary spending caps, for instance, were tailor-made to reinforce the partisan pathway by giving leaders a mechanism to develop omnibus budget packages and enforce budget discipline that might not survive in the pluralist realm of the individual committees and their interest group allies.[8]

While interest groups may hold sway in opposing cuts or tax increases, party leaders have proved adept at reframing debates to appeal to the broader values and interests served by deficit reduction. The successful reframing of debates thus changes the distribution of influence and can produce rapid and major shifts in public policy.[9]

In fact, political leaders can realize significant electoral rewards from acting on fiscal deficits. Conventional wisdom and academic theory to the contrary, intriguing studies suggest that not only have national leaders taken the initiative to pilot consolidation through the political straits, but they were rewarded electorally as well. Adi Brender and Allan Drazen used data from twenty-three nations of the Organization for Economic Cooperation and Development (OECD) from 1960 through 2003 on 164 elections. They found that governments that achieved lower deficits through policy actions actually increased the probability of their reelection. Controlling for changes in the economy, a reduction of 1 percentage point in the deficit-to-GDP ratio increased the probability of reelection for existing regimes by 5.7 percentage points. The authors attribute this surprising finding to the fact that voters do not like deficits due to their effects on future tax increases and the spending cuts necessary to finance them in subsequent years. A 2012 study done for the OECD concluded that governments sustaining surpluses through significant fiscal sacrifice were generally reelected far more often than nations slipping into deficit.[10]

In the 1990s leaders in the United States successfully mobilized broader publics that stood on the sidelines to support deficit reduction. Through three separate measures, federal deficits exceeding 6 percent of the economy were reduced, leaving four years of budget surpluses in their wake in the late 1990s. As the following shows, the patterns of partisan conflict and consensus varied across all three measures:

- Omnibus Budget Reconciliation Act of 1990: Moved by rising interest-rate pressures and the need to deflect major across-the-board cuts scheduled to be imposed thanks to the Gramm-Rudman-Hollings budget-enforcement regime, Republican president George H. W. Bush was moved to work with congressional Democrats to achieve a cross-partisan agreement. A budget summit produced an agreement that ultimately called for fiscal sacrifice by both parties. Republicans had to accept a tax increase, while Democrats had to endorse significant cuts to Medicare and other entitlements. Caps on discretionary domestic and defense programs would cover the five-year period of the agreement. The 1990 package yielded $496 billion of deficit reduction over five years. The politics were characterized as "cross-partisan" rather than "bipartisan" because a majority of House Republicans, led by Newt Gingrich, rejected the deal.

- Omnibus Budget Reconciliation Act of 1993: Known as the 1993 Deficit Reduction Act, this partisan agreement was passed through negotiations by President Clinton with his fellow Democrats who controlled the House and Senate. Not a single Republican voted for the bill in either house, and Democratic moderates defected to oppose the agreement in both houses. The 1993 act was a continuation of the framework of the 1990 agreement, with caps on discretionary spending, cuts in Medicare, and hikes on tax rates for high-income individuals. Total savings were $433 billion over five years. Of this total, $241 billion came from higher taxes, with the major share comprising higher rates for the wealthy and increased taxes on Medicare payrolls and Social Security benefits. Additionally, $77 billion came from mandatory spending savings, with Medicare constituting the bulk of these savings and the remainder coming from extending discretionary caps and debt service savings.

- The Balanced Budget Act of 1997: Chastened by the reelection of President Clinton and their loss of public standing during the 1995 government shutdown, congressional Republicans displayed new eagerness to negotiate a balanced budget agreement with President Clinton. The president was also eager to cement his legacy as a new-style Democrat, as well as set a stronger fiscal footing for such Democratic priorities as investments and possible expansions of health coverage. Coupled with this propitious political environment, the economy's growth exceeded all forecasts, delivering far higher revenues and lowering deficits in the process. The agreement provided for $204 billion in deficit reduction over five years. Unlike previous agreements, this one entirely comprised spending cuts, including Medicare provider payment reductions and continued restraint on discretionary spending. Unlike previous agreements, bipartisan consensus was enabled by significant new tax and spending programs that ate into projected savings, including capital gains tax cuts and the new State Children's Health Insurance Program.

These agreements collectively bequeathed four years of budget surpluses in the latter years of Clinton's presidency, although a booming economy facilitated by the internet technology expansion clearly lifted all fiscal boats. However, following the 2000 elections, the surpluses were dissipated by new deficits. With the CBO projecting ten-year surpluses totaling $5.6 trillion in 2001, party leaders instead succeeded this time in resurrecting deficits that have increased over the next twelve years—a fiscal swing of over $12 trillion. In the first years of the Bush presidency, tax cuts, the costs of responding to the 9/11 attacks (including the expeditions in Iraq and Afghanistan), and passage of Medicare prescription drug coverage and other domestic policy initiatives brought about deficits exceeding 3 percent of the economy. The deep recession and the countercyclical responses by both the Bush and Obama administrations hiked deficits even higher.[11]

The foregoing suggests that partisan pathways can achieve significant fiscal consolidation if there are sufficient political incentives to forge an agreement. However, when those incentives are lacking, stronger party roles in budgeting can paradoxically lead to worse—not better—fiscal outcomes. National parties have strong and compelling program and policy goals for tax cuts and spending increases that are in conflict with fiscal restraint. The changes in the congressional budget process that have centralized power for budgeting with party leaders have facilitated fiscal expansion in the last twelve years, just as they enabled deficit reduction in the previous decade.

By 2011, both parties rhetorically displayed concern about the rising deficits, as did the American public. However, party polarization has hampered the capacity of leaders in the partisan pathway to reach an agreement. President Obama and Speaker of the House John Boehner sought to reach a "grand bargain" in the summer of 2011, but this foundered on the shoals of seemingly inalterable differences between the parties over tax and spending priorities. The president and congressional Republicans were finally able to reach agreement only when a self-imposed crisis occurred, stemming from impending default prompted by the threatened failure to raise the debt ceiling. The Budget Control Act of 2011 did yield over $2 trillion in ten-year deficit reduction, primarily by placing limits on the one-third of federal spending controlled by discretionary caps. Similarly, agreement was reached on nearly $700 billion in tax increases in December 2012 only after the threatened "crisis" stemming from the expiration of the Bush tax cuts forced the hand of leaders of both parties concerned about the economic and political fallout.

Another partisan crisis in fiscal policy occurred in the fall of 2013. The failure to reach agreement on appropriations for fiscal year 2014 prompted a 15-day government shutdown, furloughing 800,000 federal employees. Party leaders were unable to reconcile differences of nearly $100 billion in discretionary appropriation levels, while Tea Party Republicans insisted on attaching conditions requiring the president's health reform to be delayed or defunded. These conflicts spilled over to the extension of the federal debt ceiling, which needed to be increased to avoid an unprecedented and economically destructive government default. Faced with the economic consequences of default and plummeting poll ratings, moderate congressional Republicans in the Senate scrambled to reach agreement with Democrats extending appropriations through three months, without halting implementation of health reform. Moreover, the debt ceiling was suspended for several months as well, permitting Treasury to meet the government's borrowing needs unimpeded.

The story of the debt-ceiling crisis is told at the end of this chapter, but this latest budget gridlock suggests that agreements will be more difficult to reach under divided government that has characterized the national government for most of the postwar period. Simply put, more polarized parties have learned to use budget issues as a central stage on which to appeal to their core constituencies at the expense of the median voter and financial markets alike. In an era where the median primary voter has supplanted the median voter as the political compass for Washington's elected officials, it is often more important for parties to be on the "right side" of the issue than to collaborate with the other side. A budget process that prized agreement and stability now has become destabilizing to the broader government and the economy.

Expert Pathway

The expert pathway has been strengthened over the years as well. Experts have become fortified by the changing composition of federal budget decisions, as well as the congressional budget process itself. The growing role of mandatory spending and the increasing interdependence of the budget with economic trends have highlighted the need for credible budget numbers and analysis using more sophisticated models to understand these increasingly complex but important relationships.

The role of experts in the process has also been enhanced because rules have replaced informal norms and political consensus as the source of restraint and institutional cohesion in the budget process. Public rules enforced by expert analysis and scoring are applied to rein in more entrepreneurial members no longer bound by traditions of fiscal norms and consensus building in budgeting. Indeed, the enforcement of the congressional budget resolution critically depends on the CBO's scoring of proposed legislation as the basis for raising points of order when individual proposals stray from macrobudgetary constraints. Underpinning the process is the perception—and reality—that the CBO numbers and scoring judgments are grounded in credible analysis and concepts.[12]

Budget scoring is not just a data-collection or estimation exercise. Rather, the real power of the CBO's expertise is associated with the budgetary conventions that are used to construct the baseline and to evaluate policy changes. Decisions on how to project the costs for such key policy reforms as Obama's health care reform or Bush's tax cuts can have major political implications for the ultimate passage of those measures. At times, a single CBO estimate can kill a proposal. For instance, a proposal with wide congressional support to have the US Air Force lease air tankers from companies such as Boeing instead of purchasing them outright foundered when the CBO reported that the leasing approach would be nearly $2 billion more costly over the long term than government purchase. The CBO also scored the leases on an "up front" basis rather than stretching out the payments over the period of the leases—thus defeating a key budgetary incentive that had made leasing seem more attractive than purchasing.[13]

While some political actors have attempted to pressure the CBO to embrace such concepts as dynamic scoring of tax cuts or incremental scoring of public-private capital partnerships, the CBO has largely succeeded in fending off these challenges with the bipartisan support of the budget committees for the most part. Budgetary experts have in fact placed their imprint on budget process reforms, succeeding in 1990 in developing the framework of the Budget Enforcement Act for budgetary decision and control and in gaining congressional passage of credit reform, an accrual-based approach to recording federal commitments for loans and loan guarantees.[14] Budget experts have perhaps even more important roles in state budgets, as Kurt M. Thurmaier and Katherine G. Willoughby suggest they constitute the hidden cluster of actors who work behind the scenes to design and frame alternatives.[15]

As other pathways struggle with budget deficits and politics, experts have become sources of credibility and legitimacy that political actors seek to borrow to fortify their positions or deflect blame. Experts serve the all-important role of mediating conflict by taking certain intractable issues out of the realm of political conflict. Thus while many could find fault with the CBO's economic forecasts, there is an unwritten agreement by both political parties that the "black box" of budgeting will be accepted by both sides. In some respect, budget forecasts and estimates are a public good for budgeting.[16] Any tampering or significant attacks erode their fundamental legitimacy and therefore their utility in containing the boundaries of conflict over resource allocations.

Beyond their roles as neutral referees, experts involved with budgeting help set the agenda of problems and solutions, to use the language of John Kingdon's garbage can model. While experts can't tell political leaders what to think, they can inform what they think about by raising the salience of key budgetary issues for national debate. For instance, budgetary experts, economists, and actuaries helped place the need to reexamine Social Security and health care on the agenda when fiscal forecasts found that they were on an unsustainable course over the long term.[17]

Of course, expert input is not definitive for budget decisions, nor should it be. However, there are times when political leaders choose to delegate sensitive decisions to expert commissions or expert-based institutions. The Base Realignment and Closure Commission is a classic textbook case where Congress used an extra-constitutional institution to save it from itself. Since closing bases in congressional districts proved to be a politically suicidal act, members of Congress established a commission appointed by the president to develop packages of base closures. Taking their cues from the Defense Department, the commission packages had to be voted on as a whole without amendments, thereby freeing members from proposing votes on their own local bases. The commission prompted hundreds of closures and relocations involving eight hundred facilities worldwide over the past two decades.[18] In 1983, Congress delegated the hard bargaining to fashion a compromise to a commission comprising key officials from Congress and the executive.[19]

These commissions worked because Congress and the president needed them to work. There was a bipartisan consensus that some policy action and reforms were essential but that Congress was institutionally incapable of making hard choices through partisan or pluralist pathways. Delegating to experts served to help avoid blame and embrace a credible forum that all could use to justify their decisions to constituents.

The expert commission model has been suggested as a way to circumvent the gridlock gripping the partisan pathway today over deficit choices. With bipartisan urging by Congress, President Obama created such a commission in 2010: the National Commission on Fiscal Responsibility and Reform, commonly known as the Bowles-Simpson Commission. The commission had six members from the House and six from the Senate, each appointed by the chambers' leadership, in addition to six at-large public members. The proposal from the commission would have saved $4 trillion from the deficit over ten years, with cuts distributed across discretionary and entitlements including Social Security. The commission also agreed to support base-broadening tax reform that would generate $1 trillion in additional revenue. The report earned the endorsement of eleven of the eighteen members of the commission, including members from both parties.[20] However, key actors in the process failed to support the commission, most notably President Obama and Rep. Paul Ryan (R-WI), chairman of the House Budget Committee. Lacking this bipartisan imprimatur, the commission's report nonetheless remains a vital agenda-building document not only for its analytical credibility, but also because it provides a roadmap for generating cross-partisan support of difficult budgetary choices. The fate of this commission also illustrates that expert-based forums cannot be expected to supplant other policy pathways if leaders fail to agree to delegate choices to these bodies.

Symbolic Pathway

The symbolic pathway has become stronger as well. Ideological think tanks and interest groups have become more focused on budget reforms as essential features of their policy platforms. For example, the Heritage Foundation and several other conservative organizations have become the champions for dynamic scoring, a process whereby the CBO would be mandated to score tax cuts by offsetting revenue losses with their prospective economic boost to growth. No credible fiscal organization supports the notion that tax cuts generate more revenue, but supply-side true believers such as Arthur Laffer have persisted nonetheless. The CBO's directors, including those appointed by Republicans as well as Democrats, have concluded that this approach is not feasible and would erode the credibility of their estimates. Rudolph Penner, a former CBO director appointed by congressional Republicans, opined that dynamic scoring would require the estimators to know in advance how the tax cut would be financed by current and future Congresses—by spending cuts, tax increases elsewhere, or borrowing.[21] Political scientists Bryan Jones and Walter Williams conclude that bad ideas such as dynamic scoring last longer than they would in markets thanks to the long time period between elections, as well as the massive borrowing capacity of the United States, which serves to postpone the fiscal consequences of ill-advised policies for many years.[22]

Such proposals as balanced budget amendments, capital budgeting, and lockboxes periodically resurface, notwithstanding their secondary effects, feasibility challenges, and threats to other competing values pointed out by budgetary experts. Dramatic reductions in federal discretionary spending caps and major tax overhauls are promised by appealing to traditional American aversion to big government and a complex tax code, without revealing the fiscal sacrifices that would be necessary to achieve these bodacious fiscal targets. Budgetary reforms carry a seductive quality that promises nearly hyperbolic fiscal benefits without requiring sacrifice or hard choices. Interested media avidly follow these developments, giving credence and greater credibility to the often-exaggerated claims for the budget reforms offered in this pathway to resolve a multitude of sins.

Most important, public officials have become increasingly attracted to symbolic budgetary proposals to position themselves on the "right side" of fiscal, tax, or entitlement policy issues. Ideas in this pathway are championed not for their technical adequacy but for their potential to appeal to widely shared values or moods. As budgetary choices become increasingly difficult, the temptation is certainly compelling to advocate symbolic solutions to budgetary choices that entail little or no apparent fiscal sacrifice. It was this environment that spawned the Gramm-Rudman-Hollings Act of 1985, which required large deficits to be eliminated over a five-year period through either legislation or a complicated formula for large across-the-board cuts across many federal programs. Because the formula excluded most entitlements and taxes, the level of cuts imposed on the rest of government was simply politically unrealistic. Moreover, the required deficit reduction was procyclical, as economic downturns would require even greater cuts to achieve fiscal balance. Gramm-Rudman was deemed by most budget professionals to be a flawed approach to budgeting, destined to fail due to its focus on unrealistic deficit-reduction targets that had no real political support.[23] Even one of the sponsors—Sen. Warren Rudman (R-NH)—called it a bad idea whose time had come.

Experts wring their hands as proposals generated in the symbolic pathway are introduced over and over again, seemingly regardless of past experience or design flaws. In an expert regime, policy learning would become institutionalized and deter backtracking but not when the symbolic pathway grips the system. Such symbolic proposals have been nicely phrased as budgetary "perennials" by Irene Rubin.[24]

Pathways and Budgetary Volatility

The pathways framework highlights the institutional and ideational roots of the budgetary volatility experienced during this period. As with other policy areas, the bases of mobilization and policy ideas have multiplied and strengthened with the institutional development and reinforcement of the four pathways to power. The pluralist pathway was the political and institutional grounding for incrementalism, as the relevant interest groups and other specialized actors in appropriations committees and agencies exercised hegemonic influence and control over discrete budgetary areas, ranging from veterans to public health to transportation.

Pluralism continues to be a strong home to narrow interests and constituencies who have always been a strength politically. However, competing policy regimes based in the other three pathways have emerged to contest for macro- and microbudgetary control and influence. The role of each of these other pathways has been fortified and reinforced by institutional developments. As each pathway has strengthened as a source of mobilization in the federal budget process, it has come to be embedded in the budget process, strategically positioned to be activated to influence budgetary outcomes. In some respects, this might be considered to be a healthy development. After all, critics of the old incremental budget process used to decry the hegemonic influence that iron triangles and narrow interests enjoyed in resource allocation. To the extent that the coexistence of pathways opens up access to more diverse interests and values, this could be viewed as a sign of vitality in a democratic budget process.

Consequently, federal budget decisions have featured episodic shifts in rules and decisions that incorporate nonincremental and idea-based forms of change and mobilization. There have been times when political decisions were trumped by broad-based values and ideologies that drove decisions in ways at odds with the stepwise and serial approach of incremental models. Major deficit reductions have been passed encompassing important new policy initiatives and budget-process reforms. Experts have gained an increasing role in guiding and informing the congressional budget process, and ideas from external policy experts have increasingly come to reframe resource allocations. The calm world of appropriations has been supplanted by mandatory entitlements whose character does not lend itself to marginal changes, particularly when small cuts from growing baselines prompt widespread mobilization. Later editions of Wildavsky's classic text recognized this shift by noting that the consensual base for budgeting had been replaced by budgetary dissensus over fundamentals.[25]

Irene Rubin has noted that the traditional notions of incrementalism prevented budgeters from seeing the changing budgetary reality taking shape in front of them. Budgeting became more complex and diverse, with parts of the budget subject to different rules and criteria. Moreover, normative budget theory featuring prominent roles for analysts and performance information gained far more traction than traditional incrementalist and pluralist thinking would have allowed.[26] While appropriations still hew to the pluralist pathway, entitlements involve heavy input from partisan and expert pathways due to their complexity and significance for macrofiscal goals and broader political constituencies. Experts in bureaucracies carry considerable influence when it comes to actual execution of budgets passed by Congress, as complex fund allocations and obligations are implemented largely out of view of actors in symbolic, partisan, or even pluralist pathways.

The tensions among pathways is reflected in greater tension between macrobudgetary totals and microbudgetary decisions due to the engagement of different pathways at different stages and levels of aggregation. Agreement on a budget resolution reached on the partisan pathway by leaders in Congress and perhaps the White House is no guarantee that the targets, ceilings, and constraints in that agreement will be honored in the subsequent allocation processes by the committees operating in the pluralist pathway. The discretionary appropriations totals in the budget resolution reflect the aspirations of party leaders for positioning as fiscal stalwarts, as well as the symbolic appeal to all members to position themselves as voting for fiscal austerity during times of deficits; both partisan and symbolic pathways are activated in voting on aggregates. Increasingly, however, observers have noted that the aggregate targets are not politically sustainable within the appropriations process. Committee members complain that they are being saddled with the unwelcome political task of either voting for major cuts or taking the blame for raising the totals at the back end of the process. Rudy Penner points to an accountability challenge from the conflicting pathways, noting that members vote for stringent spending caps as a symbolic means of proving fiscal conservatism at the aggregate while remaining free to vote large individual spending increases in the pluralist confines of appropriations.[27] The conflicts among the levels of budgeting and pathways responsible also serve to lengthen the process and prompt last-minute efforts to bridge the gap between macro restraint and micro pressures. At times, budget gimmicks emerge to paper over the tensions between macro- and microbudgeting by such actions as moving paydays across fiscal years or classifying routine and expected spending items as "emergencies" exempt from spending caps.

Possibly because of this institutional differentiation in the federal budget process, federal budgeting became far less stable and more volatile than anything the incrementalists could have envisaged. Budgetary policy veered between courting and increasing deficits in the 1980s, to mounting major deficit-reduction initiatives in the 1990s, to sustaining surpluses for four years near the turn of the twenty-first century, to renewed deficits in the 2000s. These different fiscal policies largely had their origins in the partisan pathway, but different fiscal regimes had consequences for the relative influence of different pathways. Large deficits prompted the emergence of symbolic and partisan pathways, often leading to the construction of new budget-control frameworks that limited fiscal leeway of actors in pluralist pathways. When deficits receded, pluralists came back to the fore, as central political actors loosened their control over the fiscal reigns of the budget (see figure 7.1).

In fact, the pathways compete with one another over time for control over the budget process itself. The budgetary hegemony enjoyed by one pathway prompts the mobilization of other pathways, as actors vie to advance new budgetary regimes presumably more friendly to their interests. The volatile history of budget process reform is illustrated in figure 7.2.

While the appropriations-based nature of congressional budgeting reflected the dominance of the pluralistic pathway, the Congressional Budget Act of 1974

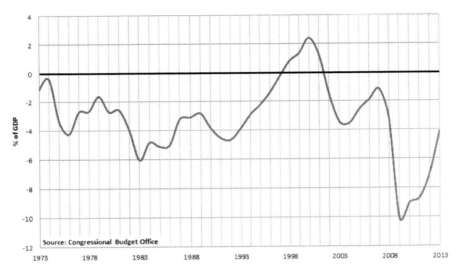

Figure 7.1. Deficits as a Share of GDP, 1973–2013

served the interests of the partisan pathway, vaulting congressional leaders into the driver's seat for fiscal policy across the entire budget. Party leaders designed the process to better compete with the influence the president exerted over the budget debate in the years before. This watershed reform required Congress to establish its own budget resolution to compete with the macrobudget issued by the president, fortified with expert-based budget-scoring rules applied by the new Congressional Budget Office. Importantly, the new process enabled party leaders to unseat appropriators from their formerly dominant role in congressional budgeting. New budget committees and a new reconciliation process gave leaders

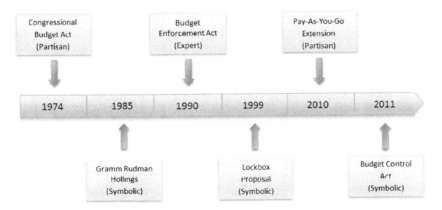

Figure 7.2. Timeline for Federal Budget Process Reform

more systematic controls over congressional committees. Nearly all major deficit reductions since that time built on reconciliation to force hard choices across a fragmented Congress.

The partisan and expert-based paths were overcome in the mid-1980s by the symbolically based Gramm-Rudman-Hollings Act. Frustrated by the inabilities of Democratic and Republican leaders to reach agreement on deficit reduction, members reached for the symbolic pathway in a desperate search for budget-ary and political salvation. As noted above, this legislation was intended to force Congress to eliminate the deficit in five years based on a highly improbable series of actions that Congress ultimately could not and would not take. While help-ing Congress align itself with the historical American norms of budget balance, it soon became apparent that mandating budget balance did not make it happen, but it did succeed in embarrassing Congress and the president with a series of annual decisions to ignore the increasingly ambitious and unrealistic cuts mandated by this budgetary regime.

Within five years of this legislation, experts and party leaders adopted the Budget Enforcement Act of 1990 (BEA), which succeeded in overturning the un-realistic and self-defeating regime of the Gramm-Rudman-Hollings Act. Unlike Gramm-Rudman, the BEA gave up on forcing Congress to eliminate the deficit itself. Rather, the new enforcement regime focused on constraining new congres-sional action over appropriations through the adoption of discretionary spending caps and PAYGO rules forcing those proposing new tax cuts or spending entitle-ments to find deficit-reduction offsets. Unlike mandated budget balance, the core concepts of the BEA have been sustained in various forms for the past twenty-three years.

However, the specific controls instituted by the BEA regime were overturned as the nation slipped into surplus, whetting the appetite of actors on the pluralist and partisan pathways for new spending and tax cuts unconstrained by deficit controls enacted years earlier. The growing prevalence of gimmicks signaled an early warning of the erosion of the legitimacy of this budgetary regime, as mem-bers increasingly colluded to evade the discretionary caps through inventive strat-egies featuring expansive use of "emergency" spending and liberal use of advance appropriations to push spending into subsequent fiscal years. While this signaled the reemergence of the pluralist pathway, party leaders battled over what to do with the surpluses. Seeking to capture the symbolic high ground, President Clin-ton sought a lockbox to prevent Congress from using the burgeoning Social Secu-rity surpluses for anything but debt reduction. For the four years of surpluses, the surpluses constituted the large bulk of the broader budget surplus. Conveniently, the lockbox would have prevented Republicans from devoting surpluses to tax cuts, just as it would have prevented Democrats from using the funds for spending priorities. While lockboxes were never formally legislated, the president succeeded in performing the symbolically powerful act of joining retention of surpluses with saving Social Security.

From 2001 during the Bush presidency, the presence of a strong conservative push for tax cuts along with the unified Republican control of Congress fostered an environment of indifference to budget process regimes. While still restrained by the absence of a sixty-vote majority in the Senate, the Bush presidency and its congressional allies found little need for budget process to implement their fiscal policies on the spending and revenue sides of the budget. The BEA formally expired in 2002, although budgetary caps on discretionary spending and PAYGO constraints on tax cuts and entitlements continued to be enforced by congressional points of order. However, because of strong control of the Congress, the president was able to steer both his tax cuts of 2001 and 2003 and the Medicare prescription drug program through Congress without any PAYGO offsets to reduce their effects on the deficit.

The absence of formal budget rules could be said itself to be the product of the partisan pathway, with a president who had determined that deficits did not matter nearly as much as more highly prized policy goals. The partisan pathway, however, was responsible for new budget controls adopted in 2010 by President Obama with the support of a Democratic Congress. The 2010 PAYGO legislation reestablished the BEA controls over new tax cuts and entitlements with several key exceptions that adhered to Obama's fiscal policy.

Finally, the latest budget process enforcement regime was the Budget Control Act of 2011 (BCA), adopted in the summer to help solve the debt-limit crisis discussed below. Republicans in Congress agreed to increase the debt ceiling in return for over $2 trillion in spending cuts over ten years. The BCA called for declining discretionary appropriations caps that would help reduce the deficit. However, beyond this, the agreement charged a new joint congressional committee with developing a package of reforms achieving over $1 trillion in savings over ten years from the end of 2011. The supercommittee's actions could range across the entire budget, including further discretionary spending cuts, entitlement reforms, and tax increases or reforms. In November 2011, the supercommittee proved to be unable to reach agreement to achieve the additional savings. Under the new law, this failure precipitated a series of automatic sequesters to fall equally on defense and domestic programs beginning in 2013. The BCA proved to be motivated by the symbolic pathway. Looking for a fig leaf to justify coming off of their deep-seated animus to increasing the debt ceiling, Republicans would need to show their Tea Party constituents that they had achieved a prized reduction in government as their price for acceding to the president. Obama had little choice but to accept these cuts, particularly since they included cuts in defense that might motivate Republicans to search for other ways to achieve the BCA's fiscal targets. While many pundits assumed that Congress and the president would find alternatives to sequestration, the party leaders could not agree on an alternative set of cuts and revenues to supplant these across-the-board cuts. In March 2013, a sequester went into effect for FY 2013, fostering across-the-board cuts in most discretionary budget accounts in defense and nondefense agencies.

In short, budget-process regimes swung widely across the four pathways in the years since the adoption of the Congressional Budget Act of 1974. In many cases, the actions stemming from one pathway motivated other pathways to countermobilize to achieve different fiscal goals and targets in different ways. This pace of policy innovation exceeds any that would be expected if the system were truly incremental or if it were truly gridlocked. Rather, the patterns reveal a policy process that has become more volatile, if not unpredictable. Indeed, the actions of one period seem to prompt reforms in other periods, as reforms taken in one pathway prompt the countermobilization by other pathways.

Concluding Observations

The presence of multiple pathways has made budget-policy and budget-process reform more prone to rapid change, more contestable, and less predictable. Rapid shifts in pathways were responsible for wide swings in budgetary policies and processes. Many would argue that such a dynamic augers well for broad-based interests not well represented in traditional pluralistic settings. It permitted and supported gains in reducing the deficit at times, while leading to higher deficits at other times.

The question is whether there is any regularity or predictability in this dynamic of pathway switching. Can we say, for instance, that narrow-based pluralist pathways will prompt the emergence of broader-based pathways as interests and values excluded are mobilized in other ways by other actors? The switching of pathways played a formative role in driving shifts of policy in agenda formation and policy formulation. Because certain frames and outcomes are promoted by different pathways, change is to be expected when the primary pathway driving an issue shifts.

The history of budget process reforms reveals that pathways have strengths and weaknesses that can help explain their rise and fall. The pluralist pathway excels in representation of organized interests, a vital function for any budget process in a democratic system. However, since there is a bias in any interest group system, pluralism has lost traction when it failed to account for all significant interests, particularly more broadly shared public interests in fiscal consolidation. The partisan pathway becomes the basis for linking budget decisions with broader constituencies and values represented by national elected officials, but those same policies are highly vulnerable to being replaced when fiscal and political realities change. Expert-based reforms are vital to enable budgetary actors to claim legitimacy and ensure that budget policy decisions influence economic and policy decisions in intended ways. However, expert rules can lose traction when they fall out of step with political values and interests. Finally, symbolic reforms have the unique advantage of overcoming partisan gridlock by promoting rapid change and responses to economic trends, but these budget arrangements can become just as quickly unwound when their hidden and ill-considered implementation challenges become manifest with experience.

Ultimately, these trends raise questions of their own that call for more research. Budgeting is a repetitive process that calls for regularity and common decision rules. Most important, it is the one policy area where decisions must be made to avoid a shutdown of government. Given the high stakes inherently involved with budget decisions, the budget process had traditionally epitomized the most routine and predictable decision-making process in government. However, as we have seen, pathway volatility has arisen to shift the rules of the game periodically, eroding the certainty, predictability, and legitimacy of the process. Given the difficult fiscal choices facing the nation in the wake of the financial crisis and the cusp of baby boomers' retirement, a credible and widely supported process will be essential to sustain the confidence and support of the publics and the markets in the future.

The Debt Ceiling Crisis: Pathways in Action

The debt ceiling emerged after World War I as a delegation of debt management to the bureaucracy from Congress. Abjuring its traditional role of approving each bond issue, Congress gave this function to experts in the Treasury, with the proviso that overall debt stay within a legislated ceiling. As the nation's finances became more complex, the expert pathway emerged as the appropriate way to manage debt financing and get the best value for money on the bond market for the government. As with state governments, a ceiling provided a continuing role for elected officials to intervene.

In reality, the debt is simply the reflection of earlier decisions to commit the government to certain spending and revenue policies. Refusing to grant an increase in debt is tantamount to individuals refusing to pay their credit cards when payment becomes due. However, the debt ceiling provides a symbolically appealing policy space that can be used by Congress to have its cake and eat it too. While we don't get to do that as individuals, policymakers can both create additional debt through spending expansions and tax cuts and subsequently position themselves as opponents of the higher federal fiscal profile arising from their earlier decisions and nondecisions.

As a result, a vote on increasing the debt ceiling has a high symbolic content and illustrates the powerful role that the symbolic pathway has come to play in federal budgeting. It has also proved to be a convenient vehicle for the opposition party to register its concern about the incumbent government's fiscal policies. Thus, while in the Senate, Barack Obama voted against the George W. Bush administration's request to increase the debt limit but as president railed against Republican efforts to refuse him the same authority. President Obama joined two of our most conservative presidents—Reagan and Bush—in pleading with Congress for debt ceiling increases. One fiscal economist suggested that the debt ceiling is, in effect, a tax on the majority issued by the minority party.[28]

Opposition to the debt ceiling gathers in both the symbolic and partisan pathways. Support arises from both partisan and expert pathways. Presidents need extensions to continue operating government programs and agencies. The failure to raise the ceiling would cause massive disruption in public administration and in the economy itself—both events that could cripple an administration's standing with the public and capacity to carry out its agenda.

Experts in the Treasury and in the markets in general understand how ruinous the failure to increase debt ceiling might be for the economy. Nearly one-third of Treasury bonds come due each year. Since there is no surplus in the budget to redeem these obligations, the Treasury must go into the market to issue new bonds to pay off the old ones—a process known as a debt rollover. If the debt ceiling is not extended, the Treasury will not be able to pay creditors when their bonds come due. This would constitute a default on the full faith and credit of the United States. While other nations have experienced such defaults, this has never happened to the United States. The perception that the nation stands behind its debts is central to the emergence of Treasury bonds as the one truly risk-free asset in global financial markets. Should doubt be raised, the interest rates that the federal government would have to pay would most assuredly increase, adding to the deficit itself.

The debt ceiling crisis of 2011 constituted a sharp conflict between expert, partisan, and symbolic pathways. The new Republican majority in the House comprised eighty-five new members, many of whom ascribed to the Tea Party label. Dedicated to reducing debt and deficits through spending cuts, they were prone to adopt extreme views on the federal role and the budget. For these members, the debt ceiling extension became a line in the sand where they could prove their bona fides to their restive Tea Party followers back home. A number of these freshmen were quoted as saying a default on Treasury bonds would be more acceptable than sanctioning the continuing growth of spending and debt that a debt ceiling extension would ratify.

In years past, the House had adopted the "Gephardt rule," which automatically increased the debt ceiling upon passage of the new congressional budget resolution. This convenient fiscal rule took the debt ceiling out of the symbolic and partisan pathways by not permitting members of the House to vote on the extension formally. However, this rule did not necessarily apply in the Senate, which could continue to obstruct the debt ceiling depending on which party held control.

This Tea Party Congress would abandon the Gephardt rule and require adoption of an increase by the full House. The House Republicans adopted what later became known as the "Boehner rule"—the debt ceiling would be increased only if an equivalent amount of spending cuts were adopted by Congress.[29] By contrast, the Obama administration advocated a "plain vanilla" extension of the debt ceiling, separating that issue from the substantive questions involved with the federal budget itself.

Speaker Boehner and his Republican majority won the debate over what the debate would be about. The debt would be raised only as part of a substantive deal involving federal spending reductions. For a time it appeared that President Obama and the speaker had indeed reached a "grand bargain" to adopt major cuts to Social Security, discretionary spending, and tax reform. However, when this fell apart, the House proved willing to bring the nation to the brink of default. Such a ruinous outcome was avoided when the administration agreed on a new plan of $2.3 trillion in spending cuts over ten years.

The Budget Control Act extended the federal debt ceiling and staved off default of the federal government but not before including major reductions in discretionary spending for defense and nondefense agencies for the next ten years. The legislation also included a budget sequester that would entail further reductions in those programs, as well as selected entitlements, if a new congressional supercommittee failed to agree and achieve more than $1 trillion in savings across the entire budget.

While having real consequences, the legislation came about on the symbolic pathway, reflecting the needs of both parties to appear to respond to rising public concern over deficits. With a Tea Party faction dedicated to opposing extending the ceiling on federal debt, Republican leaders in Congress were desperate for a symbolic way to demonstrate that they had at least attempted to achieve reductions in spending as their price for dropping their hard line on federal debt. With deficits rising to record peacetime levels during the Great Recession, the Obama administration also had an interest in appearing to support a down payment on deficit reduction, particularly since this appeared to be necessary to avoid an unprecedented federal default. The legislation was designed to incorporate a number of symbolic initiatives to show a Congress hard at work curbing the future debt of the nation, again as the price for extending the debt ceiling. The spending caps would bring spending on defense and domestic programs by 2023 to levels not seen since before 1970—a mark that most experts regarded as unworkable and unattainable. The congressional supercommittee was also a highly visible effort designed to demonstrate fealty to deficit reduction, even though it was destined to fail in a polarized Congress.

Finally, the legislation constructed a highly symbolic drama designed to stage votes on incremental debt ceiling increase to satisfy the need of Republicans to vote against higher debt, while enabling the president to increase the debt in reality. President Obama would be allowed to raise the debt ceiling in three increments over the following year and a half. Congressional Republicans would have chances to block each increase with a resolution of disapproval, but Obama would almost certainly veto it, and an override would be unlikely. Thus, under the Budget Control Act, the president was able to increase the debt to finance government while Republicans gained opportunities to vote against debt extensions and bind government spending in future years at a rate that most thought would be unrealistic.

In the fall of 2013, the need for an increase in the debt ceiling once again prompted sharp partisan conflict between the President and House Republicans dominated by Tea Party members. As discussed above, the debt ceiling issue was swept into the broader conflict over appropriations, which caused the government shutdown. Against a backdrop of impending default and precipitous drops in their poll ratings, moderate congressional Republicans seized the leadership and reached agreement with Democrats and the president on appropriations and extension of the debt limit for several months. Unlike the 2011 debt ceiling agreement, this one did not force the president to accept additional spending cuts or new budget process constraints.

Notes

1. Erik Patashnik, *Reforms at Risk: What Happens after Major Policy Changes Are Enacted* (Princeton, NJ: Princeton University Press, 2008).

2. Aaron Wildavsky, *Politics of the Budgetary Process*, 1st ed. (Boston: Little, Brown, 1964); and Richard Fenno, *The Power of the Purse* (Boston: Little, Brown, 1966).

3. John F. Cogan, Timothy Muris, and Allen Schick, *The Budget Puzzle: Understanding Federal Spending* (Stanford, CA: Stanford University Press, 1994).

4. Wilson, *Politics of Regulation*.

5. Mancur Olson, *The Rise and Decline of Nations: Economic Growth, Stagflation and Social Rigidities* (New Haven, CT: Yale University Press, 1984).

6. Paul Pierson, *The New Politics of the Welfare State* (New York: Oxford University Press, 2001), 415.

7. Roger H. Davidson, *The Post-Reform Congress* (New York: St. Martin's, 1992).

8. Schick, *Federal Budget*.

9. Frank Baumgartner and Bryan Jones, *Agendas and Instability in American Politics*, 2nd ed. (Chicago: University of Chicago Press, 2011).

10. Paul L. Posner and Matthew Sommerfeld, "The Politics of Fiscal Austerity," *Journal of Public Budgeting and Finance* 32, no. 3 (Fall 2012).

11. Pew Fiscal Analysis Initiative, *The Great Debt Shift* (Washington, DC: Pew Foundation, 2011).

12. Schick, *Federal Budget*, 56.

13. Douglas Holz-Eakin, "Assessment of the Air Force's Plan to Acquire 100 Boeing Tanker Aircraft," testimony before the Senate Commerce, Transportation, and Science Committee, September 3, 2003.

14. The 1990 BEA replaced politically unworkable deficit targets adopted under the 1985 Gramm-Rudman-Hollings Act with a more manageable set of controls focused on enforcing discretionary spending ceilings and on preventing new entitlements and tax cuts that increase the deficit.

15. Kurt M. Thurmaier and Katherine G. Willoughby, *Policy and Politics in State Budgeting* (Armonk, NY: M. E. Sharpe, 2001), 38.

16. See Phil Joyce, *The Congressional Budget Office: Honest Numbers, Power and Policymaking* (Washington, DC: Georgetown University Press, 2011).

17. Paul L. Posner, "Waiting for Godot," *Public Administration Review* 69, no. 2 (March–April 2009).

18. Government Accountability Office, *Military Base Closures and Realignments*, publication GAO-12-709R (Washington, DC: Government Accountability Office, 2012).

19. Paul Light, *Artful Work: The Politics of Social Security Reform* (New York: McGraw-Hill, 1985).

20. National Commission on Fiscal Responsibility and Reform, *The Moment of Truth* (Washington, DC: National Commission on Fiscal Responsibility and Reform, 2010).

21. Rudolph Penner, *Dynamic Scoring: Not So Fast* (Washington, DC: Tax Policy Center, Urban Institute, 2006).

22. Jones and Williams, *Politics of Bad Ideas*.

23. Rudolph Penner, *Repairing the Congressional Budget Process* (Washington, DC: Urban Institute, 2001).

24. Irene Rubin, "Perennial Budget Reform Proposals: Budget Staff versus Elected Officials," *Public Budgeting and Finance* 22, no. 4 (Winter 2002).

25. Aaron Wildavsky and Naomi Caiden, *The New Politics of the Budgetary Process* (New York: Longman, 2001).

26. Irene Rubin, "Budget Theory and Budget Practice: How Good the Fit?," *Public Administration Review* (March–April, 1990): 179–89.

27. Penner, "Repairing the Congressional Budget Process."

28. Donald Marron, "The Debt Limit Is a Tax on the Majority," *Musings on Economics, Finance and Life*, January 28, 2010.

29. Jackie Calmes, "As Debt Battle Looms, Some See No Option but to Raise Taxes," *New York Times*, May 19, 2012.

CHAPTER EIGHT

Pathways through the Political Thicket of Taxation

Long confined to the esoteric world of tax lawyers and accountants, tax policy has emerged during the past three decades as one of the most prominent and important arenas of national policymaking. Over these years, proposed and enacted tax law changes "came to dominate the public agenda," observed one key participant of tax policymaking.[1]

As tax policy became more visible and contentious, it also became more partisan. Since Ronald Reagan made large-scale individual tax cuts the core of his fiscal policy approach in 1980, cutting taxes has become the central tenet of Republican domestic policy. Tax legislation in 1981, 1993, 2001, 2003, 2009, and 2012 all elicited highly partisan and polarized responses in Congress, as well as in the broader electorate. Yet as partisan as tax policy has become, party conflict does not encompass the whole of tax politics in the contemporary era. Many major pieces of tax legislation during this same period have passed with bipartisan support, including the Tax Equity and Fiscal Responsibility Act of 1982 (TEFRA), the Deficit Reduction Act of 1984 (DEFRA), the Tax Reform Act of 1986 (TRA86), the Taxpayer Relief Act of 1997 (TRA97), and the Tax Relief and Job Creation Act of 2010.

Bipartisanship can manifest itself in other ways as well. President Obama and large majorities of both parties in Congress publicly committed themselves to extending the highly contentious Bush tax cuts for the vast majority of taxpayers, and such a policy was enacted on a bipartisan basis in the American Taxpayer Relief Act of 2012. Moreover, the *concept* of reforming federal taxes in ways recommended by most tax policy experts—by broadening the tax base and lowering tax rates—continues to draw broad bipartisan support, even though members of both political parties, and the public more generally, tend to defect in large numbers once specific tax preferences are put on the legislative chopping block. At the same time, many of these same preferences, or "tax expenditures," are rendered equally nonpartisan in times of political obscurity, when they are salient only to a handful of interests and constituencies directly affected, along with their legislative advocates and representatives.

This pattern of political diversity results in part from the shifting goals of tax policy, which have often changed abruptly from one piece of legislation to the next. The Economic Recovery Tax Act of 1981 (ERTA) was the biggest package of tax cuts in American history, offering breaks for individuals, corporations, and a welter of special interests. The very next year, TEFRA sharply reversed course, significantly augmenting revenues by raising taxes and closing loopholes. The omnibus budget acts of 1990 and 1993, as well as the "fiscal cliff" deal of 2012, all raised tax rates on the wealthy. In contrast, tax legislation passed in 1997, 2001, and 2003 cut taxes for high-income earners and introduced a myriad of special new tax breaks and incentives for a variety of purposes and constituencies.

The Tax Reform Act of 1986 (TRA) charted a still different course. Designed to be "revenue neutral"—neither increasing nor decreasing federal tax receipts— the TRA simultaneously reduced the number of tax brackets and lowered tax rates while broadening the base of taxable income by eliminating a host of "special-interest" provisions. Intended to simplify the system, making it both more comprehensible and "fair," the TRA followed the general path long favored by tax experts, working uphill against substantial political obstacles that made its passage seem implausible from start to finish.[2]

Thus the politics of taxation have proven to be complex and changeable but in ways that have hewn closely to the patterns apparent in the pathways framework. Over time the center of gravity in tax politics has shifted from the pluralist arena, which long dominated the politics of taxation, toward the partisan pathway as American fiscal policy has mirrored—and sometimes led—the broader trend toward polarized politics. Yet the TRA and the politics of tax and deficit reform in the 2000s have demonstrated both the real and potential influence of the expert pathway. And, finally, the continuing allure of a "flat tax" and the highly public campaigns for an end to the "death tax" and for a "taxpayer's bill of rights" all underscore the potential for symbolic politics even in the green-eye-shades world of tax policy.

Traditional Tax Politics and the Pluralist Pathway

Prior to the 1980s, the normal pattern of US tax politics hewed closely to the model of pluralistic, incremental policymaking. The federal income tax grew greatly in fiscal importance and complexity after its creation in 1913, but much of this was due to the cumulative effects of incremental changes over time. With the exception of changes wrought during times of war and crisis such as the increase in tax rates and development of automatic withholding during World War II, the tax system did not change in basic structure, and proposals to alter it fundamentally seldom advanced very far. In his authoritative analysis of pre-1980s tax policy,

John Witte described the standard pattern of tax politics as thoroughly incremental: "Legislative changes to tax policy usually involve marginal adjustments to the existing structure. Simple changes in parameters account for most of the modifications and most of the revenue effects. Applicable rates, bracket changes, exemption levels, standard deductions, depreciation percentages, investment credits, depletion allowances—the list of changes that can be accomplished by simply altering a number is very long. . . . Tax laws can also be easily and marginally altered by expanding or contracting eligible groups, actions, industries, commodities, or financial circumstances."[3] As a result, the income tax code grew increasingly long and complex over the course of the twentieth century, as special rules and narrowly targeted exceptions and tax expenditures proliferated.

This traditional approach to the making of tax policy can be largely attributed to distributive politics in Congress and the influence of organized beneficiary groups.[4] Interest groups with an economic stake in tax policy—which includes virtually all of Washington's thousands of interest groups—are typically well represented before Congress's tax-writing committees.[5] As journalist William Greider noted during the debate over tax reform, "every economic interest—from tobacco to insurance to labor to banks—is present."[6] Each group petitions Congress to advance or defend a set of favored tax policies, often in the absence of any oversight or counterpressure from the broader public. As Stanley Surrey noted in a classic 1957 essay on the politics of tax expenditures, "the Congressman favoring these special provisions has for the most part no accounting to make to the voters for his action. He is thereby much freer to lend a helping hand here and there to a group which has won his sympathy or which is pressing him for results."[7]

Rational-choice theory helps to explain this common, though not universal, pattern of pluralistic tax politics. The average citizen, if acting rationally, is disinclined to invest the time and energy needed to influence Congress on complex matters of taxation because the costs of obtaining the requisite information and organizing for action would almost certainly exceed any benefits. Moreover, average citizens and voters would have to overcome the free-rider problem: The benefits of policies in the broad public interest would accrue to many, including the majority of passive onlookers, while the costs of involvement would all be borne by the active few.

As a result, rational-choice theory predicts that the making of tax policy will be dominated by those organized interests able to secure advantages in tax law large enough, and narrowly defined enough, to benefit them disproportionately. Once having obtained such benefits, the same groups are expected to lobby vigorously to maintain and expand them. As economist David Davies has argued, most "taxpayers remain rationally ignorant of tax matters," while "congressional tax and finance committees are . . . virtual prisoners of highly organized, well financed, single issue, special interest groups. . . . These powerful organizations exert influence on tax laws far in excess of their small size."[8]

As in other areas of pluralist policymaking, this group-oriented process tends not to be excessively partisan in nature. Most members of Congress, regardless of party, believe it is their responsibility—and certainly good politics—to advance the interests of important groups within their constituencies. Thus Corn Belt senators of both parties support tax breaks for ethanol production, while advanced manufacturing tax credits are typically supported by both Democrats and Republicans who have high-technology manufacturers in their districts. Moreover, both parties have found strategic reasons to support the proliferation of tax expenditures. Republicans have often considered tax expenditures to be the preferred approach to advance domestic policy objectives because they provide a means of addressing popular concerns while respecting the broader partisan goal of reducing taxes, at least for some. Democrats, meanwhile, have often found the tax-expenditure approach to be the political avenue of least resistance when it comes to using public policy to address social and economic objectives.

This bipartisan pattern of pluralist tax policymaking was abundantly illustrated during the late Clinton administration, to take just one example. Given a Republican-controlled Congress, tax policy expert Sheldon Pollack noted that much of the Taxpayer Relief Act of 1997 read like "a Christmas-list of special tax provisions targeted at the constituents of the Republican Party." Noteworthy and expensive presents under the tree included a reduction from 28 percent to 20 percent in the maximum tax rate on capital gains, an increase in the exemption from the federal gift and estate tax from $600,000 to $1 million (and $1.3 million for farms and small business owners), and repeal of the corporate minimum tax for small businesses.[9] But to gain bipartisan support and the president's signature, the bill also included gifts for Democratic constituencies, including a tax credit of $500 per child (made "partially refundable" so that lower-income working parents would benefit even if they owed little or no income taxes), and eleven different education tax incentives, including a HOPE tax credit of up to $1,500 per student for each of the first two years of college.[10]

Nor was the 1997 bill a unique exercise in pluralist tax politics. Pollack notes that in a 1995 tax and budget reconciliation bill (which President Clinton ultimately vetoed due to its cuts in the Medicare and Medicaid programs),

> every Republican on the Finance Committee, save for conservative presidential candidate Phil Gramm of Texas, had some special-interest provision inserted in the Senate bill. Beneficiaries (and their respective supporters on the Finance Committee) included newspaper companies (Robert Dole of Kansas), small gas and electric companies (William Roth of Delaware, the home of the Delmarva Power & Light Co.),

water utilities and real estate developers (Charles Grassley of Iowa), college football coaches (Orrin Hatch of Utah, a close friend of Brigham Young University's football coach), life insurance companies (Alfonse D'Amato of New York), and independent gasoline marketers (Don Nickles of Oklahoma).[11]

A corporate tax break "feeding frenzy" appeared to be under way in early 2001 as well, as the George W. Bush administration prepared to launch a major effort to cut federal taxes. *National Journal* reported that business groups were engaged in a "bidding war" for favorable tax treatment, as various corporations and trade associations sought tax credits for telecommunications infrastructure, exemptions for income from stock options, favored treatment of retirement savings, and other goals.[12] In the end, however, the business community was largely frozen out of the administration's 2001 tax package, except for the research and development (R&D) tax credit. With the president already committed to a huge, $1.6 trillion package of mostly individual tax reductions, White House officials told business lobbyists to stand aside and make way for broad-based tax cuts with broader political appeal.[13] In the process, tax policy in 2001 was shifted out of the pluralist shadows and into the harshly lit arena of partisan politics.

The Bush Tax Cuts and the Partisan Pathway

As discussed in chapter 3, the traditional means by which American politics has overcome the incrementalism of pluralist policymaking and the obstacles imposed by the separation-of-powers system has occurred on those relatively brief occasions when it resembles the ideal of responsible party government. A new president who sweeps into office with large party majorities in both chambers of Congress can often mobilize the resources of office to construct a coherent legislative program and rally the public and party followers to push his agenda into law. With the rise of "conditional party government" in recent years, based on more narrowly homogeneous and ideologically polarized parties, it has become possible at times for a president with narrower support in Congress and the electorate to succeed with a similarly partisan style of policymaking.

Use of the partisan pathway to pursue important tax legislation has become increasingly common over the past three decades. The trend was launched with Ronald Reagan's election in 1980 on a platform of dramatic tax cuts. Since that time, the concept of allowing any federal tax increase has become anathema to conservatives and, increasingly, to virtually all Republicans in Congress. Consequently, polarized, partisan coalition building has played a crucial role in many of the most prominent pieces of tax legislation of the 1980s, 1990s, and 2000s. For example, the final House vote on President Reagan's program of tax cuts in 1981 divided the parties more sharply than any other tax vote going back to 1921.

This was true even after Democrats, instead of steadfastly resisting Republican tax cuts, caved on the core fiscal and philosophical issues and joined Republicans in a bidding war in which the Democrats' tax bill matched Republican tax cuts almost dollar for dollar.[14]

Similarly, the politics of Bill Clinton's 1993 tax and deficit-reduction package was almost purely partisan in character. Assembled by his administration as a result of a campaign pledge to reduce the mounting deficit, his package of tax increases and budget cuts resulted in bitter partisan fights in Congress. Senate Republican leader Bob Dole (R-KS) said the bill had earned Clinton "his place on Mount Taxmore," while a Republican House member claimed "the Clinton tax bill will drive a stake into the heart of [our] economy."[15] House speaker Tom Foley (D-WA) complained that Republicans were marching in "lockstep."[16] Indeed, the legislation failed to attract the support of even a single Republican on any of eight critical votes in the House or Senate.[17]

The final conference bill on the Omnibus Budget and Reconciliation Act of 1993 passed the House by a whisker, 218-216, but only after one freshman Democrat was convinced to change her vote and only after days of "feverish" lobbying by the administration and top Democratic leaders. The Senate, as Barbara Sinclair observes, also passed the final bill "by a hair. The vote was 51-50, with Vice President Gore casting the deciding ballot as he had [earlier]. No Republican in either chamber voted for the legislation. Speaker Foley had been right. The Republicans had marched in lockstep, but the Democrats held together enough to prevail."[18]

The dynamics of the partisan pathway in tax legislation can be seen in the politics of the 2001 tax-cut legislation sponsored by President George W. Bush. Following up on his campaign proposals, he and his administration developed a massive tax-reduction package estimated to cost $1.6 trillion over ten years.[19] The centerpiece was an array of individual income tax rate cuts, with the bottom rate sliced from 15 percent to 10 percent and the two highest rates pared in stages from 39.6 percent and 36 percent down to 33 percent. The total cost of these rate reductions was estimated at $724 billion over ten years. However, because they were gradually phased in, the estimated cost of the rate cuts in the second decade was expected to be much larger still. Another costly item was the phasing-out and ultimate repeal of the estate tax, with an estimated ten-year cost of $236 billion. Other provisions in the administration's tax package included doubling the child care tax credit ($162 billion), a reduction in the "marriage penalty" ($88 billion), allowing nonitemizers to deduct charitable contributions ($80 billion), and making the R&D tax credit permanent ($23 billion).[20]

Although this package closely mirrored the president's campaign proposals, its design and political packaging were the subject of considerable debate between the new president and his Republican allies in Congress. Given the close margins of Republican control in the House (221-211, with two independents) and the

Senate (50-50, with ties broken by Vice President Dick Cheney), congressional leaders initially wanted to advance the package in pieces, with the most popular components taken up first.[21] On the other hand, conservative activist groups maintained pressure for an expansive and aggressive tax-cutting approach once Bush won the election.[22] Once the White House decided to adopt a base-focused political strategy for moving forward administration legislative proposals, satisfying such conservative tax groups became a top priority.[23]

As required by the Constitution, tax-cut legislation began in the House, where Republican leaders pushed for even larger cuts than the president proposed in order to enhance their future negotiating position with the more moderate and evenly divided Senate. This required aggressive tactics, however, which set the stage for often bitter partisan conflict. Republicans began pushing the president's proposals through the House just two days after he formally unveiled them before a joint session of Congress and before Congress adopted the budget resolution.[24] This jeopardized chances for bipartisan support for the legislation, since the Blue Dog Democrats—who wished to avoid a return to federal deficits—insisted on passing the budget first. Nevertheless, the White House and Republican leaders were "determined to maintain the momentum for passage."[25] "The victory is to get it done, to get it passed," proclaimed Speaker Hastert.[26]

Consequently, House leaders decided to move the legislation in four separate tax bills. A modified version of the president's costly plan for rate reductions was taken up first and quickly passed the House Ways and Means Committee on a party-line vote of 23-15 on March 1, 2001.[27] The bill passed the full House on March 8 by a vote of 230-198.[28] Only ten Democrats supported the bill, and not a single Republican opposed it. The remaining three bills—the Marriage Penalty and Family Tax Relief Act (a bill that expanded child-care tax credits and addressed the marriage penalty issue), the Death Tax Elimination Act (which phased out the federal estate tax over a ten-year period), and the Comprehensive Retirement Security and Pension Reform Act of 2001 (which increased the contribution limits for individual retirement accounts and the deferral of income invested in 401k and other retirement plans)—enjoyed more Democratic support, but many Democrats complained that they were frozen out of legislative design.

The real challenge facing the Bush administration's partisan adoption strategy came in the Senate, however. Here Republicans controlled the evenly divided chamber only because Vice President Cheney broke the tie vote to organize the Senate. In addition to Republicans' lack of a working majority, many Senate moderates of both parties had qualms about the size of the president's proposed tax cuts, especially in light of the prospect for a return to federal budget deficits. Consequently, unlike in the House, the Senate strategy was built around the budget process. This entailed including the tax reductions in the budget resolution and in a subsequent reconciliation package that was immune from filibuster, thereby requiring only fifty votes for passage in a chamber that was evenly divided.

Even assembling a simple majority in the Senate was a daunting task, however. Democrats favored tax cuts totaling roughly $800 billion, about half the size of Bush's request. Several moderate Republicans shared concerns about the size of the administration's tax-cut package, and they feared that a slowing economy would erode projected surpluses.

Although the president insisted that the size of his tax-cut package was "just right" and not negotiable,[29] this insistence began to unravel when the Senate's most liberal Republican, Sen. Lincoln Chafee (R-RI), defected and refused to support a tax cut that large.[30] Ultimately he was joined by two other Republican moderates, who voted with Democrats on a key amendment to the Senate budget resolution limiting the tax cuts to $1.2 trillion, plus another $85 billion in retroactive tax cuts for economic stimulus.

This reduction in the size of the tax-cut package was fiercely opposed by the White House and its conservative allies. House leaders had declared that $1.6 trillion was the minimum they would accept, while many conservatives pressed for larger cuts.[31] Conservative groups began demanding that Chaffee be punished by the Senate Republican Conference. Moreover, groups such as Americans for Tax Reform and the Club for Growth began running television ads in wavering members' districts and threatening future primary challenges if moderate Republicans did not toe the party line.[32] President Bush also began to campaign for his larger tax-cut package in the districts of moderate and conservative Democrats from states that Bush had carried in the election. This included the home of the ranking Democrat on the Senate Finance Committee, Max Baucus of Montana.[33]

In the end, however, these campaigns were unable to generate the necessary votes for the president's full package, and a budget resolution limiting the tax cuts to $1.2 trillion passed the Senate by a vote of 51-49.[34] This was raised to $1.35 trillion by the House-Senate conference committee, which prepared the final budget resolution adopted by the full Congress.[35]

Passage of the budget resolution established the maximum size of tax cuts, but the actual legislation to reduce taxes became part of the subsequent budget-reconciliation bill. The House had already passed its tax legislation prior to adopting the budget, but it readopted legislation reducing tax rates to demonstrate its seriousness about top rate reductions and for parliamentary reasons.[36] Although Senate moderates had successfully forced compromises in the budget resolution that reduced the overall size of the tax-cut package, the chair of the Finance Committee, Sen. Charles Grassley (R-IA), was under great pressure to accommodate the president's original goals within the smaller fiscal window. This was achieved through a variety of budgetary gimmicks, such as back-loading the tax cuts (by phasing in marginal tax-rate reductions and other costly provisions more slowly). In addition, many of the bill's tax reductions were designed to sunset in the final year. For example, the per-child tax credit was gradually raised from $500 to $1,000 over the period of 2001 to 2010, but it was then scheduled to fall back to $500 in 2011.[37] Similarly, the marriage penalty, estate tax, and retirement plan contribution provisions became progressively more generous through 2010 but returned back to 2001 levels in 2011.

Although denounced by most independent analysts as "a joke" and "an outright fraud,"[38] the sunsetting provided Senate moderates with the illusion of fiscal responsibility while serving the president's political objective, rewarding upper-income voters in the Republican base.[39] It also provided a partisan agenda of future battles to make the tax cuts "permanent."

Tax Reform and the Expert Pathway

Compared to other policy areas, the tax domain includes an unusually extensive, well-informed, and highly committed professional community of experts in positions of considerable influence. Its members can be found in the Treasury's Office of Tax Policy and on the staff of the unique Joint Committee on Taxation, as well as at the Congressional Budget Office, the Congressional Research Service, the Brookings Institution, the Urban Institute, and elsewhere. Most of these participants share a commitment to a specific view of what would constitute "good" or "sound" policy: an agreement on a set of normative "principles" that, in their view, should guide legislative action.

This expert consensus proved to be an important factor in the adoption of the 1986 Tax Reform Act. Although no complex statute is ever a pure type, the TRA is an outstanding example of the operation and influence of expert politics, which was especially important in the formative stages of the legislation. The movement for tax reform rested above all else on the shared conviction of knowledgeable experts in and outside of government that the federal income tax system had grown indefensible from the standpoint of professionally salient values. It was too complex, inequitable, and economically inefficient. Further, by the mid-1980s there was widespread agreement among tax specialists on the basic features of an improved income tax system: It should be horizontally equitable, investment neutral, and administratively efficient. As Joseph A. Pechman had demonstrated in the 1950s, all three goals could be attained by broadening the tax base—by eliminating or reducing special tax treatment and preferences and subjecting more income to standard tax rates—and then lowering those standard rates.[40]

This professional consensus was especially important in shaping the first draft reform bill in 1985, dubbed Treasury 1. This initial Treasury plan was an astonishingly pure expression of expert views made possible by the secrecy with which it was developed and Treasury Secretary Donald Regan's insistence that the process be insulated from political pressures. "Political considerations were irrelevant," he had told his staff.

Although this draft reform was never formally proposed as legislation by the Reagan administration, it—rather than existing tax law—became the standard against which subsequent proposals were measured. The basic contours of the administration's bill, as well as the final TRA—base broadening, reduced rates, revenue and distributional neutrality—all were fixed at this early stage. Expert consensus also accounted for the removal of a large number of the poor from the tax rolls, a particularly costly feature, and for the sharp hike in the corporate tax rate, which helped to pay for lower individual rates.

As one would expect, professional ideals of tax reform were less dominant in the nitty-gritty negotiations of the legislative process, but they were still influential. Because the vast scope of the reform initiative overwhelmed members of Congress and many lobbyists, an enormous number of seemingly technical issues were left to be decided by the Joint Tax Committee's staff. The staff also exercised life-or-death power over countless alternatives considered by decision makers, by controlling the critical revenue estimates.

The continuing influence of expert-driven policymaking, as well as its limitations, were apparent during another engagement with comprehensive tax reform twenty years and many newly adopted tax preferences later. Building on his earlier success at tax cutting, President George W. Bush announced a new effort to reform the tax system in the fall of 2004. Following President Reagan's lead, he announced his intent to achieve a revenue-neutral simplification and rationalization of the tax code, a project that once again received wide endorsement from many tax professionals across the political spectrum. Unlike Reagan, however, who relied on his Treasury secretary and staff, Bush appointed a commission (the President's Advisory Panel on Federal Tax Reform) with bipartisan and expert credentials to lead the development of proposals, a process that would enable him to distance himself from the report should the political fallout be too intense.

The new tax reform panel was cochaired by two former senators, Republican Connie Mack from Florida and moderate Democrat John Breaux of Louisiana. Among its nine members were leading experts on tax policy and administration, including James Poterba, a leading public finance economist from the Massachusetts Institute of Technology, and Charles Rossotti, a highly respected former commissioner of the Internal Revenue Service (IRS).

The difficult challenges facing the panel were magnified by the growing presence of the alternative minimum tax (AMT) in tax policy. Originally designed in the 1960s to reach wealthy taxpayers who paid no taxes, this tax was scheduled to cover more than fifty million Americans over the next ten years and create a new source of burden and complexity for many taxpayers.

The AMT issue was seized by the reform panel and economists inside the Treasury Department as a trigger to initiate a broader review of the economic efficiency of tax expenditures and other features of the tax code. The report they issued recommended paying for the repeal of the AMT with a series of major re-forms in the tax treatment of health care and mortgage interest expenses and state and local tax payments.[41] These tax expenditures were the largest among the 120 tax expenditures in the income tax system and drew widespread condemnation by economists due to their distortionary effects on economic investment choices.

The report itself received wide praise in the expert community, and its recom-mendations have perennially been supported by experts. However, the targeted tax expenditures were also among the most politically sensitive items in the tax code. The commission's recommendations were quickly attacked by a wide range of interest groups, from the real estate lobby to health care insurance groups to unions. President Bush all but abandoned the commission's report within a short period after its issuance, and the experts' reform ideas were shelved to await the next reform opportunity.

Tax Policy in the Symbolic Pathway

Policy experts are most concerned with the actual substance of policy. For most, the key questions are: Is it economically efficient? Can it be effectively adminis-tered? Is it equitable? But tax proposals are frequently advanced for other reasons as well. Programs may be designed around a popular misconception or to take ad-vantage of a political opportunity. Sloganeering can sometimes dictate substance; framing can direct form and function. In short, bad ideas as well as good ones become law—in tax policy as elsewhere.[42] And they often do so via the symbolic pathway.

Some symbolic ideas are advanced solely for the purpose of position taking. For example, in 2002 the Republican-controlled House of Representatives passed a bill abolishing the Internal Revenue Code. A Republican spokeswoman con-fessed that the bill was never expected to pass the Senate and become law. The hope was mainly that it would "make some [Democrats'] lives miserable for de-fending the current tax code."[43]

On the other hand, symbolic coalition building can also drive important and consequential legislation. The transformation of the estate tax into the so-called death tax provides a case in point. From the standpoint of many tax policy ex-perts, the drive to eliminate the tax—which succeeded in 2001—made little sense.[44] There were few beneficiaries from this change, and the fiscal consequences were substantial. The debate itself seemed utterly removed from reality. Many of the strongest advocates for the change, including many farmers and small busi-ness owners, would have been little affected by it. Many others could have been exempted from the tax by adjusting its thresholds for inflation. But a successful campaign to transform what had been a technical provision of the tax law for many decades into a morally repugnant assault on basic American values dramatically altered the political playing field.

In their analysis of the politics of estate tax repeal, Michael Graetz and Ian Shapiro conclude that "stories trump science."[45] Opponents of repeal developed reams of technical, economic analyses that contradicted many of the claims made by proponents of abolishing the tax. But they lacked a compelling narrative that made a normative or moral case for the tax. In contrast, Graetz and Shapiro argue, "the rhetoric of death—the endlessly repeated image of the tax collector and the undertaker hovering together around the death bed—helped. But what really put death tax repeal over the top were the stories: an amalgamation of tear jerkers and model citizens who fulfilled the American Dream through their efforts and ingenuity. With these [stories], the repealers had the fairness angle covered. They had gained the high moral ground."[46]

Here and elsewhere in tax policy, the entire arena has been greatly shaped by popular resentment of taxation and, especially in recent years, an exaggerated distrust or fear of the IRS itself. The federal income tax, which had long been considered the most productive and "fairest" of all taxes by both experts and the public, has come to be widely condemned and reviled.

Consequently, flat-tax proposals have become a popular standby in presidential politics, from Steve Forbes's proposal in 1996 to elements of Herman Cain's "9-9-9" plan in 2012. While it is true that the theoretical idea of taxing consumption rather than income has a lengthy intellectual pedigree, the main attraction of the flat tax is the promise of simplicity: a tax return so short that could fit on a postcard, according to its initial popularizers, Robert E. Hall and Alvin Rabushka. Unfortunately for the proponents of such plans, the popular appeal of the idea usually erodes once it becomes clear that the low flat rate comes at the price of eliminating popular deductions for home mortgage interest and charitable contributions and that such plans tend to shift the tax burden down the income scale to lower wage earners.

Even the promised simplicity of the flat tax tends to be greatly overstated. Indeed, two writers for the *Wall Street Journal*, the same publication where the Hall-Rabushka plan first made its appearance in a March 1981 article, have cautioned that the flat-tax debate is surrounded with exaggerations and myths:

> First, none of the most highly publicized flat-tax plans being peddled by politicians today really are flat. . . . Second . . . it is virtually impossible for anyone to predict with precision how the flat tax will affect you or the nation. . . . [Furthermore], some smart people think that the flat-tax proposals are flawed ideas that sound great in theory but just won't work. . . . What is on the surface a highly appealing idea is really a very

complex proposal to scrap a system that has served us well—perhaps not as well as we would like—and replace it with an entirely new and untested system whose impact is largely unpredictable.[47]

Adding to these and other objections, the political obstacles facing change, the economic and financial uncertainty that would result from a wholly new tax system, and the enormous technical difficulties in transitioning from our present income tax to a flat-rate consumption or income tax, it is hard not to view the flat-tax question principally as symbolic position taking rather than a significant effort at practical reform. Douglas R. Sease and Tom Herman add:

> We all know rationally that taxes are absolutely necessary to the functioning of our government. Yet we resent the levels at which we are taxed, we feel inadequate in the face of the complexity of the tax system, and we fear the agency that administers that system. Politicians play on those resentments and fears to win or keep office and they are playing especially loudly these days. As a consequence, Americans can expect tax policy to be at the forefront of the political process for many years [and that the] debate will often be rancorous, confusing, and emotional.[48]

Yet, in the tax arena as elsewhere, seemingly symbolic positions designed to attract political support and aid in building coalitions can, when adopted, have serious substantive effects. This was apparent during the 1986 tax reform debate, as the Reagan administration's plan made the transition from the offices of experts in the Treasury Department to the political arena of legislative proposal. At the behest of the Treasury secretary, the tax rate structure for the president's reform plan was altered from the more awkward sounding 16-28-37 initially devised by staffers into the appealing and easy-to-remember 15-25-35 rate structure. And yet this seemingly simple change of a few percentage points involved tens of billions of dollars when applied to the entire labor force, requiring a scramble for compensatory revenues and last-minute tax law changes elsewhere in the code. Similarly, key components of Reagan's initial 1981 tax proposals—the "10-10-10" rate reduction over three years and the "10-5-3" plan for depreciation of buildings and various types of equipment—were chosen for symbolic rather than economic reasons. "They had a certain flair to them," Eugene Steuerle writes, "and gave the illusion that the complexities of the tax law could be described in simple terms."[49]

Conclusion

Over the past thirty years, the direction of federal tax policy has wavered and wobbled from one enactment to the next, and the politics of these laws have varied as dramatically as their content. How should we account for this volatility in the policy process in an established field long and quite accurately characterized as "highly incremental"?[50]

In tax policy as elsewhere, it is helpful to look at the policymaking process strategically, from the standpoint of actors trying to build a coalition of support for their policy proposals. Operating within a network of distinct but interconnected pathways of power, actors in the system encounter alternative avenues by which to advance their aims. Each of these pathways tends to appeal to particular actors in the policy system who seek to steer issues onto a path most conducive to their success. Strategically minded actors may attempt to borrow a successful decision-making technique from another pathway or to switch tracks altogether, but they are likely to change the overall style of policymaking in the process.

Partly because different tax-policy enactments over the past thirty-odd years have followed different routes to passage, both the processes responsible for these laws and their substantive content have tended to vary one from the next. The Revenue Act of 1978 saw Congress seize the tax-writing initiative from the Carter administration and construct a modestly sized but loophole-laden bill that epitomized the workings of interest group pluralism.[51] Three years later ERTA, a much larger and far more comprehensive tax-cut package, was passed by Congress, reflecting the power of a popular president to seize an issue, expand the scope of conflict, and mobilize his party and the media to help advance it. The characteristics of expert-driven reform were highlighted in the Tax Reform Act of 1986, while the politics of symbolism took center stage in the congressional actions of 1997 and 1998, which culminated in measures for "taxpayer relief" and "IRS reforms" that were anathema to most tax professionals in or close to government. When Republicans gained control over both Congress and the White House in 2001, they turned once more to the partisan pathway as the most effective vehicle for enacting a controversial program of large tax reductions.

As demonstrated earlier in chapter 6, this pattern of pathway contestation and switching occurs across the range of federal domestic policymaking, not merely within the fiscal arenas of tax and budgetary policy. That is even more apparent in the following chapter, which examines the politics of the vast architecture of federal policies that affect state and local governments.

Notes

1. C. Eugene Steuerle, *The Tax Decade: How Taxes Came to Dominate the Public Agenda* (Washington DC: The Urban Institute Press, 1992).

2. The most detailed account is Conlan, Wrightson, and Beam, *Taxing Choices*. See also Timothy J. Conlan, Margaret T. Wrightson, and David R. Beam, "Policy Models and Political Change: Insights from the Passage of Tax Reform," in *The New Politics of Public Policy*, Marc K. Landy and Martin A. Levin, eds. (Baltimore: Johns Hopkins University Press, 1995), 121–42.

3. Witte, *Politics and Development*, 244–45. For a more recent analysis of the politics of tax expenditures, see Howard, *Hidden Welfare State*.

4. Surrey, "Congress and the Tax Lobbyist," 1145–82.

5. For an excellent analysis of group and corporate lobbying over the tax code, see Godwin, Ainsworth, and Godwin, *Lobbying and Policymaking*.

6. William Greider, "Taxes behind Closed Doors," *Frontline*, no. 411 (Boston: WGBH Transcripts, 1986), 5.

7. Surrey, "Congress and the Tax Lobbyist," 1175.

8. David G. Davies, *United States Taxes and Tax Policy* (New York: Cambridge University Press, 1986), 285–86.

9. Sheldon D. Pollack, "The Politics of Taxation: Who Pays What, When, How," paper prepared for delivery at the 1998 annual meeting of the American Political Science Association, Boston, September 3–6, 1998, 13.

10. "Reconciliation Package: Tax Cuts," in *CQ Almanac 1997*, 53rd ed., 2-30-2-38. (Washington, DC: Congressional Quarterly, 1998), http://library.cqpress.com/cqalmanac /cqal97-0000181033.

11. Pollack, "Politics of Taxation," 12.

12. John Maggs and Peter H. Stone, "Tax Cut Fever," *National Journal*, February 2, 2001, 326.

13. Ibid., 329.

14. Ibid., 137. See also Michael Graetz, *The Decline and (Fall?) of the Income Tax* (New York: Norton, 1997), 124–26.

15. Quoted in Sinclair, *Unorthodox Lawmaking*, 167, 170.

16. Ibid., 172.

17. George Hager and Eric Pianin, *Mirage: Why Neither Democrats nor Republicans Can Balance the Budget, End the Deficit, and Satisfy the Public* (New York: Random House, 1997), 223.

18. Sinclair, *Unorthodox Lawmaking*, 4th ed., 172–73.

19. The administration originally estimated its proposals would cost $1.3 trillion over ten years, but Congress's Joint Committee on Taxation pegged the cost at $1.6 trillion. The administration, following custom, accepted this figure for legislative purposes.

20. "Congress Cuts Deal on Taxes," in *CQ Almanac 2001*, 57th ed., 18-3-18-9 (Washington, DC: Congressional Quarterly, 2002), http://library.cqpress.com/cqalmanac/cqal01 -106-6380-328318.

21. Mike Allen, "Bush to Forge Ahead with Agenda: Taxes, Education Big Priorities," *Washington Post*, December 14, 2000.

22. Glenn Kessler, "Tax Cut Compromise Reached," *Washington Post*, May 2, 2001.

23. Donald Lambro, "Bush Signals the Right," *Washington Times*, January 18, 2001.

24. Quoted in Juliet Eilperin, "Few Democrats Are Likely to Back House Tax Bill," *Washington Post*, March 6, 2001. See also George W. Bush, "Address before a Joint Session of the Congress on Administration Goals, February 27, 2001," *Weekly Compilation of Presidential Documents* 37, no. 9: 351–57.

25. Eilperin, "Few Democrats Are Likely."

26. Ibid.

27. US House Committee on Ways and Means, H. Rpt. 107-7, "Economic Growth and Tax Relief Act of 2001."

28. *CQ Almanac 2001*, 187.

29. Ibid., 134; and Glenn Kessler and Helen Dewar, "Senate Scales Back Bush's Tax Cut," *Washington Post*, April 7, 2001.

30. Susan Crabtree and Mark Preston, "Chafee Giving GOP Heartburn," *Roll Call*, April 2, 2001.

31. Susan Crabtree, "Tax Rhetoric Divides GOP," *Roll Call*, March 19, 2001.

32. Dan Morgan, "No Recess in Political Ad Season: Issue Spots Follow Lawmakers Home," *Washington Post*, April 14, 2001; and Alexander Bolton, "State Leaders Pressure Senators," *The Hill*, May 9, 2001, 1.

33. Mike Allen and Glenn Kessler, "Bush to Back Larger Retroactive Tax Cut," *Washington Post*, March 22, 2001.

34. *CQ Almanac 2001*, 5–9.

35. Susan Crabtree, "Shut Out Senate Democrats Denounce Behind-the-Scenes Budget Compromise," *Roll Call*, April 23, 2001.

36. Sinclair, *Unorthodox Lawmaking*, 4th ed.

37. US Congress, Joint Committee on Taxation, *General Explanation of Tax Legislation Enacted in the 107th Congress*, Joint Committee Print JCS–1–03 (Washington, DC: Government Printing Office, 2003), 10.

38. Clive Crook, "How to Take a Flawed Tax Bill and Turn It into a Joke," *National Journal*, June 9, 2001, 1707–8.

39. Robert Greenstein and Isaac Shapiro, *Who Would Benefit from the Tax Proposal before the Senate?* (Washington, DC: Center on Budget and Policy Priorities, 2001).

40. See Joseph A. Pechman, "Erosion of the Individual Income Tax," *National Tax Journal* 10 (March 1957). Summaries of key reform proposals appeared in *A Citizen's Guide to the New Tax Reforms: Fair Tax, Simple Tax, Flat Tax*, Joseph A. Pechman, ed. (Totawa, NJ: Rowman & Allanheld, 1985).

41. President's Advisory Panel on Tax Reform, *Final Report*, http://govinfo.library.unt.edu/taxreformpanel/final-report.

42. Jones and Williams, *Politics of Bad Ideas*.

43. Janet Hook, "House Passes GOP Proposal to Kill Tax Code," *Chicago Sun-Times*, July 18, 1998.

44. Due to a budgetary gimmick that was intended to make the 2001 tax cuts appear smaller, the estate tax sprang back to life in 2011.

45. Michael Graetz and Ian Shapiro, *Death by a Thousand Cuts: The Fight over Taxing Inherited Wealth* (Princeton, NJ: Princeton University Press, 2005), 221.

46. Ibid., 229.

47. Douglas R. Sease and Tom Herman, *The Flat-Tax Primer* (New York: Viking, 1996), 19–20, 26.

48. Ibid., xiii–xiv.

49. Steuerle, *Tax Decade*, 40.

50. Witte, *Politics and Development*, 244.

51. See ibid., 207–17.

CHAPTER NINE

The Pathway Dynamics of Intergovernmental Policymaking and Reform

Because intergovernmental relations intersect with virtually all fields of domestic policymaking in the United States, explaining the political dynamics of intergovernmental policy and reform is both challenging and informative. As with budget and tax policy, federal policymaking toward state and local governments has been characterized by periods of stability and bouts of sudden change, instances of both high salience and low visibility, cases of interest group dominance and seeming impotence, and bipartisanship here and bitter partisanship there.

Consider, for example, the enactment, proliferation, and reform of federal grants to state and local governments. Nearly a thousand separately authorized categorical grant programs address issues ranging from community policing to state adoption services to urban mass transit, with many programs sponsored or supported by Democrats and Republicans alike. Yet at various points over the past fifty years, this system of categorical aid has come under attack, with hundreds of programs proposed for consolidation or termination in occasional waves of reform. Often these consolidation efforts have been part of a broader partisan agenda involving reforms and cutbacks in federal activity extending well beyond the categorical grant structure.[1] The Contract with America in 1995 was one prominent example; the "new federalism" agendas of presidents Nixon and Reagan were others. But at other times, the grant consolidation movement has been advanced by policy and management experts in the intergovernmental arena, such as the former Advisory Commission on Intergovernmental Relations (ACIR) and the Government Accountability Office, with few partisan overtones.

As with federal fiscal policies, the pathways-of-power framework can prove helpful in making sense of such widely varied processes and outcomes. Consequently, the next section of this chapter examines the role of pluralistic politics in the federal grant-in-aid system. This is followed by an exploration of partisan coalition building and the politics of comprehensive federalism reform. The role of symbolic politics in the adoption of federal mandates is taken up next. The politics of expertise in the intergovernmental arena is analyzed in the following section of the chapter. Finally, insights from the pathways framework are used to explore the evolution of intergovernmental politics over time.

The Pluralist Pathway and the Proliferation of Categorical Grants

In the realm of intergovernmental relations, the politics of many categorical grants provide almost textbook examples of the pluralist-incremental model of policymaking. As of 2009, the Congressional Research Service counted 953 separately authorized federal grant programs to state and local governments.[2] This number has grown relentlessly over the past fifty years, sometimes in rapid spurts, other times more slowly and incrementally. Occasionally the number of grants has been reduced and consolidated into block grants during short bursts of reform, only to begin growing once again in the aftermath of the reform effort. For example, there were 132 categorical grants in 1960, 397 in 1967, 539 in 1980, down to 404 in 1982, back up to 608 in 1994, down to 570 during the 104th Congress in 1995, and on to 716 in 2003.[3] A handful of grants are very large—the largest twenty provide three-quarters of all grant funds—but most are small. There are twenty giants and hundreds of pygmies among the population of federal grant-in-aid programs.

In recent years legislative earmarks have also proliferated, often to deliver specific projects to the constituencies of members. From an intergovernmental perspective, earmarks constitute microcategorical grants, where nationally elected officials—members of Congress in particular—intervene in communities with highly specific projects. While such earmarks often take the form of infrastructure projects, they also can consist of services in such areas as juvenile delinquency and welfare-to-work projects.

Earmarks grew exponentially during the late 1990s and early 2000s. A series of congressional reforms after 2007 succeeded in reducing their numbers from the peak years, though still at historically high levels. For example, while a major transportation bill in the early 1990s (the Intermodal Surface Transportation Efficiency Act of 1991) had three earmarks, a subsequent incarnation of this program—the so-called SAFETEA-LU—had more than three thousand earmarks. In some cases, these projects are developed by members in coordination with state or local leaders, while in other cases they reflect independent political entrepreneurship by members of Congress operating more unilaterally in their home districts in alliance with interest groups and other client organizations.

A primary reason for the growth of both earmarks and small categorical grants is that they provide a way for legislators to demonstrate effectiveness to their constituents—their ability to "bring home the bacon," as it were. The classic explanation for this was provided by David Mayhew in his analysis of congressional reelection strategies. Two principal strategies, he argued, were advertising—"any effort to disseminate one's name among constituents in such a fashion as to create a favorable image"—and credit claiming—"acting so as to generate a belief . . . that one is personally responsible for causing the government . . . to do something." Both strategies can be advanced through the provision of "particularized benefits."[4]

Both the adoption of narrow categorical grants and the provision of earmarks within both large and small grant programs allow members of Congress to obtain particularized benefits that correspond to their own constituents' needs: local infrastructure projects, an education initiative, a community health center, and so forth. Such grants also enable members to be identified with a specific program or project for advertising purposes: announcing grant awards, appearing at ribbon cutting ceremonies, and the like. As Mayhew expressed it, "the only benefits intrinsically worth anything . . . are ones that can be packaged. . . . Across policy areas generally, the programmatic mainstay of congressmen is the categorical grant. . . . It supplies goods in small, manipulable packages."[5]

With hundreds of members of Congress each trying to craft or support legislation that will provide assistance to their districts or please a supportive interest group, district-based electoral politics is a powerful driver of both earmarking and grant proliferation. It is also a driver that is reinforced by another feature of pluralistic policymaking: policy segmentation. There are far too many policy issues, each with its own complexities and potential ramifications, for any one set of political decision makers to master. Consequently, the vast majority of policy decisions are decided by smaller sets of decision makers within a policy subsystem or issue network.[6] Congressional committees and subcommittees often function as semiautonomous centers of decision making on matters of limited national scope or salience, and members of Congress often self-select committee assignments to correlate with individual policy interests and constituency needs. The result is a legislative architecture in which farm state members dominate the agriculture committees and oversee the construction of grant programs to rural communities, urban members fill the Committee on Financial Services, where grants for community development programs are developed, and so forth.[7] At the same time, the limited jurisdiction of congressional committees shapes the way that members of Congress are able to respond to broader issues of public interest. A member of the House Education and Workforce Committee who wishes to demonstrate concern about environmental degradation might do so by sponsoring a grant program that promotes environmental education, while a colleague on the committee with a large military constituency might focus on grants that promote the hiring or training of veterans.

The end result of this combination of electoral incentives, diverse social and economic interests, and legislative architecture has been to promote the promiscuous growth of the federal grants in aid. According to an analysis by the Office of

Management and Budget, there were 169 separate grant programs in health and human services in 2003 and another 144 for education and labor.[8] Such programs range from special education and vocational education grants for students in high school, adult education programs for dropouts, intensive education and training programs for at-risk youth, apprenticeship support programs for business and labor, job readiness training for the unemployed, work support services for those on welfare, and so on.

Politically, the enactment of the Firefighter Investment and Response Act of 2000, described in chapter 2, illustrates many of the characteristics of pluralistic policymaking in the intergovernmental arena. It began as an act of policy entrepreneurship by an interested member of Congress, accumulated support from affected interest groups and other members of Congress, and eventually wound a complex course through the legislative process, launching a new level of federal support for a predominantly local government function.

A similar route along the pluralist pathway was taken during the enactment of the Brownfields Revitalization and Environmental Restoration Act of 2001, which created a $1 billion program of grants to state and local governments for cleaning up industrial sites.[9] The bill was first introduced in February 2001 by Sen. Lincoln Chafee, chairman of the Senate Environmental and Public Works Subcommittee on Superfund, Waste Control, and Risk Management. It was intended to address the environmental cleanup needs of small and low-income communities that lacked the resources to deal with polluted and abandoned industrial sites. Like most other cases of pluralist policymaking, the Brownfields Revitalization Act was heavily shaped and refined within the congressional committees of jurisdiction. In this case the chairman of the full Environment and Public Works Committee, Sen. Robert Smith (R-NH), negotiated an amendment that increased the states' role in certifying cleaned-up sites and reduced the EPA's authority to second-guess states' determination. The amended bill attracted support from most of the major affected interest groups, the nation's governors, and the Bush administration and passed the Senate by a unanimous vote of 99-0.[10]

The House of Representatives, partly in response to heavy lobbying by small business interests, unanimously passed a bill that focused more on granting small businesses relief from liability lawsuits for small amounts of dumping and for cleaning up polluted sites. House Republicans also sought to further enhance the states' role in regulating brownfields sites while diminishing the role of the EPA. This legislation also passed with overwhelming bipartisan support.

A House-Senate conference committee was required to reconcile the differences between the two bills, and here yet another interest group conflict erupted. Labor unions insisted that cleanup projects funded with federal funds be subject to the provisions of the Davis-Bacon Act of 1931, which requires the payment of "prevailing" (often union scale) wages. Ultimately, language satisfying labor unions, small business interests, state and local governments, and the Bush administration produced a final bill that passed both chambers unanimously.

The Partisan Pathway and the Politics of Intergovernmental Reform

The historical pattern of utilizing the partisan pathway for instituting significant policy change can be clearly seen in the politics of federalism and intergovernmental policymaking. This is evident both in cases of large-scale expansion of federal responsibilities vis-à-vis the states and in recurrent efforts to reform the intergovernmental system. Doing big things in national domestic policy often equates to major changes in intergovernmental relations, since constitutional, political, and administrative constraints on the federal government virtually require the assistance of state and local governments in policy design, finance, and implementation.

For example, the modern era of cooperative federalism was ushered in by Franklin Roosevelt's New Deal, which dramatically expanded the federal government's role in domestic social welfare policy. Lyndon Johnson's Great Society initiatives were widely touted as a new form of "creative federalism," quadrupling the number of federal grant-in-aid programs and greatly expanding the federal role in education, health care, community development, social services, and poverty reduction. More recently, Barack Obama invoked the theory and rhetoric of "new nationalism" in laying out a comprehensive rationale for extending the federal government's role in health care, economic recovery, infrastructure development, and financial regulation.[11]

In each of these cases, the power of the partisan pathway was harnessed in order to enact a policy agenda so substantial as to alter the contours and behavioral dynamics of the intergovernmental system as a whole. Major policies in each case were advanced by coherent partisan majorities after considerable partisan debate and conflict. Indeed, each initiative was preceded by an important election that altered the partisan balance of power in Congress and changed perceptions of power in Washington and the country at large. Roosevelt's landslide victories in 1932 and 1936 brought Democrats to power in both the House and Senate. In the wake of President Kennedy's assassination in 1963 and President Johnson's landslide election in 1964, huge new Democratic majorities were elected to Congress in 1964. President Obama's broad 2008 victory brought more Democrats into the House and, briefly, helped Democrats gain a filibuster-proof majority in the Senate.

While these prominent cases all relied upon the partisan pathway to advance major expansions of federal authority, the same has also been true for many of the most prominent attempts to reform, reconstruct, or roll back the federal role in intergovernmental relations. Conceptually other pathways might provide avenues for federalism reform as well. Impetus for reform has often come from expert and professional sources in government and public administration seeking to increase the efficiency of an overly complex intergovernmental aid system. These prescriptions for reform are what Lawrence Brown has called "rationalizing policies"— products of a government-led search for solutions to government's problems. Bipartisan support has also come from the nation's mayors and governors, who tend to advocate for greater flexibility in the use of federal funds regardless of political party. But increasingly since the 1970s, the most energetic efforts to seek comprehensive intergovernmental reform and to overcome the fragmentation and entrenched interests of the categorical aid system have utilized the resources of the partisan pathway.

The origins of this approach began during the Nixon administration. Nixon's new federalism agenda sought to promote an alternative to the centralized and fragmented policies of Johnson's creative federalism through a combination of no-strings revenue-sharing grants to states and localities, block grant programs to provide additional flexibility for broad functions such as education and transportation, and greater use of direct payments to individuals, thereby bypassing or limiting the discretion of federal bureaucrats. Despite periods of sharp partisanship during the Nixon years, however, Republicans never enjoyed a majority in either house of Congress, so the requisite conditions for successfully employing the partisan pathway were lacking. Where Nixon had success in enacting portions of his new federalism agenda, it was accomplished ultimately by mobilizing bipartisan coalitions and supportive interest groups behind revenue sharing, community development, and job-training block grants.

The politics of federalism became very different under Ronald Reagan. He openly professed an agenda designed to roll back the welfare state in general and the Great Society and New Deal specifically. Significant portions of this conservative ideological agenda were successfully enacted in 1981 through a novel intersection of the partisan pathway and the new politics of budget policymaking. His budget proposals that year succeeded in creating nine new federal block grants, terminating or consolidating 139 federal grant programs, and reducing projected domestic spending by $131 billion over four years.[12]

Reagan accomplished this through a classic execution of the partisan pathway. It began with his landslide electoral college victory in 1980, which allowed the new president to claim a popular mandate for his policy program. His victory also helped Republicans gain control of the Senate and a working conservative majority in the House. These election results made use of the partisan pathway an appealing option for the 97th Congress, and the Reagan administration was able to utilize it effectively. A solid phalanx of Republicans voted almost unanimously on all of the key votes on block grants, budget cuts, and tax-reduction proposals—most of which were carried out through the budget reconciliation process in Congress—and a sizeable number of conservative Southern Democrats went along for fear of the president's political strength in the rapidly realigning South.

As the following case study makes clear, a similar partisan strategy was employed on behalf of the budget reduction and federalism reform initiatives of the Republican 104th Congress in 1995. And the strategy was likely to be employed once again by Mitt Romney and Republican leaders in Congress had Republicans won the presidency and control of Congress in 2012. Enactment of the so-called Ryan budget by House Republicans in 2011 on an almost perfect party-line vote set the table for precisely this result.

This would be a dramatic change from the expansionary policies of the Obama administration, but such is the historical pattern of partisan-pathway politics. Election victories give one party an effective working majority in Congress, allowing it to push through a broad agenda of policy initiatives that have often built up over years of being stymied in pluralist politics. Congressional majorities then shrink as the political pendulum swings the opposite direction, and majoritarian strategies lose their viability and appeal.

Such partisan majorities are vital to the coalition-building style of the partisan pathway. While significant intraparty conflicts and disagreements often frustrate national party leaders on major issues, cohesion among majority party factions can allow major legislative victories even when the majority party's margin in Congress is slim. This was evident in the Republican-led House of Representatives from 2001 to 2005 when, despite narrow majorities, major tax cuts, Medicare expansion, and energy legislation were passed with extraordinary levels of party unity. Party unity scores for the two major parties in Congress, which measure the cohesion of party members on contested votes, have risen markedly since the early 1970s.[13] Other research has found greater ideological coherence among members of Congress of the same party, especially on core partisan issues.[14]

As indicated in chapter 3, partisan policymaking in the United States has several distinctive characteristics. In contrast to the segmented and publicly opaque process seen with categorical grants, the partisan form of intergovernmental policymaking tends to emerge on a limited number of highly visible, highly conflictual issues that are capable of uniting the different factions making up each major party. As noted above, the lead actors in this style of policymaking are the president and party leadership in Congress, who possess the resources needed to build and maintain the large coalitions on which partisan policymaking depends. If the majority party maintains its unity and controls both chambers of Congress as well as the White House, it may quickly pass a broad policy agenda that has been years in the making.

Such unity rarely lasts, however, so the partisan pathway historically has been an intermittent approach to public policy formation. In large part this is because large and unified partisan majorities in Congress have generally proved to be short-lived. Roosevelt lost his working control of the Congress by 1938. Johnson's domination of Congress ended after the 1966 midterm elections, when Republicans picked up forty-seven seats. Republicans won the White House in 1968, and the civil rights legislation and cultural liberalism of the Great Society began a process of partisan realignment in the South. As a result, the next great political wave carried Reagan into the White House, Republicans into control of the Senate, and conservatives into effective control of the House of Representatives after Republican electoral successes in 1978 and 1980. Again, the election results made use of the partisan pathway an effective option in the 97th Congress as the Reagan administration won passage of major budget and tax reductions pushed through by a political phalanx of Republican unity on key votes in Congress.

Seeking a Republican Revolution in the 104th Congress: A Case Study of the Partisan Pathway

While use of the partisan pathway to reshape the national government's role in federal–state relations has generally been a presidential strategy, congressional Republicans' attempt to utilize the strategy in 1995 provides an informative case study of the strengths and limitations of the partisan pathway in intergovernmental relations. Republicans took advantage of an electoral tsunami in the midterm elections of 1994 to win control over both the House and Senate for the first time in forty years. Under the leadership of House speaker Newt Gingrich, the new Republican majority consciously employed the partisan pathway, moving rapidly to enact a policy agenda with far-reaching implications for American federal governance. The Republicans' program centered on a bold plan to reduce federal spending, cut federal taxes, trim federal regulations, and balance the federal budget within seven years. Among the specific changes in intergovernmental programs that they proposed were plans to consolidate or eliminate 283 federal grant programs, including bilingual education, summer youth-employment programs, and the low-income energy-assistance block grant, replacing them with over a dozen new block grants for Medicaid, cash welfare, child protection, nutrition, Native American programs, job training, education, housing, law enforcement, and rural development. By one estimate, the proposals would have consolidated grants covering 75 percent of federal assistance, with major block grants for public assistance and Medicaid.[15]

Had it been successfully enacted and implemented, this partisan agenda would have fulfilled Speaker Gingrich's stated goal of a "Republican revolution." And the partisan pathway provided the route along which the self-styled revolutionaries traveled.

Legislatively, most of the key initiatives of 1995 were developed and advanced through the congressional budget process. Allen Schick observed that "efforts to balance the budget, cut federal taxes, terminate or curtail hundreds of programs and agencies, redesign farm price supports, change Medicare and Medicaid, renegotiate the relationship between Washington and the states—all were driven by [the] budget resolution."[16] A partisan budgetary strategy made sense substantively, since many of the policy objectives sought by the new Republican majority were fiscal in nature. But, in addition, legislating through the budget process carried important procedural advantages that maximized the strengths of partisan coalition building and limited the minority's opportunities for obstruction, especially in the Senate.

The budget resolution passed by the House in May 1995 marked the high-water mark of reforms in the 104th Congress. It proposed to cut projected federal spending by more than $1 trillion over seven years. This included real cuts of $190 billion in nondefense discretionary spending (a category that includes most federal grant programs, as well as direct federal operating expenses). This figure would have reduced such discretionary spending by 12 percent below 1995 levels and 30 percent below the baseline level of projected federal spending in 2002, assuming regular program growth for inflation, population increase, and the like.[17] Other cuts included $187 billion in previously scheduled Medicaid spending over seven years, $288 in Medicare, and $35 billion in cuts to various welfare programs, with part of the proceeds intended to go toward tax cuts of $353 billion over seven years.[18] This dramatic program passed the House on a nearly perfect party-line vote of 238-193. All but one Republican voted for the Republican budget, and all but eight conservative Democrats voted against it.[19]

The Senate passed its version of the budget resolution on May 25, 1995, again largely along party lines. Every Republican voted for the resolution, while all but three Democratic "deficit hawks" voted against it. The overall shape of the package was similar to that passed by the House, but it reflected the more moderate makeup of the Senate as well. The Senate's tax-cut package was smaller, as were its Medicare and Medicaid cuts. Moreover, fewer federal programs were slated for elimination, consolidation, and structural reform. For example, only one department (Commerce) was targeted for elimination, fewer programs were suggested for termination (100 versus 283), and fewer block grants were detailed in the committee report.[20]

The House-Senate conference split many of the differences between the two chambers on taxes and entitlements, but the proposed changes to the intergovernmental system remained substantial. Both chambers agreed to seek cuts of approximately $190 billion in discretionary spending and assumed that funding for many grant-in-aid programs would be deeply cut or eliminated (including the Community Development Block Grant program, preventive health, the Appalachian Regional Commission, and mass transit operating subsidies). In addition, the final budget resolution agreed to create new block grants for Medicaid, welfare, rural development, public housing, and job training. This final budget resolution passed in the Senate on a straight party-line vote of 54-46 and in the House by a vote of 239-194, with Democrats in the latter unanimously opposed and all but one Republican—from a heavily Democratic district—voting for passage.

For all of the energy and attention that goes into it, budget resolutions are only a promise that Congress makes to itself. They establish parameters and convey procedural advantages within Congress, but they do not by themselves change laws or spending levels. Those actions require the president's signature, and when partisan control of the government is divided, as it was in 1995 when Bill Clinton occupied the White House, the limits of utilizing the partisan pathway became apparent.

The challenges of divided government became evident in the appropriations process. The appropriations committees were responsible for meeting the reduced discretionary spending targets in the budget resolution. The new Republican majorities on these committees began the process of budget cutting by making reductions in spending for the fiscal year already under way. These "recission" bills reduced previously authorized spending levels by $13.3 billion, which included zeroing out several intergovernmental programs entirely (e.g., homeless adult literacy grants, summer youth-employment grants).

Larger cuts were made in the thirteen regular appropriations bills for the next fiscal year. Significant spending cuts were made in many areas, including housing and urban development programs, which were cut nearly 25 percent below postrecession 1995 levels, and environmental programs, which were cut by 21 percent.[21] However, budget cuts were only the most visible part of the Republican appropriations strategy in 1995. The new majority in the House sought to use the appropriations process to force structural changes in government as well—to use "appropriations to pass policy." For example, a program or agency's authorization might remain on the books, but the lack of funding would effectively terminate it. House Appropriations Committee chairman Bob Livingston (R-LA) put it this way: "All we have to do is put a zero next to a particular line in an appropriation bill. It doesn't matter what the Senate or what the President does. . . . We may not have the power to spend money [all by ourselves], but we do have the power to withhold it."[22] And many, mostly small programs and agencies were zeroed out. This was the fate of the ACIR, for example, which was forced to close down when its funding was eliminated—even though its authorizing statute was not repealed. The same fate befell other small programs such as the Urban Parks and Recreation Fund, the Pension Fund Partnership, and Dropout Prevention Demonstration grants.

The termination strategy was carried to its fullest extent in the House-passed version of the Labor-HHS-Education appropriations bill, which zeroed out eleven programs in the Department of Labor, sixty-six in the Department of Health and

Human Services (HHS), and ninety-three in the Department of Education.[23] But despite its appeal to self-styled revolutionaries, the limits of this termination strategy soon became apparent. Enacting appropriations bills with these budget levels required approval by the Senate and the president. One was difficult, the other nearly impossible. For example, some of the fiscal and policy changes under consideration for the Labor-HHS-Education appropriations bill were so controversial that the Senate was unable even to pass its version of the bill, much less reach agreement with the House and the president. Indeed, the effort was so partisan and controversial that hardly any appropriations bills had been enacted by the deadline of October 1, 1995—the beginning of the new fiscal year. This forced Congress to pass a short-term continuing resolution (CR) to fund the government while appropriators worked to pass regular funding (or "defunding") bills for the year. By the time the CR expired in November, only six of the thirteen regular appropriations bills had been signed into law. Most of the rest were in serious trouble. President Clinton vetoed several when they were sent to him in December, including the Commerce, Justice, State, Judiciary bill; the Interior Department appropriation; and the Veterans Affairs, Housing and Urban Development, and Independent Agencies appropriation. All were vetoed because of partisan differences over spending levels and conflicts over policy issues such as the termination of the Commerce Department and changes in environmental programs. These vetoes, when combined with the Senate's failure even to pass the Labor-HHS-Education appropriations bill, meant that legal spending authorization for over half of all federal domestic activities was still lacking months into the fiscal year.

If the Republicans' political strategy had been successful, this failure might actually have advanced their cause. House Republicans hoped that a House refusal to fund particular programs would be definitive. But President Clinton refused to sign bills that contained unacceptable provisions, even at the risk of shutting down entire agencies.

And shutdowns are precisely what happened. Without signed appropriations bills or temporary extensions, entire departments and agencies were forced to close their doors. What is more, government shutdowns occurred not once but *twice* between November 1995 and January 1996. In the interim, public anger at the government's failure to perform its most basic tasks was directed at the Republican Congress, which had, after all, claimed to be promoting revolution. By January the shutdown strategy was acknowledged to be a failure, and it was eventually replaced by negotiations over an omnibus appropriations act for all of the remaining unpassed appropriations bills. This omnibus bill, H.R. 3019, was signed by the president on April 26, 1996—halfway through the fiscal year—and it marked an end to the bitter financial battles of the 104th Congress.

In the end, the Republican revolution of 1995 illustrates both the strengths and weaknesses of the partisan pathway. Sweeping reforms were successfully rammed through the House on near party-line votes, often in record time. Living up to initial promises, the entire legislative framework of the Contract with America was voted on within the first hundred days of the 104th Congress. In the process, party leaders aggressively used the tools at their disposal to keep their sometimes restless troops in line. Committee chairs were appointed on the basis of party loyalty and legislative energy; senior Republicans on major committees, including Budget, Appropriations, Judiciary, and Commerce, were skipped over in favor of more vigorous and dependable colleagues. Frequent party caucuses were held to discuss problems and rally support, and interest group allies were engaged to help write bills quickly and to keep the pressure on rank-and-file members to stay the course. Speaker Gingrich became a ubiquitous presence on talk shows. All in all, it was a partisan tour de force that scored dramatic victories in the House. Such is the potential of the partisan pathway.

If ours were a parliamentary system of government, "Prime Minister Gingrich" would have accomplished his mission. But the partisan pathway is more challenging in a system of shared and divided powers. Legislating in our system requires involvement from both ends of Pennsylvania Avenue, and the White House was controlled by a Democrat. President Clinton controlled the political, bureaucratic, and public relations resources of the White House, and he used them to great effect in the budget showdown with Congress. The comprehensive reform agenda of the House largely failed as a result.

The Symbolic Pathway and Federal Mandates

As the previous cases make clear, policymakers and program advocates have often succeeded in building support for their federalism-related initiatives by relying on interest group and partisan strategies. Yet neither of these pathways can effectively explain the adoption of many other intergovernmental programs. This is particularly true of federal mandates—laws and regulations that prohibit state or local actions or require states or localities to carry out some federal policy. Typically they are accompanied by inadequate federal funding or none at all. According to the Advisory Commission on Intergovernmental Relations, such mandates became increasingly common during and after the 1960s, growing from just two in the 1950s to over sixty by the 1990s.[24] Although comparable data is unavailable after the ACIR was abolished in 1995, subsequent data collected by the Congressional Budget Office and interest groups such as the National Conference of State Legislatures confirm the creation of many additional unfunded mandates since the mid-1990s.[25]

Whatever the precise numbers, mandates, as well as congressional legislation that preempts state and local activity in a given policy area, have become increasingly important elements of contemporary intergovernmental relations.

Nonetheless, the creation of many of these laws cannot be fully understood by pluralist, partisan, or expert politics. This includes mandates such as the Asbestos Hazard Emergency Response Act (AHERA), which required the removal of asbestos from local school buildings; the Personal Responsibility and Work Opportunity Act of 1996 (welfare reform); the Family Educational Rights and Privacy Act, which requires schools to protect the privacy of students' educational records; and the Endangered Species Act. Unlike programs in the partisan pathway, each was enacted with broad bipartisan support, both in Congress and among the general public. Unlike policies in the pluralist stream, many were passed quickly, with difficult policy issues and trade-offs postponed until after their enactment. Interest groups tended to play a secondary role during legislative consideration, and often the objections by powerful interest groups were dismissed or ignored by Congress. At the same time, few represented the results of expert consensus, and some were opposed by policy professionals who favored an alternative solution or approach.

Rather, the politics of many federal mandates closely resemble the key elements of symbolic politics. Mandates are often based on simple, sometimes simplistic concepts that are easy to grasp and to convey to the general public. Save the bald eagle. Impose strict time limits on welfare. Raise the drinking age. These are just a few examples connected with mandates related to endangered species, welfare reform, and a uniform national drinking age. However, the ease of distilling these issues into simple slogans obscured more nuanced issues of policy design and implementation. Should all endangered species, from an obscure liverwort and snail darter to the iconic eagle and gray wolf, be treated equally and without consideration of costs and benefits in federally funded projects? Should exceptions to rigid time limits on welfare be considered during times of high unemployment, when there are few jobs available to those on welfare? Should federal highway funds be withheld from states that refuse to raise their drinking age, even at the risk of reducing highway safety in other respects?

Like other cases of symbolic policymaking, the politics of federal mandates are often driven by the powerful emotional content of the issues involved. Welfare reform encapsulated working-class resentment against suspected freeloaders, and President Clinton's embrace of the concept is what most defined him as a "new Democrat." For its part, AHERA was portrayed and perceived as an emergency measure to protect vulnerable schoolchildren from deadly asbestos raining down on their classrooms. It was passed at a time of escalating concerns about the long-term health effects of asbestos exposure but with little consensus about the merits of costly removal versus simply sealing the asbestos in place. Similarly, the passage of legislation mandating equal access to public transportation for disabled passengers was driven in part by the stories of handicapped veterans who were unable to access needed public services at the local level.[26] In the case of these mandates and many others, the politics of legislative adoption could be easily distilled into simple issues of right and wrong, for which only one choice appeared to be morally or politically viable. This was the "mandate millstone" dilemma posed by former congressman and New York mayor Ed Koch in chapter 5.

Given the power of the political ideas propelling new mandates, these issues often divide the intergovernmental lobby—the national associations of mayors, governors, state legislators, and others—as well. Research has shown that the intergovernmental lobby is most effective when it is unified in support of or opposition to a given policy.[27] Although local elected officials no longer enjoy the level of influence they once held in a decentralized party system, they still can be a formidable political force when fully unified. They are experienced politicians with their own bases of political support within the constituencies of members of Congress. Moreover, one might expect them to be unified in their opposition to federal mandates, and they sometimes are. All mayors and governors tend to agree that unfunded federal mandates are problematic in the abstract. All prefer to have maximum flexibility to utilize both federal and local resources according to their own jurisdiction's needs and local political sentiments.

But the high valence content associated with federal mandates often means that mayors and governors are divided on the issues. They, as well as members of Congress, often face what Mayor Koch described as an impossible choice. No state or local official can afford to be seen—or portrayed by a future political opponent—as callous about the needs of disabled Americans or indifferent about protecting the health of innocent schoolchildren. Moreover, especially in an era of increased partisan polarization, many state and local officials may feel bound to support the goals of federal mandates out of ideological conviction or political necessity. Consequently there was virtually no effective state or local opposition to the enactment of AHERA, even though it constituted an unfunded mandate estimated in the billions of dollars. Nor was there united opposition to raising the minimum drinking age or the workfare requirements in welfare reform. The mandate millstone was fashioned with considerable state and local complicity—or in some cases enthusiastic support.

Megan's Law: An Emotion-Laden Bill Races down the Symbolic Pathway

Megan's Law requires that state and local law enforcement agencies provide public information about the release and location of convicted sexual offenders. It passed Congress in 1996 in the wake of a horrific incident involving a seven-year-old girl named Megan Kanka, who was sexually assaulted and brutally murdered by a neighbor. The neighbor was a twice-convicted sexual predator who lived with two housemates who were also convicted sex offenders.

Following this incident, a community-notification bill was introduced in Congress by Rep. Dick Zimmer (R-NJ), who represented the district where the girl lived. This bill amended the Jacob Wetterling Crimes against Children and Sexually Violent Offender Registration Act of 1994 to *require*, rather than permit, the release by state and local governments of relevant information to protect the public from sexually violent offenders. Its legislative history reflects the powerful appeal of the idea involved.

The bill had only a single day of hearings before the House Subcommittee on Crime before being passed by voice vote and reported to the full committee. Only two witnesses testified: Representative Zimmer and Kevin Di Gregory, the deputy assistant attorney general. A month later, the full Judiciary Committee ordered the bill reported without amendment by another voice vote. The measure passed the House of Representatives in May 1996 on a recorded vote of 418-0. Two days later it passed the Senate by unanimous consent and was sent to President Clinton on May 13, 1996. On May 17, 1996, Megan's Law was signed by the president and became Public Law 104-145.[28]

This race through Congress does not mean that there were no substantive issues involved in the legislation. Although not costly, the bill imposed an unfunded federal mandate on state and local law enforcement agencies, and it gave them limited flexibility in dealing with sex offender notification. Moreover, the legislation posed an important issue of constitutionality, with some federal courts and legal scholars arguing that the measure violated the "double jeopardy" and "ex post facto" clauses of the Constitution.[29] However, few members of Congress were willing to carefully consider this issue, and in the end none was willing to oppose the legislation. The act promised to "do something" about a horrific problem, its politics were driven by the tremendous visceral force of the issue, and members of Congress acted as though they had no choice but to vote for the legislation.

The Expert Pathway and Intergovernmental Policy

In intergovernmental affairs as elsewhere, the growth of complexity in technology, the economy, and government has greatly increased the demand for expert knowledge and technical competence. The need for in-depth knowledge and technical expertise has often placed professionals and policy experts in positions of prominence, both inside and outside of government. Indeed, American intergovernmental relations have often been characterized as a system of "picket-fence federalism," in which policy professionals at the federal, state, and local levels engage in closer relationships and share greater common interests with their counterparts in other levels of government than with elected officials or fellow employees in other agencies within their own level of government. State and county public health officials work closely with, receive funds from, and communicate continually with their federal colleagues in the Public Health Service and Centers for Disease Control and Prevention; federal, state, and local transportation officials share professional outlooks, best practices, and financing across all levels of government; and so forth. In fact, these professional and financial relationships are so strong that specialized policy networks have been denounced as "vertical functional autocracies" by budget officials and others responsible for priority setting and program coordination within individual levels of government.

Although the picket-fence federalism metaphor is often used to describe the functioning of implementation networks, given the right circumstances the experts and professionals who populate these policy communities can also shape or influence the design and enactment of intergovernmental policy as well. For example, Daniel Patrick Moynihan traced much of Lyndon Johnson's War on Poverty to "the professionalization of reform."[30] Seeking to launch a rapid assault on the problems of poverty, the president and his White House staff turned the design and execution of the war largely over to the experts in the field. Similarly, Samuel H. Beer noted that, throughout the 1960s and 1970s, policy and program professionals routinely took the lead in designing and establishing new programs: "People in government service, or closely associated with it, acting on the basis of their specialized knowledge ... first perceived the problem, conceived the program, initially urged it on the president and Congress, went on to help lobby it through to enactment, and then saw to its administration."[31]

Shifts in the role of the federal government since that time have not diminished the appetite for policy information and analysis. Although the opportunities for "breakthrough" federal policies have diminished since the Great Society, they have not disappeared, as the enactment of the Affordable Care Act in 2010 illustrates. Moreover, when issues of program cutbacks and devolution have been placed on the policy agenda, policymakers are often preoccupied with what Lawrence Brown calls "rationalizing policy"—that is, revisions and reforms to the major initiatives of the past. Government programs create their own political and policy momentum as policymakers are beset with demands to modify, revise, revisit, "fix," and fill gaps in such critical programs as Medicare, Medicaid, and education.[32]

Brown argues further that the rationalizing agenda catapults policy analysts and technical staff into more a prominent position, since they are the experts who have the greatest understanding of evaluation research and greatest command over the technical details of program design that are so critical to rationalizing debates. In contrast to the lobbyists' search for analysis that bolsters preexisting group interests, Brown contends that government comes to the table in rationalizing debates armed with its own agenda as government officials increasingly become central in seeking intricate solutions to government-caused problems. This is not to say that partisan and group positioning does not occur on second-order issues such as controlling health care costs, easing transportation congestion, and addressing public health threats. Rather, the relative weight of influence often shifts in the direction of experts who assume more prominent roles in defining the problem and in mediating and legitimizing policy solutions.

Consequently, expertise is often sought by legislators in pursuit of their own policy and electoral objectives. It can both give direction on what to do—on the means of solving problems—and provide legitimacy for politically favored choices. The Intermodal Surface Transportation Efficiency Act was a good example. It was a significant reform of federal highway and transit programs that equalized treatment of different transportation modes, expanded the role of metropolitan planning organizations, and enhanced consideration of environmental and community concerns.[33] All of these reflected changes in approach endorsed by many transportation experts.

As noted in chapter 4, expert solutions often require a long lead time, as complex ideas and proposals are developed, shaped, debated, and evaluated according to expert criteria and professional norms. Once ideas achieve the level of expert consensus, however, their effects on policy change can be very rapid. Such was the case with the standards movement in education policy in the 1980s and 1990s. Bipartisan support for the passage of the No Child Left Behind Act of 2002 rested heavily on the emergent professional consensus, at both the state and federal levels, that stricter standards for elementary and secondary educational performance, as well as greater reliance on standardized testing as a tool for measuring student progress, held the greatest promise for improving the American educational system.

Waivers and the Politics of Expertise

Over the past twenty years, intergovernmental relations in several fields have been reshaped by the aggressive use of federal waiver authority—to such an extent that some have used the term "executive federalism" to describe the current era.[34] In programs such as Medicaid and welfare where the law has allowed for the consideration of waivers, states can request that certain legislative and administrative rules and requirements be waived for specific purposes: changing the mix of services available to welfare clients, expanding coverage under Medicaid, making greater use of home-based care, and so on. Federal and state executives and agency experts negotiate to develop uniquely structured "demonstrations" in a given state. William and Carol Weissert describe it in this way: "Waivers . . . delegate initial review procedures to bureaucratic agents restrained by very few criteria; demand little oversight and feedback; empower the states to design and implement policies in broad furtherance of national goals; involve substantial give and take between state and federal bureaucrats; and persist for years. These features share many of the qualities of (what) should be called 'intergovernmental licenses.'"[35]

In some instances, waivers have led to the fundamental restructuring of federal-state programs, as in the case of welfare reform experiments in Wisconsin and Michigan in the 1990s and utilizing Medicaid as a basis for expanding health care services to the uninsured in Oregon, Tennessee, and Massachusetts. In such high-profile cases, state governors, secretaries of Health and Human Services, and even presidents may be intimately involved in the negotiations. In many other cases, however, the bulk of negotiations is carried out by program specialists within the federal and state agencies. Roughly forty Medicaid waivers were granted annually during the 1990s, for example, and seventeen states had comprehensive Medicaid waivers granted between 2001 and early 2005.[36] As Saundra Schneider has observed, the negotiation of such waivers places considerable demands on the technical resources and administrative capacity of the negotiating states:

> Section 1115 (Medicaid) waivers are "administratively intensive." For example, they require a state to submit documentation on how it will determine the budget neutrality of its projects, how it will capture service utilization data for all persons served by the project, and how it will evaluate the overall impact of the demonstration programs on the health status of participants. More important, states must possess the necessary expertise and capabilities to implement these projects once they have been developed and approved. Indeed, one of the most obvious lessons learned to date is that implementation of these comprehensive health-care reform initiatives is difficult and complex. Section 1115 waivers require states to improve their claims-processing capabilities, to collect more and better enrollment and . . . patient care data, to revise their enrollment and marketing processes, to deliver services to different population groups, and to perform more effective oversight and evaluation of their efforts. All of these changes require states to assume a host of new, administrative functions.[37]

Implications for Intergovernmental Policy Formulation

Characterizations of intergovernmental policy in the United States tend to group policy development into a single general category. Those who define the system as cooperative tend to focus on grants as the primary strategy used to knit federal, state, and local governments together in vertical collaborations seeking common goals. Others define policy in more coercive terms, arguing that the system has taken a turn toward a more insistent and exclusively federal orientation, with state and local governments serving in subordinate roles implementing federal mandates and policies. Still others contend that our system has become more cyclical, with states emerging as key policy leaders during times of national policy conservatism or gridlock.

While often not explicit, each of these theories, in effect, is premised on a political model specifying the political relationships among the actors in our federal system undergirding these authority patterns. The pathways through which policy is formulated have a major influence on policy decision making and results. The different pathways tend to favor different actors and values, and policy actors attempt to steer the framing of issues, coalition building, and institutional design in ways that capitalize on the pathways that best promote their goals and interests. The pathways in no small part determine the balance of power in any intergovernmental system for specific programs and policies.

As in fiscal policy, there are multiple pathways active in our system at any one period, producing intergovernmental policy that varies across policy areas, as well as policy eras. William Gormley argues that multiple forms of federalism coexist in the same era.[38] Thus regulatory federalism, cooperative federalism, and devolution all could be found in congressional and executive actions in recent years with regard to our federal system. In the same period when new block grants were being formed through welfare reform and SCHIP, additional mandates for driver's licenses and education standards were also being imposed on the states.

Particular intergovernmental policies bear the strong imprints of the pathways that shape their origins, which also influence the roles adopted by state and local officials in the legislative process. Policies advanced through the pluralistic pathway tend to have particularistic and distributive features, as epitomized by the categorical grant. State and local officials often serve as active claimants and cheerleaders for such policies, even when such pluralism manifests itself in highly prescriptive forms of national policy influence. The partisan pathway is productive of more significant change in intergovernmental policy, but the direction is determined by which party and ideologies have working majorities. In some of these cases, state and local government officials work in alliance with their partisan colleagues in Washington. For example, many of the nation's Republican governors have worked hand in hand with Republicans in Congress to oppose key elements of the Affordable Care Act, including a major expansion of the Medicaid program for low-income families that would bring massive new federal funding into their state.

As discussed earlier, many mandates are often passed as part of a veritable policy stampede to embrace compelling values that have acquired uncontested valence status. State and local officials are not only disarmed by the broad appeal, but many collaborate with federal officials to support these programs as well, either to claim credit for climbing aboard an irresistible bandwagon or to insulate themselves from political opponents. For the most part, symbolic pathways have been used to mobilize support for new policy initiatives imposed on states and localities with little deliberation or consideration of implementation realities and costs. However, at times those concerned about mandates can conscript the symbolic pathway to gain support for restraint. During the early 1990s, for instance, state and local officials succeeded in mounting a successful media campaign against unfunded mandates, featuring "unfunded mandates day" events throughout the nation. The campaign bore fruit when both parties embraced mandate reform, leading to passage of the Unfunded Mandate Reform Act of 1995.

The expert pathway is often associated with intergovernmental policy cooperation across governments. The epitome of cooperative federalism entails professionals and experts at various levels of government working together cooperatively, sharing a consensus on policy goals and the actions needed to achieve outcomes. While implementation may spark conflict and controversy in its early stages, over many years a maturation process sets in where policy professionals across all levels of government become partners in joint administration of programs by virtue of shared goals, education, experience, and trust.[39]

Thus, intergovernmental policies are as diverse as the pathways that bring them to life. Moreover, secular changes in institutions have promoted greater potential for pathway shifting in our system than ever before. Although state and local officials are an important set of actors, they are only one among an increasingly broad range of forces and interests seeking to achieve their policy goals through the intergovernmental system. In an earlier time, state and local governments had far greater influence and leverage over policymaking in our federal system. As late as 1960, the position of state and local governments in the federal system was protected by decentralization of the party system itself. National office holders, be they presidents or congressmen, owed their nominations and political allegiances to state and local party leaders, embedding a sensitivity to the prerogatives of state and local officials in fundamental political incentives. In such a context, the partisan pathway was biased to favor the interests of decentralized actors in the federal system.

Since the early 1960s, the party system has changed dramatically, leading to the unraveling of the constraints that bolstered the position of states in the system. Our political system has evolved into one in which candidates for national office assemble their own coalitions to compete for nominations and elections. Interest groups and the media have eclipsed state and local parties as gatekeepers of candidate recruitment and legitimation; national elected officials have converted from being ambassadors of state and local party leaders to independent political entrepreneurs anxious to establish their own visible policy profiles to appeal to a diverse coalition of interest groups, media, and an increasingly independent base of voters. Far from an alliance, the relationship between congressional officials and state and local elected colleagues from their districts resembles more of a competition among independent political entrepreneurs for money, visibility, and votes.

These nationalizing trends were echoed and bolstered by other trends in our political system and the broader economy. The growth of national media institutions focused on Washington created a powerful resource for those groups wishing to nationalize problems and issues, and reporting increasingly sought to find national dimensions or applications for state and local problems or solutions.

The advent of lobbies representing broad, diffuse interests—the so-called public-interest groups—has fueled national policy advocacy as many of these groups have settled in Washington rather than the states.

The consequences of these trends for intergovernmental policy are profound. Until recently, state and local governments could rely on the partisan pathway to protect their positions in the federal system and ward off nationalizing forces intent on centralizing policy. However, thanks to the centralization and nationalization of our electoral system, state and local governments have had to compete for influence across all four pathways. Unlike in the past, however, they are no longer accorded status as cosovereigns that merit special deference but are rather one among the multitude of interests competing for access, leverage, and influence in a highly contestable system. Interestingly, as the national political system dethroned the governors and mayors as kingmakers for national political officials, the state and local governments opened significant lobbying offices in Washington, reflective of their shift from a presumptive position of influence in the partisan pathway to a suitor in an ever more competitive pluralistic pathway. To be effective in this pathway, state and local governments generally need to be united and to join with other powerful interest groups in the pluralist pathway.[40]

However, as these trends took shape, state and local officials were increasingly unable to speak with one voice. Partisan differences eroded the ability of state and local government organizations to take positions on issues that cleaved along partisan lines, such as welfare reform in 1996. Their once central position in the partisan pathway had disintegrated to the status of a player who was often immobilized on major issues that generated the most intense partisan controversy. State and local officials often took different positions on the pluralist pathway, reflecting the different interests and views of state and local elected officials and the specialists in the agencies responsible for implementing major federal programs. It was not uncommon to see governors testifying against their own state agency heads at congressional hearings on the reauthorization of such legislation as special education and environmental mandates. Similarly, the expert pathway could pit state and local government experts and bureaucrats against their nominal political superiors as they worked in alliance with expert counterparts at the federal level. Finally, state and local elected leaders often were swept up in the same symbolic waves that gripped national officials, which sometimes led them to support new national mandates and policies that proved to be costly and challenging for their own jurisdictions to implement in later years.

Despite these trends, state and local governments remain important actors in our system. If only as agents in a principal–agent relationship, states have important advantages in information, skills, and authority desperately needed by makers of federal policy to achieve successful outcomes. Moreover, as noted above, state and local governments can use a multiple-pathway system to countermobilize and force a reconsideration of original policy goals during the implementation process, as the costs and consequences of federal policy ideas become more apparent and compelling than the purported benefits. Indeed, the initial impetus for national policy ideas often comes from states and localities themselves, serving in their time-honored role as laboratories of innovation. Capitalizing on their greater relative political cohesion, state and local governments are often able to act with greater speed than national leaders mired in gridlock from pluralist and partisan pathways.

However, their loss of influence is most poignantly reflected in the federal expansion of state-led innovations. Owing to their position as laboratories for emergent policies, state policy innovations become seized upon by national actors in all four pathways who are constantly searching for new ideas and solutions. Rather than gain presumptive influence from this process of policy expansion, states often find that their own hard-won policy reforms prompt a new wave of preemptions and mandates. Far from a system that celebrates diversity, national policy actors ranging from policy advocates to business view state innovations as either reasons to reproduce policies across all fifty states or reasons to preempt those policies. In either case, states lose control as other actors across pathways use state-led innovations to opportunistically gain leverage in national policy debates.[41]

In this way, state and local governments' position has eroded in a system with multiple pathways to power. Not only must these officials face a formidable array of contenders for influence in each pathway—they must also face each other. Due to the systemic repositioning of their influence in the multiple pathways, states have been unable to build on their strategic position in our system to regain their former presumptive influence in national policymaking. Our federal system has changed irrevocably, and the pathways framework helps to illuminate why.

Notes

1. Conlan, *From New Federalism to Devolution.*

2. Robert J. Dilger, *Federal Grants in Aid: A Historical Perspective on a Contemporary Issue*, report no. R40638 (Washington, DC: Congressional Research Service, 2009), 6.

3. David B. Walker, *The Rebirth of Federalism: Slouching toward Washington* (New York: Chatham House, 1995), 16, and unpublished data for 2003 from the Office of Management and Budget.

4. Mayhew, *Congress*, 49, 52, 53.

5. Ibid., 129.

6. See, for example, Freeman, *Political Process*, rev. ed.; Cater, *Power in Washington*; Seidman, *Politics, Position, and Power*; Ripley and Franklin, *Congress, the Bureaucracy, and Public Policy*; and Heclo, "Issue Networks and the Executive Establishment."

7. For a description of this same process within the appropriations subcommittees, see Adler, "Constituency Characteristics," 104–14.

8. Office of Management and Budget, "The Number of Federal Grant Programs to State and Local Governments: 1980–2003," unpublished data, Budget Analysis and Systems Division, Office of Management and Budget, February 2004.

9. Public Law 107-118.

10. "Congress Clears Brownfields Bill." In *CQ Almanac 2001*, 57th ed., 9-11-9-12 (Washington, DC: Congressional Quarterly, 2002), http://library.cqpress.com/cqalmanac /cqal01-106-6390-328777.

11. White House, Office of the Press Secretary, "Remarks by the President on the Economy in Osawatomie Kansas, December 6, 2011," www.whitehouse.gov/the-press-of fice/2011/12/06/remarks-president-economy-osawatomie-kansas.

12. See Conlan, *From New Federalism to Devolution*, chapters 7 and 8. In 1982, the Reagan administration also engaged in serious negotiations with the nation's governors over a controversial "sorting out" plan that would have ended most federal aid programs in education and welfare in exchange for nationalization of the joint federal-state Medicaid program. However, this initiative was never formalized and submitted to Congress.

13. Sinclair, "Dream Fulfilled?," 129–31.

14. Lindaman and Haider-Markel, "Issue Evolution," 91–110.

15. Paul L. Posner and Margaret T. Wrightson, "Block Grants: A Perennial but Unstable Tool of Government," *Publius: The Journal of Federalism* 26 (Summer 1996): 87–110.

16. Allen Schick, "The Majority Rules," *Brookings Review* (Winter 1996): 42.

17. Pauline Abernathy, *Congressional Budget Plans Deep Cuts in Non-Defense Discretionary Programs* (Washington: Center on Budget and Policy Priorities, 1995).

18. See "GOP Throws Down Budget Gauntlet." In *CQ Almanac 1995*, 51st ed. (Washington, DC: Congressional Quarterly, 1996), 2-20-2-33, http://library.cqpress.com/cqalma nac/cqal95-1099934.

19. Ibid.

20. See US Congress, Senate, Committee on the Budget, Concurrent Resolution on the Budget: Fiscal Year 1996, S. Rpt 104-82, 104th Cong., 1st sess., and *CQ Almanac 1995*, 24–32.

21. *CQ Almanac 1995*, 1334.

22. Quoted in Jeff Shear, "Power Loss," *National Journal*, April 20, 1996, 876.

23. H.R. 2127, H. Rept. 104-209.

24. US Advisory Commission on Intergovernmental Relations, *Federal Regulation of State and Local Governments: The Mixed Record of the 1980s*, report no. A-126 (Washington, DC: ACIR, 1993).

25. See, for example, Congressional Budget Office, *A Review of CBO's Activities in 2011 under the Unfunded Mandates Reform Act* (Washington, DC: CBO, 2012), and National Conference of State Legislatures, "Mandate Monitor: Catalog of Cost Shifts to States," www .ncsl.org/issues-research/budget/mandate-monitor-catalog.aspx.

26. Katzmann, *Institutional Disability*.

27. Posner, *Politics of Unfunded Mandates*; and Troy Smith, "Intergovernmental Lobbying," in *Intergovernmental Management for the 21st Century*, Timothy Conlan and Paul Posner, eds. (Washington, DC: Brookings Institution Press, 2008).

28. Congressional Research Service, Library of Congress, "Bill Summary and Status, H. R. 2137," http://thomas.loc.gov/cgi bin/bdquery/z?d104:HR02137:@@@R.

29. US Congress, House Committee on the Judiciary, Megan's Law: Report together with Additional Views to Accompany H.R. 2137 (H. Rpt. 104-555, 1996), 9.

30. Daniel P. Moynihan, "The Professionalization of Reform," *The Public Interest* 1 (Fall 1965): 6–16.

31. Samuel H. Beer, "Federalism, Nationalism, and Democracy in America," *The American Political Science Review* 72 no. 1 (March 1978): 9–21.

32. Brown, *New Policies, New Politics*.

33. Robert Jay Dilger, "ISTEA: A New Direction for Transportation Policy," *Publius* 22, no. 3, (Summer 1992): 67–78; and Paul G. Lewis and Eric McGhee, "The Local Roots of Federal Policy Change: Transportation in the 1990s," *Polity* 34, no. 2 (Winter 2001): 205–29.

34. Thomas Gais and James Fossett, "Federalism and the Executive Branch," in *Executive Branch*, Aberbach and Peterson, eds., 486–522.

35. Carol S. Weissert and William G. Weissert, "Medicaid Waivers: License to Shape the Future of Fiscal Federalism," in *Intergovernmental Management for the 21st Century*, Timothy Conlan and Paul Posner, eds. (Washington, DC: Brookings Institution Press, 2008).

36. Weissert and Weissert, "Medicaid Waivers," 160.

37. Saundra K. Schneider, "Medicaid Section 1115 Waivers: Shifting Health Care Reform to the States," *Publius* 27, no. 2 (Spring 1997): 106–7.

38. William T. Gormley Jr., "An Evolutionary Approach to Federalism in the U.S.," paper presented at the annual meeting of the American Political Science Association, San Francisco, August 31, 2001.

39. Paul E. Peterson, Barry G. Rabe, and Kenneth K. Wong, *Making Federalism Work* (Washington, DC: Brookings Institution Press, 1986); and Robert Stoker, *Reluctant Partners: Implementing Federal Policy* (Pittsburgh, PA: University of Pittsburgh Press, 1991).

40. Paul L. Posner, "The Politics of Coercive Federalism," in *Intergovernmental Management for the 21st Century*, Conlan and Posner, eds.

41. See Andrew Aulisi, John Larsen, Jonathan Pershing, and Paul Posner, *Climate Policy in the State Laboratory* (Washington, DC: World Resources Institute, 2007).

CHAPTER TEN

Conclusions

Models seek to order and simplify reality. Ideally, good models
should provide satisfying explanations of public policy and be
congruent with reality.
—Thomas Dye, *Understanding Public Policy*

Most of us carry implicit models about the policy process from the political debates of our time. Very often the process is one of the few things all can
agree on. Fox News and MSNBC may portray the world in starkly different terms,
but the policy process comes in for bipartisan calumny: It is messy, chaotic, gridlocked, biased, and unresponsive. Most advocates are armed not only with elegant
policy prescriptions, but also with "process reforms" seeking to bring about more
rationality and order in how we consider competing claims—reforms that often
serve the purpose of locking in their preferences for years to come.

The process at times deserves the criticism heaped upon it in the public dialogue, but one thing is certain: The policy process cannot be viewed from a single
lens or bottom line. Policymaking is too diverse and complex to be summed up in
a single slogan or explanation. Partisan polarization may aptly describe what led
to the government shutdown of 1996, but it cannot help us understand how policymakers in the same year were able to come to agreement across party lines to
adopt reforms of welfare and agriculture subsidies. The role of entrenched financial interests can explain the failure to pass accounting and financial regulatory reforms in the late 1990s or boom years of the housing bubble but not the enactment
of Sarbanes-Oxley accounting reforms in 2002 or Wall Street reform in 2010.

How can we characterize a process that can veer from months or even years of
gridlock and grinding stalemate to swift and significant change and reform? How
can we provide a way to more systematically understand a process that is given to
such volatility and unpredictability?

In this book we have sought to portray policymaking in terms that reflect the
diversity of mobilization and outcomes that has come to characterize policymaking today. In taking on this project, we first had to abandon the search for a single
lens through which to view the policy world. Political science in the past has often
tried to formulate comprehensive theories that provided a one-size-fits-all model

to cover all major policy decisions. While such models were often stimulating, we have learned over time that they failed to capture and portray the more differentiated way that policy ideas germinate and take root in government today.

The concept of policy pathways was developed to provide a more diversified set of tools to understand a more Janus-faced policy process. Steering clear of a single overarching explanation or process, we found the pathways model to be a more satisfying way to understand the fluid and fast-moving world of contemporary national decision making.

In this final chapter we reprise the pathways model, showing how it builds on emerging theories of the policy process but also how it covers ground that others have left unplowed. We draw out the key lessons and takeaways from the model itself and suggest implications that the model reveals for the policymaking process and the potential for democratic systems to institute major reforms in long-standing policy areas. We conclude by showing the new insights about policymaking that can be derived from using the pathways model as a new unit of analysis to understand policy decisions.

The Difference That Pathways Make

There is a bottom line for this book: Pathways make a difference in our ability to understand, and perhaps even predict, policy outcomes over a range of public policy areas.

When assessing whether the model is successful in this task, we need to compare this model with others that seek to explain policy decisions. For years political scientists hewed to models of the policy process anchored in the world of interests, with policy firmly ensconced in stable pluralist domains dominated by interest groups and specialized policy officials. Major policy change that did occur flowed from major presidential regime shifts, often coming in the wake of historic party realignments. These models were in fact quite helpful in understanding policymaking dominated by groups in iron triangles where established interests ruled the policy roost. Farm and veterans policy faithfully reflected the premises of these models for years. The presidential policy punctuations provided a satisfying way to understand the emergence of waves of policy reform that occurred in the New Deal and the Great Society.[1]

Even today major work in political science still chalks up major policy change to what we call the partisan pathway. Political scientists such as John Aldrich and David Rohde acknowledge that while only a minority of legislation is partisan, the most important legislation generates partisan conflict.[2] However, our findings suggest that even for the major policy decisions we have studied in this book, the partisan pathway—while increasingly important—by no means accounts for the whole of policy reform.

David Mayhew's work on divided government offers a different, iconoclastic view for political science. Identifying the major laws passed by Congress in the postwar period, he has discovered that major policy change was passed more often with bipartisan support than through divisive partisan conflict characteristic of the partisan pathway.[3] Mayhew suggests that bipartisan majorities came to embrace major new policy reforms due to a combination of supportive policy moods and competition among the parties to claim credit for supporting new ideas gaining traction in the public. While provocative, these mechanisms still featured party leaders as the critical actors, using strategies leading to agreement rather than gridlock and conflict to court political support and approbation.[4] However, he does not go further to posit alternative ways that policy ideas come to gain traction in our system.

In this book we have argued that the pathways model provides a more satisfying and empirically based model capturing the diversity of ways that policymaking unfolds in our contemporary political system. While all models are attempts to simplify complex realities of decision making, this one seeks to systematically incorporate the complex and fluid ways that ideas and interests interact in our dynamic political system.

In the numerous cases that we have analyzed, the pathways provided a valuable lens for understanding the evolution of policies over time across key policy arenas. Each pathway is associated with systematic differences in the patterns of political influence and the scope of policy outputs. If we know something about the pathway governing a policy, we can more deeply understand how that policy came to the agenda and the nature and direction of change it represents. The particular pathway that primarily shapes an issue's fortunes powerfully affects the types of actors who are empowered to play roles in agenda formation and decision making, as well as the kinds of questions that are viewed as legitimate to raise. Terms of debate that might be legitimate for one arena may not be so when the issue switches paths, as different kinds of claims and arguments are appropriate for different pathways.

Groups that succeed in one pathway can be disarmed and outflanked when the issue shifts to other pathways with different forms of mobilization and appeals. Arguments and strategies pursued by narrowly based producer groups appropriate for pluralist pathways lose their appeal when the issue switches to the expert or symbolic pathways, which operate by different rules and respond to different values. Raising concerns about the costs of new regulatory proposals may be legitimate in the pluralist realm, but such arguments tend to fall on deaf ears when broad-based movements advancing new regulations sweep over the system. The symbolic pathway elevates the benefits side of the policymaking equation as the dominant, and sometimes only, dimension deemed to be politically legitimate. When the issue shifts to other pathways, groups hustle to adapt their strategies, arguments, and communication channels as they seek to become relevant to the new policy reality. Thus, groups such as the NRA that have dominated in the pluralist pathway had to develop their own public media institutions to better compete in the symbolic realm that gun control advocates had exploited.

We have shown that each pathway features different ways of framing issues and problems. Actors in the pluralist pathway emphasize policy feedback, anchored in complaints by program clientele and interest groups about existing policies, as the principal modality for defining problems. Policy actors in the expert pathway, as might be expected, put a premium on indicators and data. The characteristic mode of policy discovery in the symbolic pathway is crisis. Alarmed discovery of problems, whether real or imagined, helps mobilize large mass publics behind a different way to frame and conceptualize policy problems.[5]

Pathways are anchored in institutions, and one of the telltale signs of shifts in pathways is when the institutional venue for a particular issue changes. When the primary arena for determining the overall congressional priorities for federal discretionary spending shifted from the appropriations committees to budget committees and leadership negotiations with the president, this major change signaled a shift in pathways from pluralist to partisan realms. The change ushered in new actors and decision rules for budgeting that altered the nature of budget outcomes. Appropriations committees tended to make marginal changes in small increments from last year's spending levels, while the party leaders' focus on the broader deficit and competition with the president prompted them to take a broader and longer-term view that often resulted in more significant changes in federal spending.

Pathways have been shown to generate distinct ways to organize conflict and consensus around issues. Incremental change and policy stasis can be expected in the pluralist pathway. Dominated by groups with a large stake in existing policy frameworks, the pluralist pathway channels conflict into narrow and incremental realms. The partisan pathway, on the other hand, is geared for major conflicts, reflecting the significant fault lines that divide the parties and the more significant policy proposals that take root in this pathway. Leaders seek to reach beyond the existing paradigms governing issue networks to redefine issues and coalitions, often unsettling existing arrangements and interests.

Symbolic and expert pathways can also result in major policy changes and reforms, but conflict arising from these arenas is often more muted. Policies framed in these two idea-based pathways generally prompted widespread support from parties once they took hold on the agenda. Indeed, when ideas became compelling, both parties typically scrambled to endorse the idea to either claim credit or avoid blame. The 2001 USA PATRIOT Act illustrates how a potentially controversial policy reform involving significant civil liberties challenges nonetheless garnered nearly unanimous agreement, as leaders from both parties scrambled to use their votes on the bill to reassure the electorate of their fealty to protecting "the homeland" from terrorist attack.

We do not pretend that pathways represent the only variable shaping decision making. Technological innovations, economic shifts, election returns, changes in social mores and demographics, and institutional reforms are only a few of the variables that influence policy change or stasis in our system. Pathways, however, help structure the influence of these fundamental exogenous and endogenous forces on the policy process.

For instance, the Federal Agriculture Improvement and Reform Act of 1996—the Freedom to Farm Act—was given its impetus by a combination of an improving farm economy, which made farmers wealthier and reduced the rationale for federal subsidies, and the advent of Republican congressional leaders whose support of farm subsidy reforms long advocated by most economists would help them achieve their cherished goals of deficit reduction and federal deregulation. These internal and external variables shifted the issue from the pluralist pathway, which had long resisted major subsidy reform, to the expert pathway where analytically based ideas gained new traction. This pathway shift left its institutional footprint as the farm reform bill was removed from the House Agriculture Committee—the bastion of the pluralist pathway—to the friendlier confines of the House Budget Committee, which was eager to act on the advice of free-market economists.

In essence, pathways serve multiple roles in shaping policy debates and outcomes. On the one hand, the placement of issues into different pathways is influenced by a host of political and institutional factors, as discussed above. But each pathway also acts as an independent variable that helps govern policy decisions through very different structures of political incentives, decision rules, and relationships among policy actors. As shown throughout this book, if we know the nature of the pathway that drives a policy issue, we have a far deeper understanding of the reasons for policy decisions or inaction.

The Tax Reform Act of 1986 illustrates the point. Many factors have been put forward to account for this fundamental shift in tax policy that nearly every pundit in Washington said could not be done only a year before.[6] Presidential leadership, the persistent role of experts holding a candle for comprehensive reform, and a coalition of groups seeking pecuniary advantage were some of the factors. But any analysis of the reform would be incomplete if it did not recognize the impact that shifting the decision arena and rules—what we call pathways—had on the reform outcome. The cynics were right that reform would never happen—if the traditional institutions and decision rules of the pluralist pathway held sway. However, they missed the potential breakthrough that would come when the pathways changed to feature a combination of policy experts working in league with competitive and opportunistic party leaders. The story of policy reform can be told by reference to the traditional combination of individual factors often associated with policy change, but the game-changing force was the shift in pathways that these variables helped bring about. In short, the pathways themselves are greater than the sum of their variables.

The Policy Change That Pathways Promote

We developed the pathways model as a way to better understand a policy process that has become far less predictable and more varied and volatile than is typically represented.

The model better equips us to understand the varied ways that change sweeps over the system. As we have shown throughout this book, the partisan pathway no longer serves as the only avenue for achieving nonincremental policy changes in the American system of government. Expert and symbolic pathways have emerged to play a major role in policy change.

However, those pathways that offer the greatest potential for change are also those that have the greatest difficulty in sustaining the policy reforms they usher in. As noted in chapter 6, the idea-based pathways have the poorest record of sustaining their reforms over the longer term. By contrast, the pathway with the greatest policy stability is the pluralist pathway, which is the most resistant to change. This outcome is likely due to the different starting points, attention span, and resources available under each pathway. Pluralist actors typically have greater resources than others, and they also have greater ability to pay attention to policy details and proposals over a long period of time. Also, it is less resource-intensive to protect an existing status quo than to spend energy promoting change in existing arrangements.[7] By contrast, actors on the idea-based pathways have more episodic engagement with the policy process. Having exhausted resource and energy on policy change, they often move on to other targets, unable to sustain the intensity once a policy is on the books.

The switching of pathways played a formative role in driving shifts of policy dimensions in agenda formation and policy formulation. Because certain frames and outcomes are promoted by different pathways, change is to be expected when the primary pathway driving an issue shifts. Indeed, our cases suggest that policy actors engage in deliberate strategies to steer issues into pathways most congenial to their interests and ideas. Pathway switching occurs more often in cases when there is both competition across pathways on a given policy issue and less cohesion within each pathway. Thus when experts disagree, parties are divided, or interest groups conflict, the door is open for other pathways to gain an ascendant role in driving policy change

Transformations of public policy often result from the switching of policy pathways, both from narrow pathways to broader ones, leading to nonincremental reforms, but also when narrower interests recapture policy from broader publics.

This process of issue expansion and contraction is familiar to political science. E. E. Schattschneider postulates that policy can be transformed when the scope of conflict expands from narrow to broader constituencies.[8] The issue-attention cycle posited by Anthony Downs, on the other hand, provides support for countermobilization and issue contraction. In his view, policy reform is ushered in on a wave of enthusiasm when the benefits receive far more attention than the costs, but reform sputters as costs become more apparent and salient, and pluralistic groups recapture the agenda.[9]

Our work also suggests that pathway shifting is endogenous to the pathways themselves. That is to say, each pathway has its own unique political liabilities, not only undermining their effectiveness in achieving policy outcomes but also paving the way for the countermobilization of actors through the emergence of other pathways. This dynamic produces a dialectic conducive to change but often in uncertain directions and magnitude. For instance:

- The pluralist pathway tends to undermine itself because of its lack of inclusiveness and inability to achieve broader policy goals. Policy or political failure can prompt the rise of the partisan pathway if leaders decide to embrace broad-based constituencies as a major strategy. Alternatively, pressures building within the pluralist pathway can engage the symbolic pathway, building off entrepreneurial leaders, media exposure, and others who seek to expand the scope of conflict, in a process first described by Schattschneider.[10]

- The symbolic pathway can sow the seeds of change when its initiatives prove either ineffective or counterproductive. Symbolic politics has the potential to produce policy outputs that, in their haste and rush to judgment, exclude certain important interests and expert contributions to feasibility. Over time, as the safe drinking water case shows, these interests and experts reassert themselves by shifting the issue to pluralistic or expert pathways.

- Experts can get out of step with the values of broader publics, party leaders, or leading interest groups, prompting the emergence of competing mobilization pathways. The expert pathway has been shown to produce policy outputs that are difficult to sustain politically over time, as affected interests gather their forces and reassert themselves by shifting policy to the pluralistic pathway. Expert advice to save the budget surpluses accumulated in the late 1990s was soon ignored as party leaders on both sides were pressed by restive publics to use fiscal slack to cut taxes and increase spending.

- Party leaders can undermine their position when their policy regime excludes key groups and priorities. Partisan pathways also are vulnerable to countermobilization by the other party and gridlock, which can frustrate the enactment of any policy. This can lay the groundwork for subsequent emergence of expert and symbolic pathways to address public issues in a more consensual or expeditious manner. For instance, the passage of 1985 Gramm-Rudman-Hollings legislation requiring a balanced budget was a symbolic and ultimately unworkable process "fix" that emerged from the failure of party elites to achieve substantial deficit reduction through the partisan pathway.

While each pathway makes its own unique mark on a policy's fortunes, the future of a policy is also shaped by the ways the combinations of pathways are engaged. Policies supported by multiple pathways tend to move more quickly through the process than policies anchored to a single pathway, perhaps reflecting the bandwagon effect that sweeps over the entire system when a policy goal has gained compelling status. However, we have also found that multiple pathways can halt progress to policy change when they work at cross purposes by incubating opposing perspectives.

Other studies have characterized policy change by using a broader sample of all policies on the agenda in our system.[11] The work on lobbying by Frank Baumgartner and his colleagues, for instance, studied a broad sample of all policy decisions in given years. They found that the status quo is the modal response of the system in any one period of time, although when changes occur they tend to be significant, not incremental.

Since the cases we have selected represent major policy change, our findings are somewhat different but complementary. We do not pretend that our cases constitute a random sample of all policy decisions. Rather they are representative of all major changes in eight significant policy arenas. They may be policy expansions or contractions, but they tend to be the more salient issues that are likely to attract attention across several different actors and pathways. What is surprising from our cases of policy change is how frequently *major* changes occur in the eight policy areas we have examined. For both health care and tax policy, seven major policy reforms were enacted in each area in a time period of twenty years. Far from a generational event, this suggests that major policy change occurs much more regularly than the literature on policy process and change heretofore suggests.

Institutional Change and Pathway Volatility

Secular changes in institutions have promoted greater potential for pathway shifting in our system than ever before. More competition among interest groups in the pluralist pathway, more media outlets and policy entrepreneurs vying for audience share in the symbolic pathway, greater engagement by experts in policymaking, and more competition among elected officials anxious to use policy issues to fortify their standing with various publics have all served to heighten the potential for policy change. Greater competition among these actors prompts actors to switch pathways to gain strategic advantage. As closed iron triangles have broadened to become more competitive issue networks, competing groups have incentives to expand the scope beyond existing venues and pathways to reach for support from other arenas.[12] In this way, the groups promoting gun control, frustrated with the NRA's dominance in the pluralist pathway, succeeded in moving the issue to the partisan pathway by mobilizing President Clinton to make the issue a major plank of his early administration's policy priorities, culminating in passage of the 1993 Brady Bill.

The system is now positioned to encourage more pathway switching in more directions than have traditionally been recognized. While the jump from interests to the party sector has been well known, the greater accessibility of ideas and symbolic appeals as bases of legitimation and mobilization is a more recent development. Moreover, all actors in the system have become skilled at utilizing the major pathways to power. Broader and more diffuse interests, traditionally viewed as being represented by parties, have become more organized and adept at plying the pluralist pathway.[13] This development was clearly not contemplated by traditional theories, suggesting that such groups would be hampered by free-rider and intensity problems in attempting to gain a foothold in the universe of organized groups. Narrower interests have also sought to use pathways beyond the pluralistic confines to capitalize on the legitimacy that experts and symbolic ideas can confer to their claims. Thus the NRA and health insurers alike have expanded their capacity to appeal to broader publics by making their cases in more symbolic terms and by augmenting their capacity to use modern media to reach and mobilize broader publics. The tobacco lobby was only one of many groups seeking to tap the expert pathway to defend itself against scientifically based attacks by commissioning its own studies of smoking and health.

These developments have wide-ranging consequences for the pathways themselves, as well as for the rate and direction of policy change. Each pathway has become more contestable. Many applaud this development for the pluralistic pathway by noting that issues once characterized by policy monopolies have now been transformed by the representation of a wider range of interests, resulting in a more open and competitive issue network. The contestability of symbolic pathways has produced more volatility as one compelling idea that may have attracted broad support can be replaced nearly overnight with another competing notion. The contestability of the expert pathway is demonstrated by the proliferating range of scientists, economists, and policy analysts employed by contending interests. Although reflecting the newfound power of professional ideas and knowledge, this development also challenges the credibility of expert communities. The expert community has leverage due to professional consensus about the external environment and the impacts of policy proposals on that environment. Contending groups can succeed in undercutting that consensus by promoting the appearance that other ideas, regardless of their absolute professional or scientific standing, have legitimacy.[14]

The parties have become increasingly polarized, leading to increasing partisanship in Congress. Nearly half (45 percent) of our cases since 2000 have followed the partisan pathway versus 24 percent of policies in the period from 1981 to 1999. Certainly the partisan pathway continues to serve its time-honored function as the platform for major policy reform, but it has also increasingly become the source of gridlock and stasis that threatens to blunt and forestall changes arising from other pathways.[15] In 2012 alone, standard policies on the pluralist pathway to reauthorize farm subsidies, transportation programs, and military spending, which would have been politically irresistible in the past, became bogged down when leaders on the partisan pathway insisted on blocking changes that could upset their ideological positioning in an election year. Should this trend continue, the hegemonic partisan pathway could undermine the responsiveness and adaptability of our policy process. Many would argue we have already reached that point.[16]

Nonetheless, the other pathways remain fertile and independent sources of policy ferment and change. Nearly three-quarters of our forty-two cases and over half of the policies adopted over the past decade principally followed one of the nonpartisan pathways. Even in the contemporary era, partisan polarization is only part of the story of the making of public policy.[17]

Overall, these forces have produced a set of policy outcomes that are both more volatile and less predictable because policies are more prone to jump tracks more often. When more pathways have the potential for being mobilized, policy change becomes both more possible but also more uncertain. Traditional expansions of scope and mobilizations of broader interests bear policy fruit, only to inspire countermobilizations by other interests using other pathways. The symbolic and expert tracks are becoming increasingly more productive in raising issues on the agenda, and this provides an alternative form of legitimation to both incubate and enact new ideas. But because they raise the stakes and other actors have the facility to play in that game, these ideas can become neutralized by different framing and counterproposals. As we have observed, policy reforms ushered in on these idea-based pathways have proved difficult to sustain as established interests wait in the wings to countermobilize and, ultimately, reinforce the old policy order.

The implications of this warrant more consideration. Fluidity in the policy system can clearly be a good thing in certain ways. A system more open to change can be more responsive to shifts both in interests and in ideas. Notable cases of policy reform—tax reform in 1986, farm reform in 1995, No Child Left Behind in 2002— are the by-products of a system where policy pathways are both more accessible and more interconnected.

Greater competition within and between pathways can be productive not only of policy change, but also of policy that is better aligned with ever-changing public values and interests. Such a process gives incentives for greater mobilization and engagement of broader publics in policy decisions that vitally affect their interests. Indeed, most of us would embrace such a fluid process compared with the one that was the theory and reality of fifty years ago: a process tightly controlled by strong interests with only halting capacity to reach to broader publics and recognize shifting public values and ideas.

Ideally, perhaps, good public policy should be the product of all four pathways. Each brings unique comparative advantages to policymaking. The pluralist pathway recognizes the unique standing that intense interests should have in shaping policy decisions. The partisan pathway balances out intensity through outreach to broader publics that may not be as well organized or positioned. The symbolic pathway ensures an alternative route for new ideas with broad appeal to those with widely shared values to expand the parameters of debates. And the expert pathway helps ensure that policy contests will be informed by research and ideas held by those who most closely study public policy problems and outcomes.

Given the important normative values contributed by each pathway to "good" public policy, it is heartening that the process is more fluid, featuring greater potential for shifting across pathways and greater competition within pathways. Such a fluid process seems to carry greater potential to yield "good" public policy than a process characterized by entrenched and ossified pathways resistant to change. However, the greater competition within and among pathways can also carry less positive outcomes for policymaking. A volatile policy process can be destabilizing and lead to a rush to judgment as policy pathways veer from one form or mobilization and issue framing to another. Coalitions and policy consensus anchored in time-honored policy consensus can quickly become undone when policy shifts to the symbolic pathway, prompting ill-considered and poorly informed policy that has not been leavened through the painstaking coalition-building processes of deliberative democracy. On the other hand, competition can lead to gridlock, as evenly matched interests and ideas fail to gain traction and broader support. Whether they are those of closely contested interest groups, experts, parties, or media, conflicting perspectives can ultimately foster paralysis among elites and broader publics alike, leading to years of prolonged stasis.

Notes

1. David Brody, *Critical Elections and Congressional Policy Making* (Stanford, CA: Stanford University Press, 1988); and Baumgartner and Jones, *Agendas and Instability in American Politics.*

2. John Aldrich and David Rohde, "The Logic of Conditional Party Government: Revisiting the Electoral Connection," in *Congress Reconsidered*, 7th ed., Lawrence C. Dodd and Bruce I. Oppenheimer, eds. (Washington, DC: CQ Press, 2001).

3. David Mayhew, *Divided We Govern*, 2nd ed. (New Haven, CT: Yale University Press, 2005).

4. For a contrast to Mayhew that recognizes the potential for partisanship and divided government to contribute to gridlock, see Binder, *Stalemate*.

5. Anthony Downs, "Up and Down with Ecology: The Issue Attention Cycle," *The Public Interest* 28: 38–50.

6. Conlan, Wrightson, and Beam, *Taxing Choices*.

7. Baumgartner et al., *Lobbying and Policy Change*.

8. Schattschneider, *Semi-Sovereign People*. See also Baumgartner and Jones, *Agendas and Instability in American Politics*.

9. Downs, "Up and Down with Ecology."

10. Schattschneider, *Semi-Sovereign People*.

11. Baumgartner et al., *Lobbying and Policy Change*.

12. Heclo, "Issue Networks and the Executive Establishment."

13. See Berry, *New Liberalism*; Walker, *Mobilizing Interest Groups*; and Skocpol, "Advocates without Members."

14. Naomi Oreskes and Erik M. Conway, *Merchants of Doubt: How a Handful of Scientists Obscured the Truth on Issues from Tobacco Smoke to Global Warming* (New York: Bloomsbury Press, 2010).

15. Binder, *Stalemate*.

16. Ronald Brownstein, *Second Civil War: How Extreme Partisanship Has Paralyzed Washington and Polarized America* (New York: Penguin, 2008).

17. Sinclair, *Party Wars*.

Appendix:
Analysis of Pathways Designations

In this appendix we discuss how we selected the primary paths for each of the forty-two policy cases. Many of the cases had multiple paths at work, and judgment was called for in determining which was primary. We have chosen what we believe to be the most important policy decisions in eight domestic policy fields since 1980 (when idea-based politics became recognizably more prominent), supplemented as needed by a stratified selection of cases that permits adequate representation of each pathway. This generated a nonrandom but systematic sample of policies reflecting the application of expert knowledge of multiple cases in eight policy arenas.

We understand that these areas are not representative of all policy outputs and decisions during this period. Many, such as veterans' benefits, have undergone little change, and others may have shifted in limited ways contained within a single pathway. However, our objective here is not to classify the universe of policy outputs by pathway, but to better understand the dynamics of policymaking and policy change using the pathways model as a basis for insight.

What follows is an explanation for how we determined which pathway was the primary driver for mobilization for each of the forty-two policy cases. As the narrative suggests, multiple pathways were often involved in some of the most important policy decisions, but we sought for each one to determine which pathway was the most influential in shaping the political support for the ultimate decision. While the primary political actors involved in a decision can give clues about the pathways responsible, the actor alone does not provide a definitive test for determining the actual pathway most responsible for mobilizing support. Thus, for instance, the speaker of the House was a primary player in moving the 1996 Freedom to Farm legislation, but the principal basis for mobilization was not the partisan pathway. It was the expert pathway, where the speaker was able to adroitly draw on the broad policy consensus among economists about the wastefulness of farm subsidies. Accordingly, we classified pathways based on the primary strategy used to mobilize support for the legislation in each case.

Health Care

1988 Medicare Catastrophic Care Act: Expert

The formative proposal was developed by experts within the Department of Health and Human Services and championed by Secretary Otis Bowen. It received the support of President Reagan and both parties in Congress but was widely viewed at the time as Secretary Bowen's initiative. (After the House and Senate reached agreement on the conference bill, Bowen said it had his support, but he couldn't guarantee support by the president.) It reflected long-standing consensus on the part of health care professionals about the gaps in Medicare financing. The bill's reliance on income-adjusted fees reflected fiscal constraints, as well as preferences on the part of many health care economists and other experts for user-fee financing. Interest groups were activated in a reactive role, but this path sent mixed and conflicting messages: AARP supported the proposal, but another group purporting to represent seniors, the National Commission to Preserve Social Security and Medicare (headed by James Roosevelt), opposed it.

Repeal of the 1989 Medicare Catastrophic Care Act: Pluralistic

Upset about the income-adjusted fee, seniors represented principally by the National Commission to Preserve Social Security and Medicare engineered a repeal of the 1988 law. A memorable moment occurred when seniors booed and chased House Ways and Means Committee chairman Dan Rostenkowski (D-IL) down a Chicago street during a public appearance, prompting a congressional bandwagon to repeal the bill with nearly unanimous votes.

1993 Clinton Health Care Plan: Partisan

The inception of this plan reflected some support from elements of all four pathways: at least some prominent business groups and children's health groups supported it, health care–financing experts provided conceptual underpinnings and rationale, and the proposal tapped widely shared symbolic values on equity and coverage. However, the principal thrust was partisan, led by a newly elected Democratic president who used the plan as the centerpiece of his early presidency both to appeal to the party's core and to expand the base of the party. Key Republican congressional leaders worked with interest group allies to countermobilize, successfully reframing the issue around the theme of government regulation and choice of provider.

1997 State Children's Health Insurance Program (SCHIP): Pluralist

The primary impetus was provided both by the nation's governors seeking higher federal matching for expansion of health care for children and public health and children's health groups. The partisan pathway also played a role, as both parties had an interest in pushing for incremental health care expansion—Clinton to claim credit for some modest health care achievement in the wake of his plan's downfall and Republican leaders anxious to work with Democrats to expand benefits in the aftermath of their comprehensive but failed attempts to reform Medicare and block grant Medicaid, which prompted partisan and interest group outcries. The proposal was developed in bipartisan fashion, with differences resolved in conference committee. The bill passed as part of the Balanced Budget Act of 1997, with over $20 billion in block grants or expanded Medicaid to the states offset by an increase in cigarette tax revenues.

1997 Balanced Budget Act Medicare Reimbursement Changes: Expert

This was part of a deficit-reduction initiative building on expert consensus about the need to tame the growth of Medicare by constraining reimbursements to health maintenance organizations and home health providers—two groups making extraordinary profits from overly generous reimbursement formulas, documented by studies by the GAO and other researchers. Medicare was among the largest programs in the budget and one that produced relatively large out-year savings from cuts in funding ostensibly falling on providers, not patients (at least initially), and yielding $386 billion over ten years. Actuaries forecast the Medicare Part A trust fund going broke in 2001, so some changes were necessary. The Clinton administration proposed reimbursement reforms, as well as funding shifts to transfer home health care from Part A to Part B. Part B premiums were also increased, but some enhancements for preventive services were added too. A medical savings account demonstration program was added in negotiations between congressional Republicans and the Clinton White House. Overall, Medicare provisions were developed in a bipartisan manner, sharply reversing the 1995 Medicare reforms where the partisan pathway prevailed, as House Speaker Gingrich attempted to mastermind comprehensive Medicare reforms against the bitter opposition of Democrats.

1999 Balanced Budget Refinement Act and 2000 Benefits Improvement and Protection Act: Pluralistic

Provider groups such as health insurers countermobilized to roll back some of the 1997 changes. Experts charged that the complaints of providers had little analytical justification and were based largely on anecdotal information. Bipartisan majorities passed the restorations. The CBO estimated that the 1999 legislation would increase Medicare spending by $27 billion over ten years and that the 2000 legislation would increase spending by a net of $82 billion over ten years.

2003 Medicare Prescription Drug, Improvement, and Modernization Act: Partisan

The Medicare Modernization Act was the largest expansion of the federal role in health care during Medicare's first forty years, and its politics became deeply partisan, especially in the House of Representatives. Changes in medical practices since Medicare's original enactment made drug coverage an increasingly important issue for Medicare recipients, and both political parties sought to win control over the issue prior to the 2004 elections. Bush administration efforts to use expanded drug coverage as a means of enticing seniors into managed-care plans stirred strong Democratic opposition, and the Senate passed legislation on a bipartisan basis expanding drug coverage in traditional Medicare plans. Politics became intensely partisan in the House, where Republicans devised legislation, without any Democratic input, that was intend to drive Medicare reform, as well as extend drug benefits. Despite some conservatives' reluctance to enact a major entitlement expansion, a modified version barely passed the House with only Republican support after a chaotic three-hour vote and considerable arm twisting. A compromise House-Senate version passed both chambers on party-line votes.

2010 Affordable Care Act: Partisan

The Patient Protection and Affordable Care Act extended health insurance coverage to tens of millions of uninsured Americans. The law capped sixty years of struggle by Democratic presidents to establish a program of universal national health insurance, and President Obama's success at passing the Affordable Care Act was considered a major political victory. It was also a highly partisan accomplishment, with Democrats providing virtually every favorable vote at every stage of the legislative process in both the House and Senate, while Republicans actively worked to block the legislation every step of the way. Following passage, the bill became a major issue in the 2010 midterm elections and contributed to Republicans gaining control of the House of Representatives.

Gun Control

1986 Firearm Owners Protection Act: Pluralist

A major victory for the NRA, this bill lifted the ban on interstate sales of rifles and limited federal licensing requirements and federal inspections. The framing was defined by the NRA and its allies in the Republican Party. Some partisan pathway engagement was reflected in the House Republican mobilization to successfully discharge the bill from the House Judiciary Committee, whose Democratic chairman attempted to bottle up the legislation. However, the final bill passed with significant support from Democrats in both the House and the Senate.

1993 Brady Bill: Partisan

The legislation reflected a successful alliance between interest groups favoring handgun control and Democratic congressional leaders. However, the partisan pathway was most influential, stemming from the actions of newly elected President Clinton who came to define the Brady Bill as an early test of his leadership. In prior years, the bill had been successfully blocked by Senate Republican filibuster and veto threats by President George H. W. Bush. For the most part, congressional votes were partisan in nature, albeit with regional differences as well. The symbolic pathway was also engaged, with former presidents Reagan and Nixon supporting passage of bill. The symbolic dimension was also reflected in congressional Republicans' perception that they also needed to have their own bill purporting to address handgun control, with a focus on instant background check systems. The pluralist pathway was kept in check, as NRA opposition was offset by increasingly effective lobbying by gun control advocates such as Handgun Control.

1994 Assault Weapons Ban: Partisan

Patterns and political behavior similar to the Brady Bill. Strong leadership from President Clinton and partisan voting in both chambers, albeit with some support from certain moderate Republicans, characterized congressional consideration.

1999 Gun Show Controls: Symbolic

This bill was primarily a response to the Columbine shootings. Both parties sponsored separate versions that addressed similar issues, including background checks on guns purchased at gun shows, gun locks, and bans on internet sales of guns. Republicans and the NRA felt compelled to develop a bill including background checks, as all actors felt they had to appear to respond to the tragedy—a hallmark of symbolic politics.

Farm Policy

1990 Farm Bill: Pluralist

This was a classic farm bill with limited changes to basic programs, as members of both parties rallied to address the interests promoted by farm organizations. Previous reforms lowering price supports were reversed. The Bush administration initially objected but acceded to interest-group pressures by supporting the bill.

1995 Freedom to Farm Act: Expert

This bill reflected the consensus of economists who sought to move agriculture away from dependence on government subsidies and toward a market orientation, with a fixed and declining seven-year schedule of transition payments to farmers. The experts' cause was adopted by the new House Republican leadership anxious to demonstrate a commitment to free-market principles and to reduce deficits. The partisan pathway was activated to support expert concepts, with the House speaker shifting drafting responsibilities from the pluralist confines of the House Agriculture Committee to the more leadership and reform-oriented House Budget Committee.

2002 Farm Bill: Pluralist

Both parties rushed to placate and aid farmers ahead of the competitive 2002 midterm elections by revoking the framework of the 1995 law and reinstating and expanding subsidies for major row crops, adding new subsidies for new crops, creating a new dairy price support program, and expanding conservation programs. In order to supplement support from farm state members, the new law maintained expansive support for federal nutrition-assistance programs.

2008 Farm Bill: Pluralist

The 2008 farm bill was the product of three years of political negotiations. The program's lack of fundamental reforms to major crop subsidy programs in a period of high crop prices, along with high spending on nutrition, conservation, and alternative energy programs, prompted two vetoes by President George W. Bush. The second veto and veto override were necessitated by a technical error in the original bill, which required correction by Congress. Both vetoes of the $289 billion legislation were easily overturned by large bipartisan majorities in Congress.

Tax Legislation

1981 Economic Recovery and Tax Act: Partisan

This major tax cut bill was President Reagan's defining policy initiative, designed to appeal to his base and reframe fiscal policy choices. Agenda formation was quintessentially presidential and partisan. The congressional process involved intense partisan competition in the House, as Democratic leaders sought to compete in a tax-cut bidding war.

1982 Tax Equity and Fiscal Responsibility Act (TEFRA): Expert

Prompted by exploding deficits and publicity about tax "giveaways" from the 1981 bill, tax and budget professionals worked with Senate Finance Committee chairman Bob Dole to engineer tax increases and reforms, partly reversing the cuts of 1981.

1986 Tax Reform Act: Expert

This was seminal tax-reform legislation inspired by an expert consensus of economists calling for a broader base and lower rates. The initial Reagan proposal, Treasury 1, was the product of expert deliberations by senior Treasury tax experts. This proposal constrained all future legislative developments and provided the political touchstone throughout the process. The pluralistic pathway engaged but was seriously constrained by business divisions on tax-reform provisions. The partisan pathway became more prominent as the bill moved through the process, reflected in the replacement of Treasury secretary Donald Regan with James Baker, prompted in good measure by the need to use Baker's considerable political skills to shepherd the bill through the process. However, when faced at key junctures with defeat, congressional leaders such as Finance Committee chairman Sen. Bob Packwood (R-OR) returned to a purer expert-approved bill in order to avoid being blamed for defeating the goal of tax reform.

1993 Tax Increases: Partisan

President Clinton steered a tax increase on higher-income brackets as part of a broader deficit-reduction package approved on a straight party-line vote in the House with no Republican crossover votes. The tax increase was defined in partisan terms, although experts helped lend urgency to addressing the deficit.

1997 Tax Relief Act: Symbolic

Leaders from both parties were moved by the growing appeal of the tax-cut agenda to engage in a bipartisan initiative to develop selected tax cuts, with an emphasis on middle-class families. The Republican agenda called for tax cuts, and President Clinton was anxious to deliver on his own 1992 campaign promising middle-class tax cuts. Provisions included a new child tax credit, higher education tax credits, and Roth IRAs. The expert pathway was largely not engaged, and the experts' perspective on this bill was summed up by former CBO director Robert Reischauer, who deemed the tax provisions to be "junk tax cuts."

1998 IRS Restructuring and Reform Act: Symbolic

This legislation began on what appeared to be the expert pathway as an outgrowth of recommendations of the National Commission on Restructuring the Internal Revenue Service. This commission made many recommendations endorsed by tax professionals to improve tax administration. The Senate Finance Committee effectively altered the tenor of the legislation by focusing on a series of high-profile cases alleging IRS abuse of taxpayers. The committee's hearings and resulting legislation reframed the debate and prompted the bill to jump to the symbolic pathway as part of the Republican effort to demonstrate commitment to reducing the burden of government in society and the economy. Tax professionals were appalled as Congress passed broad-sweeping legislation with questionable impact on tax administration. The Clinton administration shared these reservations but the president endorsed the bill because the issue had been effectively framed in valence terms that made opposition tantamount to endorsing overbearing government.

Although the final legislation did endorse many of the commission's proposals to strengthen leadership and flexibility, it specified the so-called ten sins of serious misconduct for IRS agents that could cost them their jobs, including harassing taxpayers. New taxpayer rights were added, including shifting the burden of proof in certain tax cases from the taxpayer to the IRS. Moreover, symbolic goals were embraced for electronic filing, requiring the IRS to increase such filing from the current 23 percent to 80 percent in ten years, even though serious questions existed at the time about the technical and administrative feasibility of bringing this about. The new rights and the prohibitions on harassment by tax agents had the effect of precipitating a free fall in IRS tax seizures and collections, as agents worried about being held liable under the new rules.

2001 Tax Cuts: Partisan

This was a classic example of the partisan pathway model. It was the major initiative of the Bush administration's first year, establishing $1.4 trillion in tax cuts over ten years. Although some Democrats ended up voting for the bill, Democratic Party leaders in the House and Senate were strongly opposed, and all floor votes were along party lines.

Welfare Policy

1988 Family Support Act: Expert

Late in the Reagan administration this proposal was developed within the frame of a new consensus on the value of work support and studies of state innovations in this area. The MDRC studies of these pilots were particularly influential among researchers and policymakers alike. Notwithstanding the perennial symbolic appeal of welfare reform and the presence of a president with strong conservative leanings, the bill was developed in Congress through a consensual process in the Senate led by Sen. Daniel Patrick Moynihan. The new Job Opportunities and Basic Skills training program, child care, and Medicaid transition were at the heart of this initiative designed to promote viable work strategies for welfare recipients.

1996 Personal Responsibility and Work Opportunity Act
(PRWORA): Symbolic

All pathways were engaged in the struggle over this landmark welfare reform. Experts' research contributed to a developing consensus about the failures of the current program and the design of work experiments. Yet the research on the impact of welfare to work was mixed, suggesting relatively modest results, and values often trumped analysis in developing particular provisions of the law, such as teen out-of-wedlock-birth incentives, family caps, and hard time limits for receipt of welfare payments. The pluralist pathway was engaged, particularly as reflected in the collaborative role played by the Republican governors in framing the initial proposals in the House and working with their congressional Republican counterparts in designing key provisions for the new grant. The partisan pathway was also engaged, particularly in the early jockeying as both parties sought to define themselves at the other's expense; President Clinton vetoed two welfare reform bills before he signed the third in 1996.

However, the symbolic pathway was the most formative in explaining the placement of welfare reform on the agenda, as well as its final passage. Both Clinton and Republican leaders had made early promises about ending welfare as we know it, and having stoked the fires of reform in symbolic terms, they found it difficult to back away from this rhetorical commitment. Both parties developed legislation to implement their visions, but Republicans succeeded in going further than Clinton's initial bill, and their bill better succeeded in capturing the symbolic landscape. By inspiring a competition to avoid blame for opposing a concept that had come to be framed in compelling valence terms, the Republicans inspired the kind of competitive race for public approbation characteristic of symbolic politics—a race the president ultimately had to engage in to protect his electoral fortunes that year.

2006 PRWORA Amendments: Partisan

Although the Temporary Assistance for Needy Families program created by PRWORA was popularly celebrated as a triumph of state innovation, the Republicans in the White House and the Congress were concerned that states were undermining their ideological agenda by sidestepping the spirit of the program's work requirements. Under the 1996 act, in fact, states were able to count caseload reductions occurring due to the economy and the program alike toward the program's work requirements. The 2006 reauthorization significantly increased the strength of the work mandates associated with the program. The work-participation requirements were significantly increased, with the caseload reduction credit no longer available to offset the states' compliance obligations. Moreover, the definition of work activities was narrowed, curtailing the time allowed for education or training to count toward the work requirement. Voting in Congress occurred largely along partisan lines.

Corporate Accounting Reforms

2000 Securities and Exchange Commission Reforms: Pluralistic

Reforms proposed by SEC chairman Arthur Levitt at the time would have placed restrictions on the ability of auditing firms to sell consulting services to clients for whom they also performed financial audits. The proposal was roundly opposed by a broad chorus of interest groups, including the auditing firms, the accounting industry (led by the American Institute of Certified Public Accountants), and the business community in general.

2002 Sarbanes-Oxley Bill: Symbolic

In the wake of a market-driven crisis, Congress passed a sweeping set of reforms that imposed a new oversight structure for corporate accounting and auditing.

Although the original legislation earlier in 2002 appeared to be mired in the partisan pathway, it quickly transitioned to symbolic with the failures of Enron, WorldCom, and other major companies in 2002. In one month the issue framing jumped tracks, and the symbolic dynamics took over, with leaders from both parties climbing aboard the bandwagon to avoid blame and to claim credit for protecting investors against corporate greed.

2008 Troubled Asset Relief Program (TARP): Expert

Faced with a financial crisis stemming from questionable housing loans, widespread use of derivatives, and other risky financial practices, the nation's major banks and financial institutions experienced the possibility of bankruptcies and disintegration not seen since the Great Depression. Party policymakers and the broader public were caught unaware by the sudden and massive nature of the meltdown affecting Wall Street firms, prompting delegation to a small group of financial experts at the Federal Reserve Board and Treasury Department to manage the crisis and design a federal bailout package to stem the losses. Well before the Lehman Brothers default that triggered the crisis, the experts in these agencies had already designed a fallback proposal for federal emergency financial relief to troubled institutions. When the crisis materialized, the actual legislation was revised in consultation with both parties in Congress to add significant congressional oversight over bailout operations and compensation restrictions for senior managers of financial institutions. Party leaders from both sides of the aisle supported the bill, and crisis politics intervened to push the legislation to final passage following a precipitous fall in stock prices during initial opposition to the bill in the House.

2010 Dodd-Frank Wall Street Reform and Consumer Protection Act: Partisan

This legislation was placed on the agenda as a response to the financial crisis and Great Recession of 2008. President Obama sent Congress a proposal in 2009 that included government authority to wind down the "too big to fail" financial firms, to set up a new consumer protection agency, and to regulate the derivatives market. Although these proposals faced severe opposition from the financial services industry and congressional Republicans, the House passed the bill by a vote of 223-202. All but twenty-seven Democrats voted for it, and all Republicans voted against it.

After several failed bipartisan efforts to produce a bill in the Senate, Banking Committee chair Chris Dodd (D-CT) pushed legislation through the committee on a party-line vote. On the Senate floor the bill was passed on May 20, 2010, by a vote of 59-39 with the support of fifty-five Democrats and just four Republicans.

Only two Democrats voted no. The final conference bill passed the House on June 30, 2010, in a mostly party-line vote of 237-192, with only three Republican members supporting the legislation. On July 15, the Senate passed the bill on a party-line vote of 60-39. On July 21, 2010, President Obama signed the bill into law.

Federal Mandates

1986 Safe Drinking Water Amendments: Symbolic

Legislation developed by environmental groups promised to impose over eighty new standards on local water systems, providing fallback legislative standards if the Reagan administration refused to aggressively implement the bill. Members of both parties felt compelled to support it, particularly on the heels of the Anne Burford–Rita Lavelle scandals at the Environmental Protection Agency during the early Reagan administration. Notwithstanding costs of over $10 billion estimated to be imposed on drinking water systems, legislation was passed nearly unanimously.

1986 Asbestos Hazard Emergency Response Act: Symbolic

This legislation required the nation's 37,000 school districts to inspect for and clean up asbestos in their school buildings. Beginning with research documenting the hazards of asbestos, this legislation gained momentum from the pluralist pathway, as a broad coalition of organizations representing environmental interests, school workers, and even asbestos manufacturers saw federal regulation to be in their interest. However, the major thrust for passage during the Reagan presidency with a Democratic-controlled House was the broad symbolic appeal of the issue, which made opposition by traditional Republican conservatives in Congress and the White House politically untenable. Moreover, even though they faced an estimated $3 billion in additional costs, state and local education interests were also politically unable to publicly oppose the legislation. The legislation passed nearly unanimously through both houses of Congress on its way to its signing by President Reagan.

1990 Clean Air Act Amendments: Expert

The Clean Air Act Amendments of 1990 reauthorized and expanded the nation's principal air pollution control legislation and contained significant new requirements and timetables for dealing with urban smog, acid rain, hazardous and toxic air pollutants, and ozone-destroying chlorofluorocarbons. Many of these provisions bore the strong imprint of environmental and regulatory policy experts, particularly the novel "cap-and-trade" system of marketable permits for regulating sulfur dioxide emissions from power plants. The politics of passage was aided by powerful support from leaders of both political parties, reflecting President George H. W. Bush's commitment to be an "environmental president" and Senate majority leader George Mitchell's active involvement in the legislative negotiations.

1996 Safe Drinking Water Act Amendments: Pluralist

Local governments and other water systems were mobilized following the promulgation of some of the new regulations called for under the 1986 amendments. Congress rushed to provide them with regulatory relief, sparing smaller jurisdictions from certain requirements, slowing EPA's regulatory pace, giving the agency authority to consider costs, and permitting systems to install less costly alternatives to filtration. An expanded federal loan fund was also provided to support local implementation.

1996 Defense of Marriage Act: Symbolic

The Defense of Marriage Act of 1996 (DOMA) was designed to address concerns that the recognition of same-sex marriage in one state would require reciprocal recognition of such marriages by other states, pursuant to the "full faith and credit" clause of the US Constitution. Stimulus for the proposed legislation was a 1993 decision by the Supreme Court of Hawaii in *Baehr v. Lewin*, which held that denying the rights and benefits of marriage to same-sex couples constituted gender discrimination. In response, the Defense of Marriage Act restricted federal marriage benefits to opposite-sex couples and obviated interstate marriage recognition to same sex marriages.

DOMA rushed through the legislative process, passing the House by an overwhelming margin in a little over two months, skipping hearings and committee consideration in the Senate, avoiding filibuster and extended debate on the Senate floor, and passing the Senate in identical form as in the House in order to avoid the need for a conference committee. Such speed was driven by symbolic politics. Gay marriage was a contentious and emotional social issue for both proponents and opponents of DOMA, but public opinion polls at the time of its passage showed opponents of gay marriage outnumbering proponents by more than two to one. Given such one-sided—and intensely held—views among much of the public, Republicans used their majority in Congress to push the legislation through quickly, in hopes of using it as a wedge issue in the fall elections. Democrats, however, sidetracked the partisan strategy by voting overwhelmingly in favor of DOMA themselves. In the end, the "defense of marriage" was treated as a valence issue with bipartisan support.

2002 No Child Left Behind Act (NCLB): Expert

Signed in January of 2002 by President George W. Bush, NCLB marks the most significant expansion of the federal role in education in US history. The act requires states to establish an accountability framework to assess the performance of all students in grades 3 through 8 based on state standards, with annual testing. School districts and schools that fail to make adequate yearly progress toward statewide proficiency goals will, over time, be subject to improvement, corrective action, and restructuring measures aimed at getting them back on course to meet state standards. The expert pathway provided the critical foundation for this legislation, based on a growing consensus among educational experts on the need for and efficacy of standards and testing as strategies for improving the nation's schools. National education commissions in the 1980s, coupled with innovative programs from the states, convinced national communities of education experts, as well as national party officials, that standards-based testing should be the foundation for the federal role in education.

Both parties moved to embrace this growing consensus, as Republicans dropped their traditional reservations about interfering with the prerogatives of local schools and Democrats had to leave restive teachers unions behind in moving forward. Recognizing the growing public cry for education improvement and stronger federal leadership, the parties competed to earn the public's approbation on this dimension. It was no accident that President Bush was able to find cause with Sen. Edward M. Kennedy in joining together in a bipartisan alliance to pass No Child Left Behind.

2005 Real ID Act: Symbolic

This legislation began in the expert pathway. Administrators of state motor vehicle departments, as well as the 9/11 Commission, recommended national standards to force recalcitrant states to adopt uniform security procedures for acquiring driver's licenses, which they had failed to do under voluntary compacts. Yet given that several 9/11 hijackers had used fraudulent driver's licenses to carry out their conspiracy, the issue had great symbolic potential. In the "be careful what you ask for" category, Congress responded with passage of legislation ultimately going well beyond the suggestions made by the states. Rep. Jim Sensenbrenner (R-WI), chairman of the House Judiciary Committee, succeeded in passing a stronger measure—the Real ID Act—as part of "must sign" legislation funding US troops in Iraq and Afghanistan (P.L. 109-13). The Real ID Act establishes federal standards for promoting security for the issuance of state driver's licenses, which state associations estimated would cost $11 billion over five years. The most burdensome provisions include reenrollment of all current license holders, new verification processes with original documentation such as birth certificates, and new tamperproof security features for the card itself. In addition to a strong mandate, Sensenbrenner and his coalition also succeeded in including provisions prohibiting states from issuing federally approved IDs to illegal aliens, currently the practice in ten states.

Budget Process Reform

1985 Gramm-Rudman-Hollings Act: Symbolic

Coming on the heels of a then-record increase in the federal deficit and the failure of congressional Democrats, congressional Republicans, and President Reagan to reach agreement on substantive policy actions to reduce the deficit, this bill was attached to required extension of the debt ceiling, itself an action fraught with symbolic potential. The partisan track was not significantly engaged in inception, as a coalition of moderates from both parties fashioned a proposal that galvanized support as the only vehicle available for members to register their symbolic concerns about the deficit and their resolve to do something about it. The scheme contemplated by the bill for a series of declining deficit targets enforceable by sequesters of budget authority was widely viewed by experts and even many congressional supporters as unworkable. President Reagan was largely on the sidelines and was compelled to sign it despite his reservations about the potential cuts to defense if sequesters were activated.

1990 Budget Enforcement Act: Expert

The deficit targets in Gramm-Rudman proved to be unacceptable, partly because they were aimed at a moving target—the deficit—that grew with economic downturns and spikes in health care costs in spite of the valiant efforts of budget cutters. As part of the Omnibus Budget Reconciliation Act of 1990 negotiated by congressional Democrats and President George H. W. Bush, a new set of budget procedures were agreed to by both sides and largely fashioned by budget experts in the OMB and Congress. Instead of fastening itself to arbitrary and unrealistic deficit-reduction targets, the BEA framework instituted controls primarily on new policy expansions and spending actions by imposing caps on discretionary appropriations and by developing a PAYGO regime calling for any tax cut or entitlement expansion to be deficit-neutral. This framework in fact proved to be more sustainable, serving to curb both discretionary spending and PAYGO actions at least during the deficit years, according to the CBO.

2000 Budget Lockbox: Symbolic

These proposals were advanced by leaders of both parties as the nation emerged with increasingly large budgetary surpluses. Both parties sought through the lockbox plan to prevent the other side and themselves from using the surpluses generated by Social Security for either tax cuts or new spending. The proposals generally provided for points of order to be raised against legislation that is scored by the CBO as using the Social Security surpluses for spending or tax cuts. The Clinton administration sought to increase the stakes by articulating the even more ambitious "stretch" fiscal goal of eliminating all publicly held debt by 2013. Budget experts scoffed at these proposals for violating norms of unified budgeting, setting arbitrary targets for surpluses not connected to any underlying economic rationale, and implying that the Social Security surpluses could be "parked" for a rainy day twenty years hence. To compound the artifice, the House bills required the Social Security surpluses that were "saved" to be deposited in a debt-reduction account—even though the very same level of debt reduction would occur from saving the surplus with or without this account.

Yet, in a process bearing the hallmarks of symbolic politics, both parties vied with each other to champion saving the surplus and felt compelled to vote for lockboxes to avoid being blamed for "losing" the surplus. The valence quality of the issue is reflected in the House votes, which were nearly unanimous in nearly every roll call.

2010 Statutory Pay-As-You-Go Act (PAYGO Restoration Act): Partisan

The expiration of budget PAYGO and discretionary spending caps in 2002 was said to enable President George W. Bush to increase deficits with impunity. Injected into the 2008 election debates, deficits and the need to extend the former budget controls were implanted in the partisan pathway. Looking for a way to differentiate his fiscal policy from his predecessor, President Obama grasped for renewal of fiscal rules based on the original 1990 Budget Enforcement Act. The 2010 PAYGO legislation reestablished the BEA controls requiring new tax cuts and entitlements to be offset by savings to make them deficit-neutral.

However, the Obama budget had already advocated significant tax cuts and higher entitlements through extending the Bush tax cuts for all but wealthier Americans and through continued higher payments to doctors under Medicare. Accordingly, the president wanted a bill that contained exemptions for these priorities of his. The Democratic Congress passed such legislation with majorities of Democrats in favor and unanimous Republican opposition—a classic manifestation of the partisan pathway at work.

2011 Budget Control Act: Symbolic

This legislation extended the federal debt ceiling and staved off default of the federal government but not before including major reductions in discretionary spending for defense and nondefense agencies for the next ten years. The legislation also included a budget sequester that would entail further reductions in those programs, as well as selected entitlements, if a new congressional supercommittee failed to agree and achieve more than $1 trillion in savings across the entire budget.

While having real consequences, the legislation came about on the symbolic pathway, reflecting the needs of both parties to appear to respond to rising public concern over deficits. With a Tea Party faction dedicated to opposing extending the ceiling on federal debt, Republican leaders in Congress were desperate for a symbolic way to demonstrate that they had at least attempted to achieve reductions in spending as their price for dropping their hard line on federal debt. With deficits rising to record peacetime levels during the Great Recession, the Obama administration also had an interest in appearing to support a down payment on deficit reduction, particularly since this appeared to be necessary to avoid an unprecedented federal default. The legislation was designed to incorporate a number of symbolic initiatives to show a Congress hard at work curbing the future debt of the nation, again as the price for extending the debt ceiling. The spending caps would bring defense and domestic spending by 2023 to levels not seen since before 1970—a mark that most experts regarded as unworkable and unattainable. The supercommittee was also a highly visible effort designed to demonstrate fealty to deficit reduction, even though it was destined to fail in a polarized Congress.

Finally, the legislation shifted the blame to President Obama by allowing him to raise the debt ceiling in three increments over the following year and a half. Congressional Republicans would have chances to block each increase with a resolution of disapproval, but Obama would almost certainly veto it, and an override would be unlikely. Thus, under the Budget Control Act, the president was able to increase the debt to finance government while Republicans gained opportunities to vote against debt extensions and bind government spending in future years at a rate that most thought would be unrealistic.

Index